# THE INDO-PACIFIC: NEW STRATEGIES FOR CANADIAN ENGAGEMENT WITH A CRITICAL REGION

Fen Osler Hampson, Goldy Hyder, and
Tina J. Park, eds.

sh.

SUTHERLAND
HOUSE

Sutherland House
416 Moore Ave., Suite 205
Toronto, ON M4G 1C9

First edition, November 2022

If you are interested in inviting one of our authors to a live event or media appearance, please contact sranasinghe@sutherlandhousebooks.com and visit our website at sutherlandhousebooks.com for more information about our authors and their schedules.

We acknowledge the support of the Government of Canada.

Manufactured in Canada
Cover designed by Jordan Lunn

Library and Archives Canada Cataloguing in Publication
Title: The Indo-Pacific : new strategies for Canadian engagement with a critical region / Fen Osler Hampson, Goldy Hyder, and Tina Park, eds.
Names: Hampson, Fen Osler, editor. | Hyder, Goldy, editor. | Park, Tina, editor.
Description: Includes bibliographical references and index.
Identifiers: Canadiana (print) 20220416117 | Canadiana (ebook) 20220416176 | ISBN 9781990823220 (softcover) | ISBN 9781990823237 (EPUB)
Subjects: LCSH: Canada—Foreign economic relations—Indo-Pacific Region. | LCSH: Indo-Pacific Region—Foreign economic relations—Canada.
Classification: LCC FC244.P3 I53 2022 | DDC 327.71059—dc23

ISBN 978-1-990823-22-0
eBook ISBN 978-1-990823-23-7

# Contents

# Introduction
# Fen Osler Hampson, Goldy Hyder, and Tina J. Park

THE INDO-PACIFIC region, stretching from North America to India, is home to 60% of the world's population and 20 of its 33 megacities (those with more than 10 million inhabitants). The region not only accounts for roughly 60% of global GDP but an even larger share of global growth, which means its importance as the world's economic centre of gravity is increasing with each passing year. By rights, the Indo-Pacific region should figure prominently in any discussion of Canadian trade and foreign policy, yet Canada's relations with countries across the region have never lived up to their potential, and Canadian businesses continue to underperform in the Indo-Pacific marketplace. Why this is the case, and what should be done about it, is the focus of this collection of essays by distinguished policymakers and business leaders.

The most obvious reason why Canadians, who themselves inhabit a Pacific nation, are insufficiently engaged in the Indo-Pacific region has to do with our longstanding preoccupation with our southern neighbour. The United States dominates Canada's political, economic, and cultural agenda and has done so since the end of the Second World War. Successive calls to diversify trade, beginning with the so-called "Third Option" articulated if not actively embraced by Pierre Elliott Trudeau's government in the 1970s, have had little effect. While it is true that Canadian exporters have begun to make inroads into other markets with the help of several recent trade deals—notably the Comprehensive Economic and Trade Agreement (CETA) with the European Union and the Comprehensive and Progressive Agreement for Trans-Pacific Partnership (CPTPP)—the overall impact on Canada's trade profile has been limited to date.

To make matters worse, the United States over the past decade has shown increasing interest in the Indo-Pacific—to the point where it is now arguably the U.S. government's leading foreign policy priority—but does not appear to consider Canada to be part of the region. This poses a risk not only to our relationship with the United States but also to Canada's relationships with other countries in the region, as some partners seek to work closely with the United States on their own regional strategies.

Some might wonder whether Canada's lack of engagement in the Indo-Pacific will ever change, but we believe it must—and soon. The fact that the region is gaining in economic heft—and is likely to continue doing so for the better part of this century—should be enough to instil a sense of urgency among key Canadian decision-makers in government and the private sector. Granted, the United States remains a vital engine of global economic progress, but in relative terms its importance is shrinking. What's more, the country that for decades confidently championed globalization has now turned decidedly inward. Canadians have felt the impact of rising U.S. protectionism in industries such as steel and aluminum, as well as through the imposition of ever-stricter "Buy American" rules on public procurement. Meanwhile, the surge in U.S. shale oil and natural gas production over the past dozen years has cut into demand for imported Canadian energy. On top of these pressures, supply chain disruptions caused or exacerbated by the COVID-19 pandemic and the Russian invasion of Ukraine have reinforced calls for the reshoring of U.S. manufacturing.

Before the pandemic struck, the annual GDP growth in Canada was predicted to average 1.5% over the next half century, half the pace of the previous 50 years. Persistent weak productivity growth and an aging labour force are among the biggest economic challenges facing the country, but in the post-pandemic era Canadians will also have to contend with changing global trading patterns and deglobalization. Deglobalization, however, is not a viable strategy for a relatively small economy such as Canada that depends heavily on foreign trade and exports of natural resources.

Hence, Canada must diversify its trade and investment by more aggressively pursuing new opportunities in global markets—especially fast-growing economies in the Indo-Pacific.

But for a variety of reasons, the road will not be easy. Canada's relationship with China, which appears poised to overtake the United States as the world's largest economy within a decade, remains thorny at best. While the crisis involving Huawei executive Meng Wenzhou, former Canadian diplomat Michael Kovrig, and entrepreneur Michael Spavor has been resolved, there remain deep suspicions and distrust in the minds of many Canadians when it comes to doing business with China. At the same time, Canada's relations with India—which haven't been warm since Canada cut off nuclear trade with India in the 1970s—have cooled further under Justin Trudeau's Liberal government. Efforts to negotiate a bilateral free trade agreement stalled in the last decade, though the negotiations have resumed and may receive some much-needed impetus now that Russia's invasion of Ukraine has heightened concerns about supply-chain resilience.

Elsewhere in the region, engagement by Canada has been spotty and *ad hoc*, characterized by an unwillingness to make substantial investments in building political and business relations. This is despite the fact that Canada is home to many significant Indo-Pacific diaspora populations, including 1.8 million Chinese-Canadians, 1.4 million Indo-Canadians, and 850,000 Filipino Canadians. In the 2016 census, more than six million people in Canada reported having Asian origins, representing 17.7% of the country's population. It is both surprising and disappointing that Canada's approach toward the Indo-Pacific region fails in any systematic way to mobilize and leverage these vast social networks in pursuit of stronger transnational connections.

Of course, the case for more active Canadian engagement in the Indo-Pacific region is not limited to trade diversification and commercial opportunities. Russia's illegal assault on Ukraine—and by extension the Kremlin's efforts to reshape the existing international order—are reminders that Canadians cannot afford to take global peace and security for granted. Now more than ever before, we must work together and deepen our relationships with like-minded democracies. In the context of the Indo-Pacific, Canada should pursue a *tiered approach* to renewed regional engagement that prioritizes the region's democratic countries. Canada must actively develop fuller and more productive relationships with Australia, India, Indonesia, Japan, and South Korea, covering the full spectrum of economic, social, educational, and security ties.

Other countries, not all democratic but still dynamic economically, fall into the second tier. They include Thailand, Cambodia, the Philippines, Malaysia, and Vietnam.

As this book highlights, China is in a special category. Given its vast size and importance to the global economy, China cannot and must not be ignored. Beyond being an important and growing market for Canadian natural resources, manufactured goods, and services, China is the largest trading partner of almost every country in the Indo-Pacific region. For all the talk about moving production out of China because of higher costs, COVID-19, trade tensions, and geopolitical uncertainty, the fact remains that no other country can match the scale and scope of its supply chains. Hence, Canada must seek to re-engage China with its "eyes wide open" following the largely symbolic boycott of the 2022 Winter Olympic Games. This is especially true when it comes to Chinese investment in Canada. The federal government should steer Chinese imports and investment away from sectors deemed of strategic importance for national security.

A similar principle applies to data and intellectual property. Although some have hailed Asia's new Regional Comprehensive Economic Partnership (RCEP) agreement as a significant step toward facilitating cross-border data flows, China—the first country to ratify RCEP—has adopted legislation that allows it to restrict the storage and transfer of any data that it views as a threat to Chinese national security, economic development, or public interest. In effect, China wants data to flow in but not necessarily flow out. China is also making concerted efforts to assert its IP rights globally by embedding itself in the standards-setting process and thereby shaping how new digital technologies and platforms are used. This underscores the need for Canadians to adopt stronger measures to protect our own IP.

Hoarding data is the 21st century digital equivalent of using traditional trade subsidies to seek an unfair competitive advantage. In this context, the World Trade Organization's plurilateral joint statement initiative on e-commerce, which seeks to promote openness and trust in digital trade, represents a positive first step.

China, it should be noted, has embarked on its own deglobalization strategy, which aims to reduce the country's dependence on foreign trade. However, the impact of this initiative on Canada is likely to be minimal given China's heavy dependence on imported commodities to meet the needs of its fast-growing middle class. A formal trade agreement would have little effect on Chinese purchases of Canadian natural resources and agricultural products, because global markets will set the price of such commodities.

Economic growth across the Indo-Pacific is also creating significant export opportunities for natural gas. Canada is the world's fifth-largest producer and fourth-largest exporter of natural gas, but in the absence of a liquefied natural gas (LNG) export terminal we are limited to the North American market. To take advantage of the growing demand for LNG, our governments will have to work with industry, accelerate regulatory approvals, and negotiate long-term contracts with countries such as Japan and South Korea, both of which are major energy importers and reliable partners. They can provide the capital for such projects. These countries will be looking to wean themselves from suppliers in the Middle East whose shipments must cross the disputed waters of the South China Sea, most of which China claims as its exclusive economic zone. Exercising full sovereignty over this area is a core component of President Xi Jinping's "China Dream." Japan, Korea, and others in the region are also attempting to free themselves from dependence on Russian oil and gas, but have limited short-term options. Canadian policymakers need to expedite, not frustrate, the construction of LNG export capacity on our West Coast.

Beijing's military activities in the South China Sea—and similar territorial disputes involving the Himalayan Plateau and the Taiwan Straits—are among a wide range of regional security challenges with tangible and direct consequences for Canada. The longstanding security risk posed by

North Korea's nuclear ambitions is magnified by its intermediate-range and newly developed intercontinental ballistic missile capabilities, which pose a direct threat not just to South Korea but also to North America. China's remarkable economic rise and growing diplomatic clout have shifted the balance of power in the region, aided to a degree by periods of incoherent and inconsistent U.S. foreign policy. While the countries of the Indo-Pacific boast some of the world's most extensive military capabilities, the region lacks effective institutional mechanisms for conflict resolution. The challenges to regional—and global—stability posed by border disputes, geopolitical rivalries, and ongoing piracy on the high seas have been exacerbated by the stresses and strains of the COVID-19 pandemic, cyber warfare, and the emergence of new regional and international terrorist networks.

If Canada hopes to enhance its engagement with emerging markets where democratic structures are weak or non-existent, it will require large doses of careful and pragmatic diplomacy. Even in countries that are moving in a democratic direction, democratic institutions take a long time to develop. Canadian foreign policy can be effective only to the extent that it is realistic and balanced. It is essential to work with Canada's local partners, not against them. Progress is more likely to be achieved by supporting international institutions that promote the rule of law and fight corruption.

Finally, we must recognize that some of Canada's core sectors—notably the resource extractive industries—are facing criticism domestically and internationally. The federal government will have to work with the private sector on environmental, social, and governance (ESG) criteria to demonstrate commitment to these core principles. Managing the domestic politics of ESG is a crucial responsibility of the government. Canadians themselves must understand that there will not necessarily be any quick wins in this area. It took almost 20 years for the oil sands to become technologically productive and economically viable. The development of carbon-capture technologies and other measures to alleviate climate change will also take time and a great deal of investment.

This edited book presents distinguished authors with real-life experiences in the given country or region, discussing specific opportunities and strategies for Canada's engagement with key countries in the Indo-Pacific as we look toward the next decade. It offers insightful reflections and recommendations from key policy and business leaders on the opportunities for a much deeper engagement strategy. These chapters cover a broad range of issues tied to business, trade and investment relations, military and cyber security, and politics and diplomacy. Unlike many existing studies and books, the volume provides a comprehensive road map that identifies key opportunities and priorities to deepen Canada's relations with key countries in the region.

# 2

# The Geopolitical Context

## Derek H. Burney and Fen Osler Hampson

V LADIMIR ILYICH Lenin reportedly said, "there are decades where nothing happens; and there are weeks where decades happen." The world is now living through one of those periods as the Coronavirus pandemic continues to deliver a major shock to countries around the globe, including Canada. Inflation ravages many economies, and the threat of escalation of conflicts over Ukraine and Taiwan looms ominously. But it is also true that some of the major economic and geopolitical forces affecting Canada's future have been evident for a long time, well before COVID-19 struck. To riff on Lenin: for decades things were happening that affected Canada's vital national interests, but for decades Ottawa was wedded to old ways of thinking and doing business. But if ever there was a time to break old habits, it is surely now as the global power structure seems fragile and the world struggles to deal with these challenges at a time when the global power structure seems more fragile, it is surely now. In the third decade of the 21st century, Canada must begin to think and act geostrategically. That imperative involves recognizing the intersection of economics, politics, defence, and diplomacy, which for a trading nation like Canada, are closely intertwined. In this chapter, we discuss the three core elements of a new strategic imperative that are required to shift Canada's economic interests and military commitments away from the Atlantic and North America toward the Indo-Pacific region.

*Strategic Imperative #1: Reduce Canada's economic dependence on the United States because of declining marginal gains from trade and heightened political risk to Canada's economic relations with the United States.* Canada's first major challenge is to wean itself from a continentalist mindset to one that is oriented more toward the Indo-Pacific, which has become the world's new centre of economic gravity and growth. This is even more urgent now because Canada no longer has a privileged or "special" relationship with the United States, which, in recent decades, has used its political and economic clout to bully Canada and limit its access to U.S. markets for a wide range of goods and services.

In the decades that followed World War II, Canada's economy moved into ever closer orbit with [the United States as the pre-war British Imperial Preference System yielded to a liberalized trading system under the General Agreement on Tariffs and Trade.] The ratification of the Canada–U.S. FTA (1988) and NAFTA (1993) agreements led to the removal of major tariff and non-tariff barriers to trade between Canada and its continental neighbours, reaping major benefits to all three North American trading partners. In 1980, two-way bilateral trade in goods and services represented 40% of Canadian GDP. By 2005, that figure had increased to 52% and was valued at $710 billion annually or nearly $2 billion every day, becoming the largest two-way exchange between two countries in the world. Two-way flows of foreign direct investment also accelerated: in the early 1980s the value of annual two-way flows averaged under $10 billion; by the middle of the first decade of the 21st century, they had reached $480 billion.

But the idea that the U.S. market will continue to pay limitless and ever-increasing dividends to the Canadian economy has been sorely tested by the actions of successive U.S. administrations—Republican and Democrat—over the past three decades.

The first major disruption to the relationship came in the aftermath of the 9/11 terrorist attacks on the United States. Despite efforts by the Canadian and U.S. governments to manage the border in a cooperative way, many of the initiatives that were introduced to manage border security had the opposite effect—the border became sticky and thick as red tape and other kinds of restrictions took effect. In the years that followed, the aggregate flow of goods and people across the Canada–U.S. border never returned to their pre 9/11 levels—despite a near parity exchange rate in 2011.

By the end of the first decade of the 21st century, China replaced Canada as the leading merchandise supplier to the United States (and also became the second-largest supplier to the Canadian market) as unit labour costs in Canada rose and Canadian manufacturers lost their competitive edge. In the energy sector, which accounts for almost a quarter of Canada's trade with the United States and roughly 10% of Canada's GDP, U.S. policies were increasingly inimical to Canadian interests as environmental and other groups mobilized to stop the construction of pipelines on environmental grounds. In response to those pressures, the Obama administration refused to issue a permit for the construction of the Keystone XL pipeline, which would have boosted oil shipments from Canada by more than 900,000 barrels a day and generated tens of thousands of jobs on both sides of the border. But that was simply one in a growing number of snubs and slights against Canada by U.S. policymakers and regulators. The United States procrastinated on Canada's efforts to join the Comprehensive and Progressive Agreement for Trans-Pacific Partnership (CPTPP) though ironically in the end Canada joined the "Comprehensive" TPP as it came to be known and the United States did not. "Buy American" provisions in President Obama's stimulus package to jump start the U.S. economy in the aftermath of the 2007–2008 financial crisis discriminated against Canadian suppliers, while U.S. labelling practices for Canadian beef imports cost Canadian producers more than a billion dollars annually.

The renegotiation of NAFTA sucked most of the foreign policy oxygen out of Ottawa during the Trump years leaving little time for senior government officials to focus on much else. Negotiations were bruising and difficult. The new United States–Mexico–Canada Agreement (USMCA), or what some pundits disparaged as NAFTA 0.8, kept NAFTA's dispute mechanism in place (a deal breaker for Trudeau) and Canada's supply management systems for dairy, pork, and poultry while raising North American content requirements for auto production. But the ink was barely dry on the agreement when General Motors closed one of its key plants in Oshawa, Ontario, and four others in the United States, dispelling any illusions that USMCA would lead to stability in the automobile sector. Trump's tariffs on

Canadian (and Mexican) steel and aluminum were also only removed well after USMCA was signed.

Hopes that the Biden administration would usher in a new spirit of cooperation—or, at the very least, introduce some normalcy to the relationship after the tumultuous years of the Trump presidency—have been dashed. Although Donald Trump reversed Obama's decision on Keystone, President Biden did another one-eighty turn and issued an executive order cancelling the permit for the pipeline on his very first day in office.

Canada now finds itself fighting a rear-guard action on multiple fronts with the Biden administration. In addition to the Keystone decision, which Trudeau meekly took on the chin, Biden has dithered about weighing in on Michigan Governor Gretchen Witmer's efforts to shut down Enbridge's Line 5 pipeline, which supplies much of the oil and natural gas that is consumed in Central Canada. To add insult to injury, the citizens of Maine in a statewide referendum voted overwhelmingly to reject the construction of a Hydro Quebec electric transmission line across their state, a project that was worth billions to Quebec and U.S. interests.

Canadian policies further aggravated matters. Increased regulations driven by the primacy of Climate Change slowed investments in the development of vital oil and gas resources, which are vital to our economic and export growth.

U.S. protectionism has once again reared its ugly head in President Biden's Infrastructure, Investment and Jobs Act, which is pumping $1.2 trillion into the U.S. economy in key infrastructure spending on a wide variety of projects. Buy American provisions in the Act will effectively shut Canadian firms out of contracts worth billions. There was some comfort when Congress did away with the discriminatory tax credit, which would have applied to electric vehicles manufactured in the United States only, instead of North America as a whole, as it does now. But the absence of a US carbon tax in Biden's climate plan puts Canada at a clear competitive disadvantage.

The Biden Administration doubled tariffs on Canadian softwood lumber imports shortly after the "Three Amigos" summit in November, an event that, in itself, reflected a significant downgrade to Canada–U.S. relations and more recently won a dispute over Canada's dairy policy restrictions.

Canada will obviously continue to rely on the United States as a key market that is vital to Canadian prosperity notwithstanding the many challenges it confronts in managing that relationship in an era of growing U.S. protectionism. We also need to recognize that the remaining years of a constrained Biden administration offer little promise for dramatic improvement. The United States no longer holds the key to Canada's future economic growth. That key lies with the emerging market economies of the Indo-Pacific where growth is taking place at a much faster rate. By the middle of this century, emerging markets are projected to account for 70% of the world's wealth and 60% of global trade with Asian economies accounting for 50% of global GDP and 50% of the world population.

***Strategic Imperative #2: Pursue an "Eyes Open" policy toward key emerging markets in the Indo-Pacific, especially China.*** Ten years ago, we delivered a major report entitled *Winning in a Changing World*,[1] which was based on soundings taken with senior business leaders from across the country, to the then Prime Minister Stephen Harper. Our report didn't mince words. "The global economy is changing dramatically," we said, but "Canada is not keeping pace. The Chinese, Indian, Brazilian, Colombian, Mexican, Korean, Turkish, Vietnamese, Indonesian, and South African economies are expanding at more than twice the rate of Canada's more traditional markets" and will soon account "for more than half of the world's production and consumption of goods and services." It bluntly noted that "with some notable exceptions, Canadian firms have made little progress in penetrating new markets while losing market share in traditional ones. Unless Canada dramatically ups its game and changes the way it does business, it assuredly will not be a significant player in these new markets." But it also observed that the region presents its own unique challenges for Canadian business: "The quasi-market nature of these newer global players poses unique challenges and requires innovative approaches and different negotiating, trade, and investment strategies from those Canada is now pursuing." And it urged the federal government to give its "negotiators full authority to act in the national interest, supported by a new provincial and private-sector consultative network." "As these newer players in the global economy come to invest in Canada," it also said, "we need more coherent and focused rules on foreign investment. We must identify our key sources of comparative advantage and respond to the unique challenges posed by foreign state-owned enterprises and sovereign wealth funds."

The main thrust of the report's recommendations is just as relevant today, if not more so. The most dynamic economies in the world are in the Indo-Pacific region. They are led by the two juggernauts, China and India, but also include Australia, Indonesia, Malaysia, the Philippines, Vietnam, and South Korea. Although Japan is a mature, developed economy with an aging population and has experienced sluggish growth in recent years, it is still the third-largest economy in the world and the world's second-largest developed economy. Although Canada is a signatory to the CPTPP, has signed its own free trade agreement with South Korea, and has launched negotiations with ASEAN countries, it will take more than signatures on paper to yield the benefits from a more open trading regime with some of the emerging economies of the Indo-Pacific. As other chapters in this volume detail at much greater length, upping Canada's game in these markets will require buy-in and a comprehensive trade and investment strategy that is led by Ottawa with the support of the provinces and with the active engagement of the business community.

The Australian experience is instructive in this regard. Australia's trade with Asia represents 50% of its total trade with the world with roughly one-third of that trade being with China. Australia's engagement strategy was developed in a *White Paper*, which was issued with all-party support by the Australian government in 2012. The report, over 300 pages in length, was wide ranging and covered topics such as trade, investment, education, immigration, defence, and the requirements for effective corporate governance for Australia to succeed in Asian markets. It also set out clear targets to be achieved in each sector for its engagement strategy, including a recommendation for Australian companies to ensure that at least one-third of their boards are individuals who have "deep experience and knowledge of Asia."

Although Canada cannot emulate the Australian model in every respect, the Indo-Pacific's growing demand for food, energy, minerals, education, tourism, etc., presents major opportunities for Canadian trade and investment. But it will require intense planning and systematic coordination between governments—federal and provincial—and the private sector.

However, when it comes to China, like Australia Canada will have to be especially vigilant about the risks of deepening economic ties with a country that is increasingly authoritarian and overtly hostile toward other countries and their citizens—one that openly flouts not only basic human rights, but also trade and investment principles enshrined in the World Trade Organization. Some sectors of the economy, like critical infrastructure and high tech, should simply be off limits to Chinese investors. In this respect, the green light the federal government gave to the Chinese takeover of a Canadian lithium company left many observers scratching their heads. Australia has banned Chinese companies from its 5G wireless networks because of legitimate security concerns (the United States and the United Kingdom have done the same). Canada was under pressure from its Five Eyes partners and belatedly followed suit. Calling China out for its bullying behaviour or secretive, authoritarian ways is also not risk free as the Australians have learned. When Australia called for an independent inquiry into the origins of COVID-19, which originated in China, Beijing hit back by suspending Australian shipments of coal, beef, and other commodities. Canada has likewise experienced Beijing's ire for its detention of Huawei executive Meng Wanzhou not just with the arrest of Michael Kovrig and Michael Spavor but also Beijing's suspension of Canadian canola, beef, and pork imports.[2]

As the National Bank has reported "manufacturing capital stock in Canada is the lowest in 35 years" and one of the worst among OECD countries. That affects productivity and in turn weakens growth. We need policies that will attract, not repel, investment, and a tax system that is competitive.

Pressures in the United States for reshoring investment and manufacturing and decoupling critical global supply chains for key products and services in sectors like aviation, semiconductors, rare metals and medicals devices, which run through China, will also have an impact on Canada's economic strategy and the choices it confronts. As a recent U.S. Chamber of Commerce study *Understanding U.S.-China Decoupling: Macro Trends and Industry Impacts* (2021) points out, in the investment channel alone, a U.S. decoupling strategy that led to the sale of U.S. FDI stock in China would take its toll on the U.S. economy with GDP losses approaching half a trillion dollars along with major job and output losses. But China's economy is slowing and becoming more focused internally for growth than externally.

To be sure, China will remain a crucial market for global trade and investment because of its sheer size and economic heft. It is just too important to cut loose from the global economy. In truth, China's manufacturing know-how, relative currency stability and domestic market for goods and services dwarf those of other emerging economies, including India, Brazil, and Mexico. As *Forbes'* writer Kenneth Rapoza underscores, China also has much lower corporate tax rates than its competitors, a cheaper wage structure than Brazil or Mexico, and a highly diversified manufacturing sector. Although rising wages in China are pushing the production of lower value goods to other countries, it is still highly competitive in many sectors.

The cost of moving goods within China and overseas is also much lower than other countries because of its state-of-the art ports and transportation system. On the corruption index, China is also viewed as a better place to do business than Brazil, Mexico, Vietnam, or the Philippines, where stifling regulations and outdated infrastructure pose additional obstacles.

In our opinion, Canada does not need trade agreements with China to sell what China wants from Canada, which are commodities that are fungible and the price of which is set by global markets and assuredly not China alone. As Canada discovered when China banned its canola imports, Canadian canola still found its way to China via the United Arab Emirates, which acted as a sort of third party, middleman during the dispute. The bottom line is that if China wants Canadian commodities badly enough, they will find their way there. Canada has a massive trade deficit with China because we buy more than we sell them. This also gives Canada leverage should it decide to use it. At the same time, it is important to recognize that there are major trading and investment opportunities with other economies in the region—economies where the political risks of going offside are lower but where there is still indirect access to Chinese markets because China is the major trading partner of these countries.

Equally, we should not hesitate to act in concert with others to bolster Taiwan's international status. We should strengthen trade and investment relations with Taiwan and support Taiwan's entry into the CPTPP.

*Strategic Imperative #3: Pivot Canada's military assets toward the Indo-Pacific.* Although NATO is still vital to global security, Europe is wealthy enough to attend to many of its own defence needs. Germany and France have to punch above their weight as the United Kingdom now does. Russia's threat to Ukraine is one Canada must take seriously. It provides more reason to beef up Canada's defense spending with a concrete plan to increase the size of our forces and modernize equipment, without which we are simply not credible to anyone anywhere. If NATO expands its sphere of operations to the Indo-Pacific, Canada will obviously pivot with NATO. But Canada should not wait for this to happen. China presents a much greater security risk to the Western world than Russia. As Nicholas Burns, the U.S. Ambassador-designate to Beijing said in his confirmation hearings before the U.S. Senate Foreign Affairs Committee, China poses "the greatest threat to the Western World." CIA Director William Burns has also described China as "the most important geopolitical threat we face." Between 2010 and 2020, China's military expenditures rose by 76% and the PLA's war-fighting abilities have vastly improved. By 2030, China's navy will be more modern and bigger than the United States. Statements by President Xi Jinping and other Chinese leaders characterize the United States as a declining power. China's actions in the South China Sea, Hong Kong, and its increasingly nationalistic rhetoric over Taiwan and turn toward greater domestic repression are viewed by many strategic analysts as evidence of China's belligerent intentions.

Given the importance of the Indo-Pacific region to Canada's economic future, Canada has a key stake in the region's stability as great power and regional rivalries intensify and a wide range of new security challenges such as terrorism, cybercrime, espionage, natural disaster management, transnational crime, human and drug trafficking compete with traditional security concerns. For our economic partners in the region, economics and security are two sides of the same coin. They have repeatedly told us that if Canada wants to strengthen its commercial and economic ties in the region, it has to be a much more engaged and reliable security partner.

More than ten years ago, Canada's then defence minister Peter MacKay told delegates at the annual gathering of defence ministers and security specialists at Singapore's Shangri-la Dialogue that Canada was keen to join the ASEAN Defence Ministerial Meeting-Plus and East Asian Summit forums. But the response from his interlocutors was that Canada had to show that it was a serious defence and security player in the region first before any kind of invitation would be extended. Former ASEAN secretary general, Thailand Surin Pitsuwan, was uncharacteristically blunt in his own assessment of Canada as a security partner: "Canada knows that it has been rather absent from the region," he remarked in 2012.

Little has changed in the intervening years. The indifference of our key allies to our security sensibilities was painfully brought home in September 2021 when the United States, Australia, and the United Kingdom announced a new security pact that would give Australia access to advanced U.S. nuclear-powered submarine technology to outfit their new fleet of attack submarines while strengthening security cooperation. "The AUKUS alliance," the BBC reported, "is probably the most significant security arrangement between the three nations since World War Two.... The pact will focus on military capability ... [and] will also involve the sharing of cyber capabilities and other undersea technologies." No such invitation was extended to Canada to join this new alliance and Ottawa was blindsided by the announcement.

AUKUS underscores that Australia is considered a serious defence and security partner in the Indo-Pacific. Canada clearly is not. Some key statistics are quite telling. Australia has a population of 25.8 million people whereas Canada's population is 38 million. In 2019, Australia's GDP was USD 1.4 trillion. Canada's was USD 1.7 trillion. Yet, despite being roughly two-thirds the size of Canada on both metrics—population and

GDP—Australia's military budget was 2% of GDP (34 USD billion) versus 1.4% for Canada (22.8 USD billion). Australia is committed to major
increases in defence spending over the next 10 years and boosting its air and
naval capabilities in order to prepare for a post-COVID world that, in the
words of former Australian prime minister Scott Morrison, is "poorer, more
dangerous and more disorderly." Morrison also warned that "We have not
seen the conflation of global economic and strategic uncertainty now being
experienced here in Australia in our region since the existential threat we
faced when the global and regional order collapsed in the 1930s and 1940s."
No such warnings or commitment to boost defence spending have come
out of Ottawa. Instead, all of the talk about Canada's "defence" is focused on
a seemingly endless parade of lurid allegations about sexual harassment by
senior military officers and the shabby treatment given to the veterans of the
Afghanistan campaign. Our military is declining and yet is top heavy with
generals and flag officers while woefully deficient in modern equipment.
Poor political leadership and an addiction to woke trends do not help.

As David Pugliese wrote in the *Ottawa Citizen*, the U.S. Marines have
180,000 active marines and a maximum of 62 generals. Canada has roughly
66,000 regular forces commanded by 129 generals and admirals. No wonder
the strategy or purpose of our defence force is in the doldrums. Further,
as Kim Richard Nossal points out, the writing of Canadian defence policy
by successive governments—Liberal and Conservative—is devoid of geography, or "a-geographical," other than occasional platitudes about the close
security relationship Canada has with the United States. The Trudeau
government's 2020 Defence Policy Statement, *Strong, Secure and Engaged*,
was no exception choosing to devote much of its attention to the social
welfare needs of Canada's military members and their families. As one of
Canada's most astute journalists and war correspondents, the late Matthew
Fisher, sardonically observed, "the idea that Australia is physically closer to
China is hokum. By the most obvious measure, Vancouver is 435 kilometres
closer to Beijing (actual distance 8,508 km) than Beijing is to Sydney (8,943 km).
By another measure, Sydney is only 1,000 km closer to Shanghai than
Vancouver is."

For the first time since the Korean War, where Canada played an important combat role, the country has a critical choice to make: whether to dramatically up the ante on its defence and security presence in the Indo-Pacific
by both increasing and redeploying naval and air assets in the region or to
stick with the status quo, which will not only further marginalize us in the
region, but thwart any effort to boost trade and investment ties in a part of
the world where we do not have any special relationships or preferred access.

It is quite apparent that the United States is shifting its own strategic posture in the region away from an emphasis on large land-based
forces toward highly mobile naval, air and special forces and technologically sophisticated cyber-attack capabilities, space-based intelligence
and communications systems, and missile defence capabilities. Australia
is also moving in the same direction with the modernization of its own
forces. Canada will have to decide whether it plans to follow the U.S. and
Australian lead. Although some effort has been made to increase Canada's
visibility in the region through, for example, more frequent ministerial visits, visits to local ports-of-call by our navy, and participation in joint military exercises such as the Rim-of-the-Pacific Exercise, the annual Cobra
Gold Exercises in Thailand, and joint exercises on the Korean peninsula,
developing a more permanent and robust military presence in the region
will be critical to gaining acceptance as a trusted security partner. However,
offers of military assistance must be based on close consultation with our
regional partners. And in a part of the world where personal relationships
truly matter, Canada will have to ratchet up its diplomatic and military
engagement to a much higher level than exists now. The occasional cameo
appearance by senior Canadian officials in the region won't win over many
hearts or minds.

In addition to seeking AUKUS membership, Canada should also aspire
to membership in the "Quad," which is emerging as another key strategic
grouping in the region. The Quadrilateral Security Dialogue was established in 2007 by former Japanese Prime Minister Shinzo Abe. Although
it fell into abeyance during the tenure of former Australian Prime Minister

Kevin Rudd, who worried about offending Chinese sensibilities, it has returned to prominence as reflected in bimonthly meetings of senior foreign ministry officials, joint military exercises, and the group's commitment to developing achievable policies. At their March 2021 meeting, Quad leaders reaffirmed their commitment to "quadrilateral cooperation" and striving for "a region that is free, open, inclusive, healthy, anchored by democratic values, and unconstrained by coercion." Going forward, the group will focus its efforts on addressing the "the global devastation wrought by COVID-19, the threat of climate change, and security challenges facing the region with renewed purpose" while also "promoting a free, open rules-based order, rooted in international law" for the Indo-Pacific region "and beyond."

Canada also needs to bolster its sovereignty defence in the Arctic, especially given recent activity by China and Russia in that region. The first line of defence begins at home.

A strengthened role for Canada in regional deterrence should also be accompanied by the revitalization of our own contribution to arms control and regional confidence-building measures. Arms control is an area where Canada has traditionally been a major player as our role in the creation and development of the 1970 Nuclear Non-Proliferation Treaty regime and the 1992 Open Skies Treaty between Russia and the U.S. attests. As the United States, China, and Russia enter a new arms race to modernize their nuclear arsenals and develop new weapons like hypersonic missiles[3] and ground-based anti-satellite weapons, the risks of strategic miscalculation and inadvertent escalation will heighten because of the absence of warning times to allow decision makers to act. The loss of control over military forces resulting from actions taken by local military commanders could set in motion a chain of events that political authorities cannot control or reverse. The mobilization of Europe's armies just prior to the onset of World War I after the assassination of Archduke Ferdinand in Sarajevo, which set in motion an uncontrollable chain of events, highlights such dangers even in the 21st century.

In our book, *Braver Canada: Shaping Our Destiny in a Precarious World* (2020), we argued that "Canada requires a new global strategy that reduces the country's economic reliance on the United States, opens new gateways to the markets of the Indo-Pacific region, and establishes new political and security partnerships that go beyond the framework of Canada's traditional alliances and commitments to international institutions."[4]

# 3

# The Geoeconomic Context
# Meredith B. Lilly and Amily Li

THE INDO-PACIFIC is the world's fastest-growing and most dynamic economic region. China, India, and Indonesia are projected to become the world's first, second, and fourth-largest economies in 2050.[5] The region's emerging markets of Vietnam, India, Bangladesh, Pakistan, and the Philippines are expected to have the highest annual growth, ranging from 4.3% to 5.0%.[6] These promising trends are propelled by large populations and an expanding middle class. Home to three major regional trade pacts—the Regional Comprehensive Economic Partnership (RCEP), the Comprehensive and Progressive Agreement for Trans-Pacific Partnership (CPTPP), and the ASEAN Free Trade Area (AFTA)—the Indo-Pacific is well on its way to becoming the epicentre of international trade and investment globally.

Meanwhile, Canada and its historical allies and trading partners in the United States and Europe are not expected to experience significant growth. For Canada to mitigate its lagging economic expectations, it must seize opportunities where they exist, including greater trade integration with the Indo-Pacific region. Yet, Canada must become a more consistent and sophisticated actor in the region to do so.

In the final decades of the 20th century and continuing well into the first years of the current one, Canada sought to treat trade with the Indo-Pacific region as distinct from political and security matters. This worked in Canada's favour, enabling it to grow commercial relations and destination markets for exports without linking complex political files, human rights problems, control over disputed maritime waters, or the rise of authoritarianism in some of those countries. Challenges that arose were addressed either via diplomacy or placed under formal dispute settlement via the World Trade Organization or the UN Convention on the Law of the Sea,[7] for example. Canada has long relied on such institutions to reflect and secure its national interest as both a founding country of post-war multilateralism and a middle power.

Some of the world's most powerful countries have increasingly shunned or simply ignored the rules and judgments of such international bodies.[8] Canada has been forced to reckon with a nastier and more protectionist global context in which its "boy scout" approach to multilateralism requires a tougher style.[9] Recent events have demonstrated the necessity of considering trade relations as integral to these broader geopolitical trends, from China's hostage-linked trade diplomacy toward Western countries to the United States' beggar-thy-neighbour economic policies aimed at friends and foes alike and to acknowledge the influence of Canada's choices on such issues. In addition, as economic nationalism and regional trading blocs are amplified in the wake of the COVID-19 pandemic, Canada may finally recognize the imperative of seeking proper trade diversification to avoid finding itself alone at the top of the world. It is looking to the Indo-Pacific to realize those gains.

This chapter outlines the trade and geoeconomic issues related to Canada's engagement with the Indo-Pacific as it considers the next steps for relations with the region. First, we outline the necessity of locating Canada's strategy in relation to broader U.S.–China strategic competition. Second, we examine the economic growth prospects offered by the Indo-Pacific region as Canada seeks to diversify trade. Finally, we conclude with suggestions for Canada's strategy that also reflect new values-based and resiliency goals for trade and supply chains.

## Superpowers Cast Long Shadows

Canadian engagement with the Indo-Pacific reflects a deliberate strategy to diversify trade relations beyond the United States and China. Yet, due to their market power and global influence, both countries remain central to Canada's ambitions for the Indo-Pacific.

Canada's dependence on trade with the United States has made it vulnerable to protectionist action south of the border for over a century.[10] While Canadians like to remind Americans of the balanced bilateral trading relationship of roughly \$350B (USD) in goods exports annually for each country,[11] they are less likely to mention that these figures represent approximately 75% of Canadian exports but only 15% of American ones. Although the tumultuous years of Trump have passed, President Biden has primarily maintained his predecessor's protectionist policies. For example, the Biden administration has reinforced similarly punitive duties on Canadian softwood lumber[12] and has promised tax credits for American-assembled electric vehicles designed to re-shore jobs to the United States.[13] Although Canada and Mexico would prefer to work together to build a stronger North American trading bloc to benefit all three countries, the Biden administration is more circumspect.[14] In this context, Canada feels an even greater urgency to build trade relationships beyond North America.

Meanwhile, Canada's efforts to substitute U.S. trade by expanding relations with China have faltered badly. Canada's approach to China was uneven under the Harper government (2006–2015), yet bilateral trade grew, and the two governments reached several important economic agreements. In 2016, a newly elected Justin Trudeau vowed to improve relations with China, but efforts were short-lived.[15] Relations began to sour in 2017, after Trudeau failed to launch formal free-trade negotiations during his bilateral visit, allegedly over Canadian insistence that labour and human rights provisions be part of any agreement.[16] But it was the 2018 arrest of two Canadians in retaliation for Canada's detention of Huawei CFO Meng Wanzhou that put Canada–China relations in the deep freeze.[17] China imposed bans on Canadian canola, pork and beef imports and challenged Canadian firms and investors. By the time China released Canadians Michael Spavor and Michael Kovrig more than two and a half years later, Canadian public opinion on China had reached an all-time low. The government hardened its resolve to chart a new path for economic relations with the Indo-Pacific.

## The Indo-Pacific Pivot

Canada finds itself in solid company as it seeks to rebalance trade relations with a renewed focus on the Indo-Pacific. The United States, Europe, and regional countries are all striving to launch their strategies for the region and are devoting more resources than Canada. Yet, neither Canada nor target countries in the Indo-Pacific can work independently from their respective "big brother." There can be no Canadian Indo-Pacific strategy in isolation from Canada's trade and economic relations with the United States. This means Canada must pay particular attention to American plans for the region and align its approach in sensitive areas touching on national security. Failure to do so could result in Canada finding itself blocked from trade with the United States in such places, as would undoubtedly have occurred had Canada permitted the entry of Huawei 5G technology into its wireless infrastructure.[18] With many sectors increasingly viewed through a national security lens, Canada cannot afford to gamble access to the American market for uncertainty in the Indo-Pacific, despite the region's allure.

Similarly, Indo-Pacific countries with which Canada is seeking to expand trade relations must play their chess games with China. Although none are as trade-exposed to China as Canada and Mexico are to the United States, China remains the top trading partner for most regional countries. For example, Figure 1 displays CPTPP member countries' two-way trade with select blocs as a percentage of total national trade (2019).[19] It demonstrates that, among CPTPP partners, Mexico and Canada are the odd ones out with respect to the balance of interests between the United States and China. In devising its strategy, Canada has much to learn from regional leaders such as Japan and Australia, *de facto* guardians of the CPTPP and countries with more sophisticated and nuanced approaches to China.

Given this context, Canada has some meaningful ways to assert its strategy for economic relations with the region. Below, we argue that Canada should prioritize three areas. Cognizant that Canada is not yet regarded as a significant player in the region, we seek to balance Canada's interests in the Indo-Pacific with considerations of what Indo-Pacific partners may be seeking from Canada in return.

**Figure 1:** CPTPP member countries' two-way trade as a percentage of total national trade, 2019

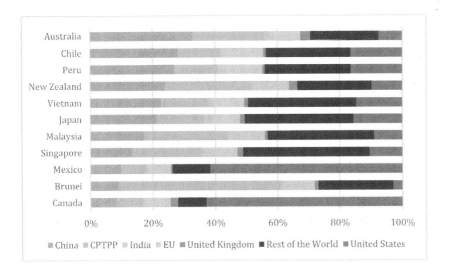

**1. Grow and Strengthen the CPTPP:** Canada's primary goal for trade should be to prioritize the CPTPP as the instrument of choice for advancing Canadian trade relations. As an ambitious, 21st-century trade agreement, the CPTPP includes strong provisions on digital governance, state-owned enterprises, labour, environment, and human rights. As part of CPTPP, Canada can work with other members to negotiate from a position of strength with new entrants to the deal. Together, CPTPP members can urge new countries to offer broad market access proposals and display high ambition on standards in state-owned enterprises, industrial subsidies, labour, and the environment.[20]

Interest in the agreement by potential new members is increasing, and negotiations with the United Kingdom have begun. Other countries expressing interest are Thailand, South Korea, and Taiwan.[21] While it is recognized that Taiwan's application presents challenges, Canada should welcome the small democracy's efforts to join, both for economic and strategic reasons. Similarly, per CPTPP rules for the accession of new members, China's application should be rebuffed until the country curbs its distortionary trade practices and makes ambitious commitments to broad trade liberalization and high standards.[22] Finally, seeking to advance trade relations in the region via CPTPP enables Canada to operate constructively in a forum where both China and the United States are absent, thereby allowing Canada to assert its interests for CPTPP enlargement.

Pushing to advance Indo-Pacific trade via CPTPP also means Canada should rethink its *ad hoc* "kitchen sink" approach to trade agreements in the region. Except for India, which Canada can easily justify developing a bilateral trade deal due to India's market size and global influence, it is difficult to defend negotiating minor agreements with regional countries outside the CPTPP structure. One exception may be Canada's November 2021 move to launch formal negotiations with the 10-country ASEAN. Canadian officials did so primarily to demonstrate a new and serious stance toward the Indo-Pacific, away from further dependence on trade with China. Given Canada's need to catch up with competitors from Europe, Australia, and the United States, and simultaneously downplay Canada's reputation for "friendly but shallow" relations with countries in the region, launching formal negotiations with ASEAN offered a clear signal of Canada's serious intent.[23]

Even so, Canada must confront the challenge that ASEAN's agreements typically do not address key provisions of Canada's modernized trade agreements such as state-owned enterprises, government procurement, labour, or the environment. Given concerns about deforestation, environmental degradation, and human rights abuses in ASEAN countries such as Indonesia, and as labour shifts away from China and toward less developed countries in ASEAN, it would be indefensible for Canada to negotiate an agreement that failed to address such issues. The marginal economic gains for Canada expected from any ASEAN deal only reinforce the need for Canada not to settle for a weak agreement. Economic analysis by Global Affairs Canada suggests that a trade agreement with ASEAN would offer Canada GDP gains of only $2.5 billion (USD), or 0.3%.[24] Nevertheless, Canada's formal engagement with ASEAN reflects broader political, economic, and development objectives beyond trade. Canada could also use the negotiations to advance those goals while nudging some members toward the more ambitious CPTPP.

**2. Link Migration with Regional Economic Success:** The Indo-Pacific region is highly populated and continuing to grow. Canada has strong services exports to offer its citizens, including international education, financial services, transportation, and tourism. Despite this, a recent study found that insufficient knowledge of the Canadian market and absent on-the-ground networks are the top two factors discouraging Indo-Pacific companies from doing business in Canada.[25] Yet, Canada can leverage its diaspora networks to build these trade relationships. For example, 15% of Canadians have ethnic ties to the Indo-Pacific region comprising East, Southeast, and South Asia.[26] Informal social networks play a significant role in accessing and developing relationships in foreign markets.[27] As such, Canadians with ties to the Indo-Pacific can play an essential role in facilitating trade and investment with Indo-Pacific markets that are considered opaque, risky, or difficult to navigate relative to traditional partners in North America and Europe.

Another often overlooked aspect of international trade is workers' economic power as they move around the globe. As the workforces of Western countries contract due to demographic transition, migration is expected to account for 80% of population growth by 2050: Canada, Europe, and the United States will compete to attract workers from high-potential countries, many located in the Indo-Pacific. As one of the few developed countries where migration continues to be embraced by citizens and political parties, Canada can partner effectively with Indo-Pacific countries on shared migration goals.[28]

In addition, Canada is a leader in negotiating temporary entry commitments in trade agreements for high-skilled individuals. It has also liberalized temporary entry visa policies through sectoral and bilateral migration programs to encourage migration in high-demand sectors, such as agriculture, health care, and high-tech.[29] For example, India is a top source country for migration to Canada. Its citizens make up 23% and 35% of all permit holders under the Temporary Foreign Worker Program (TFWP) and International Mobility Program (IMP), respectively.[30] The Indian government champions a proactive strategy to encourage foreign work in high-income countries to provide remittances income in the short term and eventually return to

India to further the country's development.[31] Similarly, Filipino immigrants represent another major category of temporary workers to Canada and comprise the primary group of immigrants in health occupations in Canada.[32] The Philippines is Canada's top destination for remittances at more than $1 billion annually.[33]

Lastly, Canada needs to revise its current international education strategy to continue attracting young people from the region and support them better while studying in Canada.[34] After the global COVID-19 pandemic wanes, global migration patterns will inevitably change. Yet, Canada must continue to encourage migration as a central pillar of its economic strategy for the region.

**3. Encourage Investment in Canada's Clean Energy:** Unlike many resource-dependent countries of the Indo-Pacific, Canada has a rich natural endowment of forestry, farmland, minerals, and energy. While countries such as Japan are desperate to develop energy solutions to improve self-sufficiency, Canada struggles to develop a national consensus on how to responsibly extract its natural resource wealth. Canada also requires foreign direct investment (FDI) to realize many capital-intensive projects. Roughly half of all investment in Canada from the Indo-Pacific region is in the oil and gas sector. Yet, the region's share of inward FDI stock remains marginal overall, increasing from 6.5% in the 1990s to only 10% by 2020.[35] Japan, the largest regional investor in Canada, would readily increase commitments if its financiers were more confident about Canada's capacity to deliver.[36] However, toxic domestic politics around pipelines and a government dedicated to accelerating the transition away from fossil fuels has rightfully earned Canada a reputation for being an unreliable destination for energy investment.

Although Canada has struggled with slow regulatory approval processes for many years, support for investment by the previous Conservative government of Stephen Harper helped maintain investor confidence that major projects would eventually proceed. The dramatic reversal by the Liberal government that followed caught some regional investors off-guard and injured bilateral relations. For example, in 2012, Malaysian energy giant Petronas made a $36 billion investment in British Columbia's Pacific Northwest LNG natural gas project, an investment approved by the Harper government, under the *Investment Canada Act*.[37] By 2017, the company cancelled the project, citing regulatory challenges and delays.[38] While the Liberal government indicates it supports clean energy growth supported by foreign investment, it must work much harder to correct both the impression and reality that major resource extraction initiatives in Canada face enormous challenges becoming operational.

This is particularly important now, as Indo-Pacific countries plan their transition from gas-powered vehicles: Canada can offer investment opportunities to fuel that transition. For example, Canada is home to a vast reserve of strategic minerals needed for electric vehicle batteries and other clean energy solutions. Due to the high cost of extraction and processing in Canada, most such minerals are currently extracted in countries with poor labour and environmental practices and subsequently sent to China, which has cornered the global processing market. Yet, as the United States and Europe become more concerned with the national security implications of this reliance on China, and as they reckon with the poor labour and environmental values reflected in those supply chains, Canada quickly becomes a strong competitor. As a country with strong labour and environmental practices, actively reflecting its commitment to clean energy through carbon pricing and research innovation, Canada is a logical destination for foreign investors motivated by these factors.[39]

## Conclusion

In this Indo-Pacific century, the region grows in vibrance and economic opportunities: Canada must approach it deliberately, consistently, and with much greater ambition. In addition to crafting a strategy focused on broad regional engagement, it is essential to understand that the Indo-Pacific is not homogenous and should not be treated as such. Home to a diverse group of emerging countries with markets, people, challenges, and opportunities unique to each country, Canada's overarching strategy and goals for engaging the region must be complemented by country-specific plans that enhance bilateral relationships. This requires serious and sustained political engagement by high-level Canadian government officials with their foreign counterparts, coupled with efforts to include provinces and territories and private sector leaders. Detailed recommendations specific to each Indo-Pacific country can be found in subsequent chapters of this book.

As Canada and other countries emerge from the COVID-19 pandemic, the need for resilience and diversification in trade relations and supply chains is apparent. While one strategy must be greater self-reliance in sectors necessary for survival, such as health, essential medicines, food, and energy, it is equally essential for Canada to diversify trade partners beyond the world's largest economies. Supply chain flexibility, realized by sourcing from alternative suppliers via secure alternative routes for goods delivery, is key to mitigating disruptions.[40] In this way, Canada and other middle powers, including those in the Indo-Pacific, can work together on supply chain resilience to support mutually assured survival.

# 4

# The Business Perspective
# Goldy Hyder

U NTIL RECENTLY, the term Indo-Pacific tended to evoke images of great powers and regional players vying for advantage—scenes of naval ships entering disputed waters, troops mobilizing, and fighter jets scrambling. Today, the term better captures a vast and growing region known for its economic dynamism. Governments, companies, and investors worldwide are increasingly looking to the Indo-Pacific region for economic and commercial opportunities.

We have entered the Indo-Pacific Century. The region is home to a large and growing middle class that will dominate global consumer demand for decades to come. There are significant opportunities for Canada within the Indo-Pacific region and many challenges—not least to Canada's long-term competitiveness. How should Canada shape its foreign and trade policy to capitalize on its strengths while minimizing potential risks?

Canada has operated in a comparatively comfortable environment for a long time. As a trading nation, the country developed an early reliance on Britain. Over time, Canadian businesses evolved to serve the burgeoning U.S. market. With the benefit of geography and supported by rules-based trade, Canadian companies have grown and flourished in a safe and stable part of the world.

But our world is changing. While protectionism is not new, the Trump Administration's loud embrace of an "America First" economic policy served as a wake-up call for many Canadian businesses. Many Canadians assumed the Biden Administration would be less inclined toward economic nationalism, but that has not proven to be the case. Canada and Canadian companies cannot and should not turn away from the U.S. market. Still, we must understand that we are facing a much less predictable bilateral trade and investment environment.

When President Trump entered the White House, some commentators suggested that Canada offset U.S. protectionism by pivoting toward China as an alternative market. Subsequent events—notably China's harsh response to the 2018 arrest in Vancouver of Huawei executive Meng Wanzhou—have underscored the risks inherent in doing business with the world's second-largest market. The message, clearly, is that Canada must continue to engage with China, but only in the context of a broader diversification strategy.

In any event, Canada's challenges go well beyond U.S. protectionism and arbitrary behaviour on the part of China. Despite the World Trade Organization's efforts to modernize the international trading system, the future of rules-based trade is not guaranteed. Hence Canada needs a Plan B that protects its trade interests. Such a plan must include a robust set of bilateral and regional trade agreements, particularly with fast-growing Indo-Pacific markets.

The good news is Canada has already established a strong network of bilateral trade agreements in the region, and work is underway to negotiate new frameworks with markets that are not currently covered.

Canada's most important agreement in the region is the Comprehensive and Progressive Agreement for Trans-Pacific Partnership (CPTPP). Complementing it is the Canada–Korea Free Trade Agreement. Canada could expand its Indo-Pacific reach further by supporting the expansion of the CPTPP, negotiating an agreement with the Association of Southeast Asian Nations (ASEAN), and reaching bilateral deals with Indonesia and India.

But more trade agreements do not necessarily mean greater trade diversification. Jim Carr, Canada's former Minister of International Trade Diversification, likened trade pacts to bridges. Governments can build them, but the decision as to whether to use them is ultimately in the hands of tens of thousands of individual companies of all sizes in every part of the country. Many of those businesses are not convinced of the benefits of pursuing new markets. The COVID-19 pandemic has disrupted trade flows but setting that aside it is unlikely Canada will hit the target it set in recent years to grow global exports by 50% between 2018 and 2025.

Trade, of course, is just one dimension of Canada's commercial relations with the rest of the world. Many Canadian companies have significant operations in the Indo-Pacific. Manulife and Sun Life each have longstanding ties in the region. BMO has been doing business in China since before Confederation. Canadian pension funds, too, have major stakes in the region. The Canada Pension Plan Investment Board has offices throughout the Indo-Pacific. Its diverse and significant regional portfolio of more than $130 billion accounts for a quarter of the fund's total assets. Many other firms have expanded to the region with great success in recent years. Yet a significant number of leading Canadian companies have not taken the leap.

In the 20th century, it was possible for a Canadian company to be a world leader simply by focusing on the North American market. That strategy is likely insufficient in the Indo-Pacific century.

For Canada and Canadian companies to remain relevant in the Indo-Pacific, we need a comprehensive regional strategy that reflects business input. Canada has succeeded in the past with a "Team Canada" approach. Business ties run deep in the region, and businesses have a stake and role to play in implementing a successful regional strategy.

Early in the pandemic, economist Larry Summers suggested that the COVID-19 pandemic could turn out to be a "hinge in history," marking the end of the American century and the beginning of the Asian century. While the United States has turned inward in recent years, the Indo-Pacific region has become increasingly integrated, at least in economic terms. The Regional Comprehensive Economic Partnership (RCEP) entered into force in 2022, creating the foundation for an integrated regional economy. Canada is currently on the outside looking in, but with a focused strategy, our country could make progress in three areas: economic growth, trade diversification, and increased regional relevance.

## Economic Growth

Much of the world's economic growth over the next several decades will occur in the Indo-Pacific region. The McKinsey Global Institute, in its *Asia's Future Is Now* discussion paper, estimates that by 2040 Asia will account for 50% of the global economy and 40% of global consumption. PwC's *World in 2050* report forecasts that China and India will be the world's two largest economies by the middle of the century, followed by the United States in third place and Indonesia in fourth. Many other economies in the Indo-Pacific will also rank highly on the list. Over the same period, the Indo-Pacific will become home to the majority of the world's middle-class consumers. The World Data Lab predicts that as many as one billion people in the Indo-Pacific will join the middle class by 2030. India and China will be the source of many of them, but South and Southeast Asia will also generate large numbers of middle-class consumers.

As the world's economic centre of gravity shifts toward the Indo-Pacific, Canada and Canadian companies must be prepared and positioned to thrive. One clear area of opportunity is e-commerce. In 2021, Ottawa-based software giant Shopify predicted that within two years, the value of e-commerce transactions in the Asia-Pacific region would outstrip that of the rest of the world combined. Chinese companies and consumers are currently driving much of this activity, but other parts of the region have significant e-commerce markets or are projected to develop major markets within the next decade.

For Canada, the Indo-Pacific also represents a major source of potential talent. A concern frequently expressed by Canadian CEOs is the challenge of recruiting talent across their international operations. The Indo-Pacific is already home to many of the world's most educated young people, as evidenced by the results of the OECD's Programme for International Student Assessment (PISA). Fifteen-year-old students across the region typically outperform their peers in Europe and North America in mathematics and science tests. In India, there are often more skilled graduates than there are suitable jobs. Canada has the opposite problem: a shortage of skilled workers in many fields. Canadian firms can therefore benefit by seeking to recruit highly skilled, foreign-trained workers.

To enhance their ability to thrive in the Indo-Pacific, Canadian companies also need more employees who are more familiar with key markets in the region. The Asia Business Leaders Advisory Council (ABLAC), a high-level group of Asian and Canadian business leaders convened annually by the Asia Pacific Foundation of Canada, has recommended a greater focus on education and workforce training to improve intercultural skills and knowledge of Asia. More frequent international exchanges, during which employees have an opportunity to work on a temporary basis in Indo-Pacific markets, would also help.

No matter how you look at the region, the growth story is compelling in comparison with Canada's traditional markets in North America and Europe. In its latest Global Economic Prospects report, the World Bank said that average annual real GDP growth in the advanced economies could slow to the 2% range in 2022. Meanwhile, emerging markets in the Indo-Pacific are predicted to grow by well over 5%, and potentially even faster in the region's three most populous countries: China, India, and Indonesia, with a combined population exceeding three billion. Canada and Canadian companies cannot risk missing out on this colossal growth opportunity.

## Diversification

Economic resiliency is an increasing concern for governments and businesses around the world, especially since the onset of the COVID-19 pandemic. This has given rise to calls for protectionism and nearshoring or onshoring in some countries. For a relatively small trading nation such as Canada, resiliency means something else entirely. Other than in a few critical areas, self-reliance is not a viable strategy for Canada. Our country must become more, not less, globally engaged.

Canada's high degree of dependency on the U.S. market used to be a strength but is now a challenge. According to Global Affairs Canada's *State of Trade 2021* report, the United States has been the destination for three-quarters of Canada's merchandise exports in each of the past five years. The United States also accounts for roughly half of Canada's direct investment abroad. That represents a slight drop over the past 30 years. However, it is still almost six times greater than the stock of Canadian direct investment in the United Kingdom, the second most important destination for Canadian direct investment abroad.

In 2018, at a time when negotiations on a new North American trade agreement had stalled, President Trump threatened to impose tariffs on Canadian-assembled cars that he said would cause the "ruination" of Canada. He might have been exaggerating, but there is no doubt that the United States has the power to inflict significant harm on Canada's economy. Many of Canada's most valuable exports, including motor vehicles and energy products, face severe challenges in today's America, in part because of the influence wielded by environmentalists and labour groups over trade policy.

Also of concern to Canadian companies is the escalating rivalry between the United States and China. Together, the world's two largest economies absorb roughly 80% of Canada's exports. Wherever possible, Canada must strive to avoid being caught in situations where it must choose between accommodating the wishes of one country or the other. Given the uncertain domestic political environments in both countries, it is risky for Canada to remain too reliant on either.

In short, Canada must balance the need to remain competitive in both the United States and China with the equally compelling need to strengthen commercial ties with other markets. Canada has competitive trade frameworks with Europe, as well as with many key markets in the Indo-Pacific. Securing high-quality agreements is an essential first step toward ensuring that Canadian firms can compete across the region. Beyond that, governments must continue their vital work to promote and facilitate trade and investment. Large businesses should be encouraged to play a more active role in helping small and medium-sized suppliers gain access to new markets.

Beyond trade, there are numerous opportunities for businesses to enhance their competitiveness by partnering with companies in countries such as Japan and South Korea. A recent LG-Magna joint venture to manufacture electric vehicle motors, inverters, on-board chargers, and related systems is an excellent example of what businesses can do to compete with larger U.S. and Chinese rivals. Such partnerships benefit from strengthening the connections between Canadian companies and integrated regional supply chains.

Being present and active in the Indo-Pacific region is more important than ever. The recently ratified RCEP agreement includes China, Japan, South Korea, Australia, and New Zealand and may eventually include India. It is the world's largest regional free trade agreement, currently accounting for almost a third of global GDP. While some analysts play down its significance due to the agreement's limited ambition, it would be to Canada's benefit to participate in what may prove to be the defining framework for Indo-Pacific trade. Whether directly or indirectly, participation would help Canada achieve its diversification objectives.

## Relevance

Canadian companies have a successful track record beyond our borders, especially in the United States. Banks, insurance companies, auto parts manufacturers, and many others have become major players in the U.S. market. The United States will undoubtedly remain an attractive place to invest, but like Canada, its share of the global economy is likely to shrink over the coming decades. Therefore, it is worth questioning whether continued success in America will be sufficient to be considered a global leader in the 21st century.

If Canada is to nurture an increasing number of global champions, more companies will need to become active in the Indo-Pacific. Some of Canada's most globally engaged firms are already working hard to build and maintain high-profile brands in the region, such as Canadian fashion brands Lululemon and Canada Goose.

Unfortunately, a glance at Canada's Financial Post 500, a ranking of the country's largest publicly traded companies, is all it takes to see that far too many of Canada's leading companies have yet to venture beyond their home market and the United States. Unless this changes soon, the inevitable result will be an erosion of Canada's global economic standing. Only 12 Canadian companies appear in Fortune magazine's most recent list of the 500 largest global companies, and most of them have dropped one or more places in the index over the past year. All the more reason why Canada, and Canadian companies, must work harder to establish a meaningful presence where growth is occurring: in the Indo-Pacific.

## Conclusion

Canada is an Indo-Pacific nation by its geography, history, and strong people-to-people business and trade ties. But we should be concerned that many other Indo-Pacific countries fail to include Canada in their regional economic strategies. Canadian policymakers and business leaders should be working together to expand and strengthen the country's interests in the region. We must recognize that the Indo-Pacific region is critical to Canada's future economic growth, its economic security, and its role as an advanced nation home to a range of leading international firms.

Canada's business community and companies of all sizes have a clear stake in a successful strategy. As Canadians learned during the renegotiation of NAFTA, we are most effective when the public and private sectors act in unison. Many Canadian companies and business groups—including the Canada–ASEAN Business Council, Canada–India Business Council, and the Canada–China Business Council—have experience and connections that could prove valuable in implementing an ambitious Indo-Pacific strategy.

# 5

# A Vital Interest for Canada
# Leonard J. Edwards

SINCE THE 1980s it's been increasingly obvious that Asia would be the world's economic engine in the 21st century. Led by a surging China on its way to "great power" status, with India not far behind, combined with Japan, Korea, plus Indonesia's huge potential, the Asian region—with almost 60% of the world population—has been steadily accruing geopolitical weight. In the years ahead, and certainly by mid-century it will become the most powerful region on the planet with a major voice in global decision-making, replacing the dominant 20th century "Atlantic" combination of Europe and the United States of America.

The brutal and unprovoked Russian invasion of Ukraine in late February, 2022, has understandably reminded Canadians of our close association with European affairs, not least because Canada's population contains the third-largest group of persons of full or partial Ukrainian descent outside Ukraine. We have responded accordingly in terms of financial, humanitarian, and military support to sustain the Ukrainian government and people in face of this most serious threat to European security since the end of the Cold War. It does not, however, change the broader strategic calculus that the future of global peace and prosperity, including the preservation of the international rules-based order and democratic forms of government, rests less in Europe than in the vast domains and varied populations of the Indo-Pacific, led China, India, Indonesia, Japan, South Korea, and Australia. If anything, events in Ukraine have reminded us that complacency and inaction can have serious consequences. Canada must take strong steps now to prepare for the even greater opportunities and contests to come in Asia.

Canada has always been a Pacific country. The ancestors of our First Nations came from Asia. Colonial explorers searched for a route to the Pacific. The Canadian Pacific Railway was partly inspired by the commercial opportunities of a transportation link between Europe and Asia. Over the past 150 years Canadians have visited, worshipped, studied, worked, taught, and holidayed in Asia. We have fought for freedom in Asia and defended Canada there. Millions of Asians have made Canada their home, to contribute and change the face of our country. In recent decades, many businesses have taken up the growing economic opportunities offered in Asia, contributing to Canadian prosperity. Successive governments have expanded diplomatic and political relationships to promote Canada's interests, values, and foreign policy objectives.

But have we done enough? Despite some high points, the truth is that over time we have responded often half-heartedly and certainly intermittently to the promise and growing power of Asia, or what is now being termed the Indo-Pacific.

While economic benefits will remain critical to Canada (especially as we diversify away from what has been a hugely beneficial but now more self-centred U.S. market), security and political developments of global significance are occurring in Asia, or arising from the exercise of Asian power. Recognizing Asia's economic weight and growing geopolitical importance, major countries far from Asian shores (such as Britain, France, and Germany) have become more active than Canada in cultivating Asian relationships and organizations, contributing to Asian security, and pursuing business as never before. For them, Asia has become a top priority.

What is Canada to do? The answer is simple but daunting: we must raise our level of effort in all of Asia to that deserving of a "vital interest" for Canada.

A century ago, as Canada began exercising an independent voice in international affairs, we made Europe and America our strategic priorities as fit our interests and the geopolitical realities of the day. Times have changed. We must now make the Indo-Pacific our leading geographic priority outside North America, along with the commensurate investments of time, energy, and of both human and financial resources. And we need a Strategy to take us there.

## Forging an Indo-Pacific Strategy: Two Leadership Challenges

In making Asia its predominant regional priority outside North America, Canada must overcome two constraints: one internal, one external. Both pose challenges for leadership.

The first is that Canadians themselves appear doubtful that their futures are particularly linked to that of Asia and the Indo-Pacific. Much of this is lack of awareness.

Canada has traditionally looked east to Europe and south to the United States, rather than to Asia. According to the 2016 Census, almost 73% of Canadians are of European ancestry. This historical identification exerts a powerful influence on priority setting in Ottawa, since electoral fortunes are especially dependent on the support of the more plentiful central Canadian voters, who live far from our Pacific shore. A public opinion poll by the Asia Pacific Foundation of Canada released in November 2020 reported that only 38% of respondents consider Canada part of the Asia Pacific region.[i]

The second challenge is that over the past decade some influential Asians have become skeptical about whether Canadian governments and businesses are really serious about Asia. They wonder if Canada's interests extend beyond the purely commercial objective of economic gain—if we are also ready to be part of the Indo-Pacific "community" over the long-haul with a stake in the future of the region, including its security in troubled times.

These doubts did not always exist. Canada went to Asia in the late 1980s and early 1990s as the region took off economically. We convinced many Asians that we saw ourselves as part of this dynamic new Asian community. Prime Minister Brian Mulroney decided Canada would be

---

[i]Canadian Views on Asia," 2020 National Opinion Poll, Asia Pacific Foundation of Canada, November 2020.

a founding member of the Asia Pacific Economic Cooperation organization (APEC) in 1989. In the 1990s, Prime Minister Jean Chrétien led a number of major Team Canada business and political missions to Asia, including to China, India, Pakistan, Indonesia, and Japan. He hosted the 1997 APEC Summit in Vancouver. Provincial leaders led delegations to Asia. Bilateral business councils were active with Japan, India, and Korea and were formed with China. The 1990s was a heyday for Canadian engagement.

Unfortunately, the 1997–1998 Asian Financial Crises sapped the vigour from Asian growth. Although it recovered after several years, Asia lost some of its shine. Some companies focused their attentions on a growing China. Following his election victory in 2006, Prime Minister Stephen Harper designated Latin America as his new government's regional priority, which over time resulted in a decline in political attention and high-level travel to the Asia/Pacific, reductions in Canada's official presence, and cuts in funding for programs for working with Asians on foreign policy, security, and development issues.

While Mr. Harper's government took a renewed interest in Asia after 2010, the cumulative effect of Canada's lower profile in Asia generally through the first decade of this century, after the burst of activity in the 1980s and 90s, has been captured in a question often asked by "old friends" in Asia: "What has happened to Canada?" Business competitors have been heard telling clients that Canadians come and Canadians go.

Overcoming these two challenges—uncertainty at home about Asia's importance to Canada and doubt within Asia about Canada's readiness to commit long-term—will require leadership from the top, as we had in the 1980s and 90s, to shape opinion in Canada and to convince Asians that Canada is serious.

With its Pacific Ocean shoreline, Canada can present itself as having an association with today's Indo-Pacific community, but we must also act the part. We have to do more than just enjoy the economic benefits. A Canadian contribution to the region's security will be a sine qua non. So will the expectation that Canada's top political and business leadership will regularly visit, and seek the views and cultivate the influence of their Indo-Pacific counterparts.

A new Indo-Pacific Strategy for Canada represents a major turning point. It resembles the period in the 1980s when we took the step toward greater economic integration within North America through the Canada/U.S. Free Trade Agreement and later the North America Free Trade Agreement (NAFTA). This time the stakes are greater, involving not only Canada's economic future, but also, at a time of global change, our long-term security and, ultimately our voice and place in the world.

## What about China and India?

Within an overall Indo-Pacific strategy, there will need to be special attention given not only to China but also to an overlooked India, now on its way to becoming Asia's second great power this century.

China's remarkable economic performance over the past four decades, joined with its assertive exercise of political weight and military power under Xi Jinping's leadership since 2013, have become dominant features on the Asian scene. Over the years these developments have tended to shift Canadian attention to China and away from the opportunities available from engagements with the rest of Asia.

The December 2018 detention in Vancouver of Huawei's CFO Meng Wanzhou at Washington's request for extradition to the United States, and the events that followed, illustrated just how dominant China had become. For almost three years China not only held Michael Kovrig and Michael Spavor "hostage" in retaliation for Canada's action, but also our freedom to exercise all our foreign policy options in response. The rest of Asia receded even further in the public mind.

With the end of the "Two Michaels"/Meng Wanzhou affair, the door is finally open to an unencumbered hard re-assessment of Canada's approach to China. It is also perfect timing for a re-discovery and re-assertion of Canadian interests, policies, and potential for action in the Indo-Pacific. Both exercises need to be in alignment and mutually supportive, with the

China strategy part of, and strengthened by, a bold and broad Indo-Pacific Strategy.

This 21st century Asia strategy must also include India and South Asia. Until recently, Canada's approaches to the region differentiated between the economically more dynamic Asia-Pacific area and South Asia. This no longer makes sense. The Indo-Pacific nomenclature recognizes South Asia's new dynamism, with India at its centre.

Coming up with a strategy for India—on the same plane as China—will be a challenge. It requires a "start fresh," putting aside the historical baggage and out-of-date impressions of India that have been part of our approach to relations with Delhi since the 1970s. We cannot afford to ignore any longer the significance to Canada of India's rise, its economic and corporate weight (which Canadians greet more positively than China's),[ii] its global influence, and its strategic importance as a counter-weight to China.

If China is the major strategic challenge for Canada in forging this new Indo-Pacific strategy, India presents the major strategic opportunity.

# The Objectives and Benefits of a Transformative Indo-Pacific Strategy

During the course of 2021, it became known that work was underway within the Canadian government on a new Asia or Indo-Pacific Strategy for Canada. Its level of ambition and its details remain unclear. Its roll out timing in 2022 is uncertain.

If it is—as it must be—ambitious and transformative, this Strategy's overall objectives could be as follows:

- First, to embed Canadian businesses more deeply in the booming 21st century Indo-Pacific economy, re-building Canada's reputation as a reliable long-term and physically present economic partner, investor, and contributor to regional prosperity;

---

[ii] "Canadian Views on Asia" National Opinion Poll, Asia Pacific Foundation of Canada, November, 2020.

- Second, to re-establish Canada's place as a member of the Indo-Pacific political community, supporting effective regional cooperation and governance, helping those countries still in need of development and technical assistance, promoting respect for human rights, and contributing to peace and stability in Asia;
- Third, to leverage the Indo-Pacific's growing influence within global decision-making as a pathway for looking after Canadian interests while promoting Canadian solutions to meeting major international challenges, such as maintaining a robust liberal global order and fighting climate change;
- Fourth, to create the best strategic position for Canada's management of its relations with Asia's 2 new "great powers": an assertive autocratic China and a rising democratic India.

An ambitious Indo-Pacific Strategy will serve Canada and Canadians in three major ways:

1. maximize the economic benefits available to Canadians arising from Canada's presence on the Pacific periphery and our access to the world's most dynamic economic region this century,
2. protect our nation's security from known and as yet unknown threats that are certain to arise in the Asian context in the decades ahead, or in other parts of the globe that engage Asian powers and interests, and
3. advance our influence in global affairs and international decision-making on matters of critical importance to Canadian interests, such as the fight against climate change and projecting the values for which we stand.

Setting this kind of framework of over-arching objectives and targeted outcomes for Canadians is just the start. New sub-strategies, priorities and activities to achieve this transformative shift for Canada to the Indo-Pacific will need to be developed and implemented. New resources will be required. Business and government will have to invest in a new generation of experts and country-specialists for deployment in positions at home and in Asia up to and including heads of offices and embassies. All this will take time.

## Business, Trade, and Technology

Economic benefits sit, as they have for 50 years, at the very top of Canada's hierarchy of interests in Asia.

While somewhat dated and pre-COVID, a 2017 Price Waterhouse (PWC) study projects that, with Gross Domestic Product (GDP) measured in purchasing power parity (PPP) terms, Asia is on trajectory to have 8 of the top 20 global economies in 2050. China and India will be in first and second positions and (after the USA) Indonesia will be fourth. Japan will still be in the top 10, while the Philippines, Pakistan, and Vietnam will move up into the top 20 joining South Korea. The PWC Study predicts that by 2050 Canada is likely to fall out of the top 20 entirely to position 22 in a virtual tie with Bangladesh and below 7 other Asian countries. This harsh projection should be a powerful incentive, while we are in a more fortunate position, to invest in strong two-way relationships with the rising Asian stars that will serve us well throughout this "Asian" century.[41]

Canada's business sector will play the lead role in our quest for success in this dominant growing regional economy of the 21st century: through marketing Canadian goods and services, exploiting investment opportunities, participating in large infrastructure projects, accessing shifting global supply chains, and engagement in high-technology sales, research, and partnerships.

To be successful in Asia, they will need to think long-term, have a local presence, be ready to work with local cultures and business practices, and exercise patience and perseverance. In Asia, the old axiom applies: "you cannot do good business with a stranger." This puts a premium on interpersonal relations from the top down, underpinned in important markets by ties between CEO groups and business associations to build trust and familiarity. In Asia "business diplomacy" pays dividends.

Canada's businesses are more likely to succeed if they have the backing of government, starting with the Prime Minister and ministers establishing trust relationships with Asian counterparts. High-level missions open doors, signal Canada's political commitment, and increase the chances that when faced with choosing between Canadian and other options Asia's elites will give Canada serious consideration.

Over its vast area, Asia's complexities often need translation, especially for newcomers more familiar with jurisdictions in Europe or the United States. Ottawa must ensure its offices are positioned, headed, and staffed at levels and with the right expertise, including a cadre of trade commissioners with deep Asia knowledge and experience. As we did for the U.S. and Mexico markets after the conclusion of the NAFTA, made-for-Asia programs should be created to assist and incent first-time Canadian businesses to leave their comfort zones and leap into competitive Asian markets.

Fortunately, Canada is relatively well positioned with many countries in terms of regional or bilateral trade agreements that improve on the World Trade Organization's Uruguay Round multilateral agreement of 1994. Others are under negotiation.

Canada's accession to the 11-member Comprehensive and Progressive Trans-Pacific Partnership (CPTPP), which came into force in 2018, without the United States following the Trump Administration's withdrawal from the negotiations that Washington originally originated, includes improved access for Canadian companies into Japan, our fourth-largest global market, as well as Vietnam, an eventual top-20 economy. We have a well-performing free trade agreement with the Republic of Korea, our seventh-largest global market. Significantly, Canada and Indonesia (a prospective No. 3 economy) announced in June 2021, that they were launching negotiations on a Comprehensive Trade and Economic Agreement (CEPA). In November 2021, Canada and ASEAN agreed to proceed with free trade agreement negotiations.

However, there are two major lacunae: we have no WTO-plus trade agreements with either China or India.

As regards China, the Trudeau Government indicated in September 2020 that conditions were no longer favourable to the launch of trade negotiations after years of on/off pre-launch discussions. Although the "2 Michaels"/Meng Wanzhou crisis is behind us, it is exceedingly unlikely the "bridge" of our bilateral relationship is robust enough to support the stress of a long and tough trade negotiation. And public opinion in Canada is against such an initiative.

However, there are two other possible avenues that would fit comfortably under our Indo-Pacific strategy. The first would be for Canada to apply to join the new Regional and Comprehensive Economic Partnership or RCEP. Completed in November 2020 among 12 Asian countries, including China and all of ASEAN (India backed out at the last minute), the RCEP is the "soft" kind of trade agreement that Canada has traditionally avoided in preference to high standard WTO-compliant arrangements covering "substantially all trade." However, countries like Australia, New Zealand, and Korea with similar preferences have joined the RCEP given the economic and political gains from this broad Asian agreement. Japan used the RCEP "umbrella" to complete its first trade agreement with China, an example we could follow.

The second avenue would depend on whether China proceeds with its application in September 2021 to join the CPTPP. While there are doubts as to China's intention to proceed, Canada could gain trade concessions from Beijing in return for Ottawa's agreement to give China access to the negotiating table (China also has to get other CPTPP members on side). Other benefits would accrue from the subsequent negotiations themselves.

After a futile decade of trying to negotiate a trade agreement with India, Canada could now benefit from a recent major change in Indian trade policy away from its allergy to opening its domestic market to outsiders. At India's initiative, talks will resume in 2022, focusing on achieving an "early harvest" of incremental steps which could eventually lead to a major agreement. We might also see if Pakistan and/or Bangladesh could be interested in a similar "incremental" approach. They are predicted in the Price Waterhouse study cited above to be in 18th and 22nd positions respectively in global GDP (PPP) rankings in 2050.

## Security, Political, and Strategic Relationships

In the Indo-Pacific, economics and security have always been closely entwined. Over the past four decades, Asia's relative stability (setting aside the conflict in Afghanistan and tensions between India and Pakistan) has facilitated remarkable economic development in the region, particularly in

China and East Asia. Asia's global significance is already huge: according to UN estimates, an astounding 42% of the world's exports and 38% of global imports were expected to pass through the Indo-Pacific in 2021.[42]

In the past decade, however, maritime boundary and fisheries disputes, Islamic extremism, piracy, and military build-ups have created new uncertainties. Much of this is China's doing. Beijing has aggressively asserted a claim to historical sovereignty over much of the South China Sea, bullying the Philippines, Malaysia, Vietnam, and Indonesia in the process. It has scuffled with India in the disputed Himalayan border areas, and sharpened its rhetoric over Taiwan. All have involved demonstrations of Beijing's growing military capabilities. China now uses harsh economic measures to discipline countries it regards as acting against its interests.

The affected ASEAN states have tried to fend off Chinese claims in the South China Sea through their own presence and a successful appeal by the Philippines to the International Court. Some have looked to their American ally for support and increased military preparedness. The Quadrilateral Security Dialogue, or "Quad," formed in 2004 among India, United States, Japan, and Australia, has stepped up its security-related activities, and in 2020 held its first military exercise in over a decade. In September 2021, the United States, Britain, and Australia announced the formation of a new security partnership in the Indo-Pacific.

In light of these events, Canada can ill-afford not to become more engaged in Indo-Pacific political/security affairs. The region will increasingly influence global decision-making and—as the primary zone of interface among the United States, China, and a rising India—the course of geopolitics.

Our first step under our Indo-Pacific strategy must be to get admission to the most important regional groupings, starting with a campaign (perhaps working with another state such as the Republic of Korea) to become a member of the Quad.

We must also achieve membership in the East Asia Summit (EAS). Prime Minister Martin's government decided not to seek inclusion in the EAS when it was established in 2005 by ASEAN. Described by Australia's government as "the Indo-Pacific's premier forum for strategic dialogue" at the leaders' level covering "political, security and economic challenges,"[iii] it involves 16 Asian participants, plus Russia, and the United States. So far Canada has not been able to get ASEAN's approval for accession, although Prime Minister Trudeau attended the 2017 summit as a "guest." We have also not been admitted to the top security forum in the region, the ASEAN Defence Ministers PLUS group. Created in 2010, non-ASEAN "Plus" participants are the United States, Russia, Korea, China, India, Japan, New Zealand, and Australia. Canada's Defense Minister was present as "a guest of the Chair" in December 2020.

A second step, which would support our campaign for admission to regional groups, would be to increase our offers to help ASEAN countries, and others, navigate through security related disputes and difficulties. We did this in partnership with Indonesia in the 1990s through a nongovernmental Workshop process on "Managing Potential Conflicts in the South China Sea." Other steps could include offering our world-class expertise in ocean fisheries management, the setting up of refugee systems and administration, designing confidence-building measures between disputants when needed, and establishing cyber-security capabilities.

As a third initiative, outside Southeast Asia, we could show more leadership on the one security issue in our extended neighbourhood where we have history, credibility, and a responsibility to speak out: the threat posed by North Korea. North Korean missiles are now capable of reaching Ottawa, Toronto, and Montreal and will use Canadian airspace to hit eastern U.S. targets. As one idea, Canada could work informally with a few Asian and possibly other countries outside the six Party Framework to find fresh ideas that could lower tensions and reduce the nuclear threat.

The most positive impact—both for the region and for Canada's security— would come from establishing an ongoing presence in the Indo-Pacific by Canada's Armed Forces, particularly from the Royal Canadian Navy, as well as other security assets, including intelligence and cyber-security personnel. Some progress has been made in sending additional and more

---

[iii] East Asia Summit (EAS), dfat.gov.au.

senior military and defence officials to Asia for exercises, networking, interchanges, conferences, training, and the UN Command in Korea. However, this is short of the strategic shift demanded by a fundamentally changing security picture in Asia and the growth in Asia's share of global military power.

Making that shift will be the toughest challenge in delivering a truly transformational Indo-Pacific Strategy for Canada. It will require a break with our historic thinking about Canada's defence priorities (particularly its embedded emphasis on the Atlantic and European theatres), a major re-allocation of resources, new and expensive investments in defence, and ultimately a 21st century Defence Plan for Canada.

Ironically, recent events in Europe—Russia's invasion of Ukraine—have now propelled Canada's government to commit to a Defence Policy Review. This review provides a golden opportunity for Canada to assess all of its longer-term security and defence needs and to set new global priorities that reflect Asia's growing predominance as the world's key strategic theatre, and Canada's responsibilities for North American defence and our Arctic frontier. While European security remains important geostrategically, Russia's actions have driven home the message to our European allies that they must now assume primary responsibility for their own defence and maintaining peace and security in Europe.

One major foreign policy initiative under Canada's Indo-Pacific Strategy should be the creation of a network of Strategic Partnerships chosen primarily from Asia's fellow democracies: India, Japan, Indonesia, South Korea, Australia, New Zealand, and the Philippines. While not a democracy, Vietnam is a rising Asian state of consequence.

Each Strategic Partnership would be "governed" by a Framework agreement with an Action Plan and overseen by regular joint sessions of Foreign, Defence, and Economic/Trade ministers and timely meetings of Heads of Government.

We would use this network to amplify Canada's voice and effectiveness in the region and on global affairs. The Partnerships could be used as consultative and coordination mechanisms, or more ambitiously to create informal coalitions for tackling regional and global challenges such as threats to security, the effects of climate change, or improving the performance of international institutions.

This network of Strategic Partnerships would also strengthen our standing in dealing with China, which prefers to deal one-on-one so as to maximize leverage from its size and power.

Finally, Canada has a strong record over decades of providing development aid, technical, and other assistance to Asian countries most in need. In many countries, such as Indonesia, this legacy of support is remembered very positively, often down to rural levels, and is part of the "Canada brand." This provides a solid foundation on which Canada can further build its reputation as a contributing member of the Indo-Pacific community. Despite the astounding economic development in Asia, there remain countries with an ongoing need for Canada's help and generosity.

## Awareness and People-to-People

While development assistance, business ties, and interpersonal contacts are important components behind public awareness of Canada in the region, much more can be done. Awareness differs from country to country: Indonesians appear to have little awareness of Canada, and vice versa, whereas those in other countries with large diaspora populations in Canada and tourism ties know us much better. Under a new strategy, studies should be done to understand better levels of awareness of Canada across the region and where efforts to advance awareness might best be focused. Indonesia appears to be one major country where special efforts are justified.

Also important is the need to improve awareness of the Indo-Pacific in Canada, especially if there is to be public support for a major shift in Canadian international priorities to the Indo-Pacific as a "vital interest." The Asia Pacific Foundation of Canada's most recent National Poll in December, 2021 reveals that Canadians "report limited general knowledge" about Asian countries. The good news is that the same poll also shows that younger Canadians are more inclined than their older compatriots to have warmer feelings toward Asia and to believe that Asia will have a positive impact on Canada. This bodes better for the future.[43]

Clearly, our new Indo-Pacific Strategy needs components that build awareness at both ends by strengthening the personal and intra-communal connectivity between Canada and Asia, between Canadians and Asians. Obviously, family connections between Asian Canadians and their home-lands are very important but non-Asian Canadians also need to be brought into the picture. Offering educational experiences through both universities and technical colleges should be an area of emphasis under our Action Plan for the Indo-Pacific strategy, plus sports and culture, all of which focus on youth and create life-long associations.

In 1997, Canada hosted the APEC Leaders' Summit in Vancouver, and in conjunction with it, an awareness-raising "Year of Asia-Pacific in Canada." After twenty five years, perhaps it is time for us to offer to host APEC again, to confirm to Asians that Canada intends to exercise its Indo-Pacific credentials, and to show Canadians that the future of the Indo Pacific will be part of their futures as well.

## Conclusion

The case for making Asia a region of "vital interest" for Canada rests on the argument that during this century Asia will become the world's dominant region in terms of all measures of power. Canada has the strategic choice of remaining locked in its more European and North American settings, or diversifying to pursue fully the opportunities available from an Asian destiny and to meet the security and other challenges that will arise.

The benefits from a bold Indo-Pacific strategy extend beyond the region. As Asia's share of global power grows, and our relative ranking declines, we can leverage Canada's membership in the Indo-Pacific community to sustain Canada's voice and influence in the international system. It will help us continue to bring Canadian views and positions to bear on matters of global significance and the working out of arrangements for meeting 21st-century challenges yet unknown.

# 6

# Canada and Australia
# Michael Small

F OR OVER a hundred years, speechwriters reaching for a handy phrase to describe Canada–Australia relations inevitably land on a family metaphor: The two countries are siblings or cousins in an Old Commonwealth family.[44] This metaphor does capture something about how the two countries see each other, but as a description of their place in the world, it belongs more to 1922 than 2022. The head of this household has long since ceased to be the original patriarch, Great Britain, and that role has passed to Uncle Sam. Except for New Zealand, which gets treated like a younger sibling, the rest of the kids have gone their separate ways. What's left of the metaphor is more sentiment than strategy. In an era of sharp geopolitical competition, strategy is what's needed now more than ever.

This chapter argues that Canada must fill the gap. Australia has had no lack of strategies that shape its foreign and defence policies, from its Australia in the Asian Century White Paper of 2012, its Foreign Policy White Paper of 2017, and its multiple Defence white papers and updates from 2009, 2013, 2016, and 2020. One need only look at the cover of the 2017 Australian Foreign Policy White Paper to grasp its focus: it shows a map of Asia with a super-imposed white circle that spans from India to Kamchatka to New Zealand, with Australia and ASEAN right in the middle. It is a screenshot of the Indo-Pacific. Canada is nowhere in this frame.

This should come as no surprise. As a thought experiment, if someone today in Australia were editing a book like this one on "Australia in the Indo-Pacific" no one would suggest that there should be a chapter on Canada. We simply do not register in that context currently in Canberra.

To understand how Australia fits into a Canadian strategy for the Indo-Pacific, it is helpful to take a more global look at how the two countries relate to each other. Imagine four concentric "rings of proximity" between the two countries, as follows.

## Ring One: Canada & Australia

The closest ring is our relationship with each other. In strict diplomatic terms, our bilateral relationship is constructive and uncomplicated. We exchange diplomatic cables and personnel between our foreign ministries. We have an agreement to co-locate missions in each other's Embassies.[45] We provide consular services to each other's citizens in countries where the other is not represented. Our armed forces have long-standing traditions of exchanging officers as part of maintaining service-to-service relationships. We have a very active bilateral youth mobility agreement. Overall, there is a great deal of breadth, but not as much depth. People-to-people ties are as important as institutional ones. Here is where the family metaphor still has some resonance. Canadians and Australians instinctively feel they understand each other, even if they have not spent much time together.

What generates energy in our bilateral relationship is that both countries regard the other as their closest natural comparator. We both have affluent, well-educated populations spread over large and often inhospitable continents. We have a common colonial founder, which gave both countries comparable political and legal institutions, a shared official language, and the same head of state. At independence, we opted for federalism to help manage the distances and differences within our borders. We are settler societies created by European migrants who actively recruit new citizens worldwide. Still, neither country has figured out how to successfully reconcile with its aboriginal peoples. We both have open, capital importing economies, which the rest of the world envies for our natural resources. Yet, most of our population live in large cities and earn their incomes from services or high technology industries that face real challenges from larger global competitors.

The result is that Canada and Australia constantly benchmark against each other in public policy. This has been going on since at least the 1970s when former Australian PM Gough Whitlam held up Canada as a frequent role model for the kind of modern Australia he was trying to build. More recently, the value of trying to institutionalize mutual learning led to the Canada-Australia Public Policy Initiative (CAPPI), signed by Prime Ministers Harper and Howard in 2007 and directed by our respective cabinet offices. This same sentiment inspired the private sector-led Australia-Canada Economic Leadership Forum launched in 2010.

What drives these initiatives is the intuition that if a given policy or program works well in one country, it could probably be adapted to work in the other one. In a world where the pressure to innovate is constant, both countries can lower the transaction costs of developing new public policies if we learn from each other's successes and failures. Foreign policy commentators tend to overlook this dynamic in the bilateral relationship because it revolves around domestic economic and social policy. But it makes Australia a point of reference for a far-wider range of federal departments, and some provincial ones, than any other country discussed in this volume.

Canada–Australia commercial relations also benefit from businesses' comfort level in operating in the other country. Each country is a second-tier merchandise export market for the other, amounting to C$4.5 billion in two-way merchandise trade in 2020, plus C$ 2.1 billion in services. Bilateral investment flows are more significant: Canada is Australia's eighth-largest destination for foreign direct investment, while Australia is Canada's fifth-largest outward investment destination and the largest in Asia-Pacific.[46] In good measure, this is because of the stable regulatory environment in both countries and the confidence investors have in the rule of law in both places. The CPTPP has removed most tariff and non-tariff barriers and ensured that a modern trade agreement is in place. The bilateral trade disputes which consumed considerable political bandwidth in the 1980s and 1990s are a thing of the past (though Canadian supply management quotas still rankle Australian free-trading sensibilities). Even Australia's action to take Canada to the WTO in 2018 over wine distribution in provincial liquor stores was resolved to Australia's satisfaction. Both sides reference it as an example of how international dispute mechanisms should work.

A shared interest in how business leaders in the other country view the world also drives private sector engagement. A look at the agenda of the Australia–Canada Economic Leadership Forum over the past ten years shows that almost all the sessions either compare performance in economic sectors that are important to both economies (ranging from energy to infrastructure, to agriculture) or they are discussions of how each country see trends in other parts of the world (the Indo-Pacific of course, but also the United States and sometimes Latin America). Bilateral relations per se attract comparatively little attention beyond introductory bromides from politicians.

## Ring Two: Five Eyes Relationship

The second circle is an informal but uniquely powerful arrangement: the Five Eyes security and intelligence-sharing arrangement among the United States, United Kingdom, Canada, Australia, and New Zealand. Its indispensable member, of course, is the United States, but each of the others makes a distinct contribution. The arrangement sustains a deep relationship of trust among these five governments around sharing vital national assets. The Five Eyes arrangement enables the daily work of more than half of the Canada-based staff in the Canadian High Commission in Canberra, representing every agency in Canada's national security community. Each of them is also accredited to New Zealand. Australia has fewer security agencies directly represented in Ottawa, but the others cover Ottawa from Washington. These patterns of representation reinforce the Five Eyes context of their work.

There are many Five Eyes meetings that rotate annually around the five member countries. While the most intense cooperation is around intelligence sharing, the same five-country formula has been applied to other areas of government. Thus, there is a long-standing five eyes conference of heads of immigration and border security, another one on citizenship, and another one on consular cooperation.

The Five Eyes relationship is the one that most connects vital Canadian national interests with Australian ones. It has enduring importance because it operates almost entirely at the level of career officials rather than politicians. Thus, it enjoys a high level of continuity between the participating governments, despite the changes of parties in power and ministers in key portfolios.

The announcement of the AUKUS agreement in September 2021, between the United States, United Kingdom, and Australia is potentially the most significant shift in the Five Eyes relationship since 9/11. All three signatories have declared that it does not represent a downgrading of existing Five Eyes cooperation, and there have been no early signals that belie that. However, AUKUS creates an inner circle of trust within the five to enable defence technology sharing and procurement in a range of critical technologies, starting with but not limited to nuclear-powered submarines. There is a clear risk for Canada that this unique relationship will turn into "Five Eyes in two tiers,"[47] with Canada parked in the lower tier, with reduced access and benefits to follow. Minimizing this risk should be a priority of Canada's Indo-Pacific strategy.

## Ring Three: Global Engagement

If we widen our focus on engaging the world, we have similar approaches to multilateralism, grounded in shared values and interests as democratic, open-market economies. Within the United Nations, Canada, Australia, and New Zealand have long supported each other's candidacies and used our respective diplomatic assets to assist each other's Security Council bids. As the second- and third-largest contributors to the Commonwealth, we work closely together to improve the performance of that organization. Australia was an inaugural member of the Ottawa group of countries that have met regularly since 2018 at the Ministerial level to look at ways to reform and revitalize the WTO. We bring similar concerns to the table in the G20. It is a natural reaction for our respective ministers and prime ministers to seek each other out regularly for bilaterals on the margins of multilateral meetings.

The bigger problem—which pre-occupies Australia as much as Canada— is that the existing institutions of global governance are not working well. The failure of the G20 to address the economic fallout of the COVID-19 pandemic is a case in point. There are many reasons for this decline in per- formance, but the rising tensions between the United States and China are prominent. As middle powers, both countries share a profound interest in defending the rules-based international order, especially when major powers act as if those rules do not apply to them. Australia was an early and vigorous supporter of Canada's initiative to build a coalition against arbitrary deten- tions. Our current mutual pre-occupation with Chinese coercive economic measures, and a longer-term concern over the predictability of U.S. foreign policy, has given Canadian and Australian leaders even more reasons to talk to each other.

In sum, Canada–Australia relations per se are in good shape when meas- ured against the first three rings of proximity. When we turn to the fourth ring, the Indo-Pacific, there is a conspicuous gap.

## Ring Four: the Indo-Pacific

This is the ring of proximity most directly relevant to this book. There is a clear differential between our two countries in the degree of attention paid to the Indo-Pacific for two fundamental reasons.

The first reason is a matter of geography. Asia has always been Australia's security backyard and the source of its most immediate security threats, from the spectre of uncontrolled Asian migration and marauding Russian Pacific fleets before World War I to the genuine threat of invasion by Imperial Japan in World War II, to periodic political instability in Indonesia, to gov- ernance failures in East Timor, Papua New Guinea and Solomon Islands, to China's rapid military modernization and aggressive territorial claims. By virtue of our geography, Canada has never faced comparable threats to our security from Asia, and it is unlikely that we ever will. For us, paying attention to this region always seemed like an option; for Australia, it is a necessity.

The second reason is a matter of economics. As important as the major Asian countries are as export markets and sources of investment for Canada, the entire Indo-Pacific in 2020 accounted for 10.5% of Canada's goods exports, while it accounts for 80.2% of Australia's.[48] Australia's twenty-nine year stretch of unbroken growth (until 2020) was fundamentally due to surging demand for its commodities from nearby markets in Asia. At the same time, Australia has been very successful in growing its export of services to Asia, especially in higher education and tourism. This gives Australia a far more significant economic stake than Canada in the region's continued prosperity; and on the flip side, a much greater economic vulnerability if supply chains are disrupted or markets closed due to political tensions or conflict.

This combination of threat and opportunity from their near neighbours has meant that Australian policymakers never take the region for granted. Diplomatically, Australia has ensured that it is an active and visible member of every Asian-centred body they can join. They were the co-founders with Korea of APEC in 1989 and took credit for convincing President Clinton to elevate it to a leader level forum in 1993. They lobbied intensively to join the East Asian Summit and succeeded in 2005. They were a founding member of the Quad, which in 2021 emerged as a key coordinating body for Indo-Pacific strategy.

Furthermore, in global fora, like the United Nations and the G20, Australia highlights its sensitivity to Asian concerns, for example, in its successful campaign for the U.N. Security Council in 2012 or its planning for its G20 year in 2014. The same focus is true of their trade policy strategies. Australia already has bilateral trade agreements with most of the region's major economies. They were an early joiner in the negotiations for the TPP and played a major role in supporting Japan's desire to reboot the agreement after the United States withdrew. At the same time, they are a member of RCEP, which includes China and their ASEAN partners. It is a hallmark of their foreign policy that they constantly try to mesh their bilateral with their multi-lateral diplomacy to advance their interests in the Indo-Pacific.

As amply documented in this book, the contrast with Canada's inconsistent engagement with the region is self-evident. Canadians seem to think that simply asserting that we are a country with a Pacific coastline and a G7 economy means we are entitled to have the welcome mat rolled out for us whenever we choose to show up. That may have been true twenty years ago, but as the stakes in the Indo-Pacific have gotten much higher, it is no longer true today. Both the previous Conservative government and the present Liberal government were surprised when their expressed desire to join the East Asian Summit and the ASEAN Defence Ministers Plus meetings were not welcomed. As Peter Jennings, the Director of ASPI, a Canberra based think-tank, put it plainly in a blog from mid-2014:

Here we come to the problem: Canberra is not disposed to support Ottawa's membership bids. The Australian perspective is that it has been difficult enough to assure our membership as an intrinsic part of the region. We back the Singaporean view ... that, at this stage, the priority should be put on the effectiveness of regional institutions rather than their inclusiveness ... The Canadian view has its own set of blinkers, which in their case goes to the amount of defence contact needed to sustain a credible level of Asia-Pacific engagement. Canadians don't accept that the price of entry to regional security cooperation is much higher than token military involvement in multilateral meetings.[49]

Canadians sometimes read reactions like this as Australian resentment against Canada seeking a presence in their backyard. Australians' natural competitive instincts (see the Olympics) can come to the fore when it comes to gaining access and influence in Asian capitals. More than one Canadian Ambassador in the region has found themselves cast by their Australian counterpart in some kind of public competition for bragging rights. And of course, we do directly compete for market-share in specific export sectors, such as higher education. But fundamentally, what Australia wants us to do is pull our weight if we seek a higher profile in the region.

What Canadians miss when they see Australians simply trying harder to position themselves in the Indo-Pacific, is the underlying strategic imperative they face. The United States will guarantee Canada's security from threats beyond North America, whether we ask them to or not. Australia operates with no such safety net. In the words of a distinguished Australian analyst, the constant, underlying theme of its foreign policy over the decades is "fear of abandonment."[50] Consequently, Australia constantly works to keep the United States engaged and committed to maintaining order on its side of the Pacific. In Australian thinking, a straight line connects the Battle of the Coral Sea in 1942 through the signing of the ANZUS Treaty in 1951, to the basing of U.S. Marines in Darwin in 2011, to the AUKUS pact of 2021.

It is also a matter of strategy that Australia now identifies China as the greatest long-term threat to their security. This reflects the sharp deterioration in their bilateral relations in just the last four years. This assessment is not universally shared in Australia: the Labour Party in Opposition strenuously criticized bellicose anti-Chinese positions taken by the Coalition government and argued for a more diplomatic, nuanced approach to the region.[51] But Labor has been careful not to criticize the AUKUS agreement itself, and when in power Labor has been just as determined to demonstrate their credentials as an ally the United States can count on. For several decades, Australian leaders from both sides of politics declared their firm intention to avoid being forced to choose between their security interests with the United States and their economic interests with China. Today, Australians feel that room for manoeuvre has disappeared, and they have decided to move even closer to the United States.

Canada instead faces what might be called a paralysis of choice. Precisely because our economic and security stakes in this region are not as high as Australia's, and other regions of the world—staring with the Arctic and NATO—have some claim on our modest defence capabilities, successive Canadian governments have avoided making new long-term security commitments in the Indo-Pacific. Canada has yet to issue any statement that explains our contribution to the security and prosperity of the Indo-Pacific. One looks in vain to find an articulation of Canada's approach to China beyond former Foreign Minister Garneau's brief public comments after the release of Michael Kovrig and Michael Spavor that Canada would, depending on the issue, "co-exist, co-operate, challenge, or compete" with China.

Studied ambiguity or fence-sitting is a time-honoured posture in Canadian public life (Mackenzie King elevated it to art form). It's not an

Australian approach to most problems. Instead, Australian policy-makers in the words of one well-placed Canadian observer, "have a remarkable appetite for strategic risk."[52] They have made their choices and are comfortable with them. They wonder when we will make ours.

## Conclusion

Every observer who looks at Canada–Australia relations comes away with the same question: why don't these two countries do more in the world together? A lack of formal architecture at the political level and the frequent turnover of Ministers in key portfolios on both sides is one reason. Our different degrees of engagement in the Indo-Pacific is another. A deeper reason is the very comparability of the two countries, located in opposite parts of the world. Each country knows the other will be there for them when they are really needed; the rest of the time, both governments are happy to regard the other as "not a problem." Instead, both governments prefer to invest more effort with bigger powers or dissimilar partners whose like-mindedness can't be taken for granted (e.g., Australia with Indonesia or Canada with Mexico).

Australia should matter to us as a benchmark for a Canadian Indo-Pacific strategy. Canada will never make the same scale of investments in the Indo-Pacific as Australia—they will always have far more skin in that game. From the vantage point of Canberra, the single most impressive investment we could make would be to increase our level of defence spending from 1.4% of GDP to bring it closer to Australia's 2.1% and to allocate more of that to the Indo-Pacific (as argued in the Geostrategic overview chapter). Given the current public mood in Canada and the present government's priorities, that seems a faint hope. But short of that ask, we can still learn some lessons from Australia about engaging more effectively in the Indo-Pacific.

First is the primacy they give to having a strategic view of the great power dynamics in the region, which they constantly keep in mind as they calculate their own diplomatic and security interventions. If you have a strategic view, other countries want to talk to you in a serious way, even if they don't wholly agree with you, in order to inform their security calculations.

Thus, a Canadian strategy for the region should be grounded in our view of how China will evolve, how the United States and its allies should respond, and where Canadian interests lie.

Second is the importance of having a publicly articulated national Indo-Pacific strategy: stated and re-stated at length in speeches by Ministers; which can be explained in host capitals by Canadian Ambassadors; and which can be analyzed and debated by parliamentarians, academics, and journalists. Since our last foreign policy review in 2005, Canada has become terrible at doing this. One looks for any coherent statement of the Liberal government's foreign policy beyond one impressive speech by Chrystia Freeland in June 2017 defending the rules-based international order. Articulating a strategy and putting it out in public not only guides our national choices, it tells other countries where we want to go. Without one, most outside observers wrongly assume we are doing nothing, and we get little credit for what we are doing.

Third, the security dimensions of our engagement with this region are seriously under-developed. Understanding the fractured security architecture in the Indo-Pacific has always been regarded as a niche activity in Canada. The last time we made a sustained contribution was through the Track 1.5 South China Sea dialogues that Canada co-sponsored with Indonesia in the 1990s. The Canadian Armed Forces, mainly through the Navy, regularly participate in major U.S.-led military exercises such as Rim of the Pacific and Talisman-Sabre. We significantly contribute to multi-national operations enforcing sanctions against North Korea. But beyond that, our very modest security contributions on a military-to-military basis in the region have little political visibility. Canada needs to pick a couple of issues—relating either to traditional or non-traditional security threats—and a couple of partner countries and make a sustained commitment to building security capacity for the long-term. The South Pacific would be an excellent place to start, given the match between their developmental priorities and ours and the weak capabilities of those states. A Canadian co-operative security program would be welcomed both by the Pacific Islands and by Australia and New Zealand. Whatever we do, the quantum of dollars spent is less important than doing it in a consistent way that speaks to Canadian capacities and local needs. That would demonstrate what the security prong of a Canadian Indo-Pacific strategy looks like.

Fourth, Canada should focus less on joining new regional security fora and more on adding value in flexible ways to existing security partners such as Australia or Japan. By doing that, we are much more likely to succeed in fleshing out Canada's role in a future Quad plus arrangement. The most significant pay-off would be to focus on making a serious contribution to the other defence technology priorities identified by AUKUS, i.e. "cyber capabilities, artificial intelligence, quantum technologies, and additional undersea capabilities.[53] We have significant capacities in those areas that could be leveraged to bring us into the new AUKUS technology sharing agreements without ever acquiring nuclear-powered submarines.

Fifth, we need to up our diplomatic game in the region by adopting the 2 plus 2 formula—joint foreign ministry and defence ministry talks—with Australia and others. Australia has used this formula for decades with the United States; they started doing the same with the United Kingdom and Japan around 2010, and they do so now with all of their major partners. Australia has floated versions of this idea with Canada for over ten years but, somehow, Global Affairs and National Defence can't get their heads around sharing a common agenda and speaking to their respective interlocutors in a joined-up way. Developing this habit amounts to table-stakes for being taken seriously on Indo-Pacific issues.

Sixth, we need to invest more in our analytical capacity inside the Canadian government to understand developments in the region. It is striking that Australia's lead analysis agency—the Office of National Assessments—has more than double the staff of its Canadian counterpart. Building this capacity should also involve being more open to a constant exchange of ideas with the private sector, academic institutions, and think tanks. Strengthening this kind of capacity in Global Affairs, in DND, and PCO is incredibly cheap compared to buying new military hardware. The structures required to recruit and develop these skills have always been there. Over time, what has atrophied is the appetite in Ottawa of senior decision makers for absorbing intelligence assessments and diplomatic reporting. But there is no point in increasing our tempo of high-level political-military talks or strategic dialogues if we have few insights of our own to bring to the table.

Finally, our greatest under-developed asset for deepening relations with regional partners like Australia is our proximity to the United States. Canada has always focused on managing our crucial bilateral relationship with the United States. But outside the realm of macroeconomics, less time is spent standing back from the cross-border fray and thinking about where the United States is headed as an economy, a society and a polity and how that will affect Canada and the rest of the world. It is astonishing that while there is a very well-funded U.S. Studies Centre at the University of Sydney, there is nothing comparable at any Canadian university, despite our geographic proximity and our far deeper economic relationship with the United States. Given the 2016 and 2020 elections results, it is obvious that the consensus positions that guided U.S. foreign policy for decades have been substantially weakened, and the continuity of U.S. foreign policy is now in some doubt. This is not a happy fact for Canada, Australia, or any other close U.S. ally to acknowledge. But not talking about it will not make it any easier to manage. If Canada has a region, it is North America. Our perspectives on how to relate to our local superpower will be of interest to interlocutors far beyond our backyard.

# 7

# Canada and China
## Jeff Nankivell

O F ALL the bilateral relationships treated in this volume, the trajectory of the Canada–China relationship may be the one about which there is the least certainty in making predictions for the next decade.

For a start, there is the question of what kind of China the world will see in 2030. The total physical closure of China since early 2020 to foreign visitors—and, exceptionally among countries, even to many long-term foreign residents seeking to return—raises fundamental questions about how to open Xi Jinping's China will be when COVID-19 eventually ceases to be a justification for border closure.

This trend away from openness, already at a level not seen since the late 1970s in terms of the treatment of foreign journalists, is putting many other critical connections to the rest of the world at risk. For example, while the evidence of China's universities moving to constrain foreign research partnerships and other exchanges is mixed, it seems likely that party authorities will be much more selective in allowing such partnerships and exchanges in the coming years. They will be subject to more restrictions in areas such as field of study and choice of partners. And if pursued seriously in practice, the new Party doctrine of "Dual Circulation," suggesting parallel drives for self-sufficiency at home and export dominance abroad, has the potential to lower the trajectory of China's commercial relations with many countries.

Both China and the United States will continue military buildups. The United States will step up its alliance-building efforts in Asia. There will be decoupling in specific areas of high-technology research and development and U.S.-imposed embargos on tech inputs (goods and services) to PRC-linked buyers by American companies and by foreign companies with American companies' business ties. That said, based on evidence to date,[54] and unless protracted war in Ukraine leads to a hard global division between American and Sino-Russian client states—outside of some high-tech industries, it is unlikely that we will see a general disengagement from China by corporate America, and the U.S. administration is likely to continue to seek to pry open China's market to U.S. exports.

For Canada, this means any engagement strategy formulated now will need to have built-in flexibility to accommodate shifts in critical aspects of its operating environment. For example, a more thoroughgoing U.S. embargo of a wide range of technologies may dramatically constrain the choices available to Canada's government, research institutions, and firms when working with partners in China. In this context, companies, business organizations, their supporting public institutions, and governments will need to make ongoing assessments of the medium- and long-term implications for them of any such decoupling trends in the United States and among our other allies.

## Why Does Engagement with China Matter?

It is hard to imagine how Canada could have a successful Indo-Pacific engagement strategy without effectively managing its relationship with China. China is simply too big a player in the region, with enormous and still-growing influence across all spheres of business, technology, politics, security, public health, and climate action.

Readers will no doubt already be aware of some basic facts, based on recent trends and reasonable assumptions: at some point in the next decade, China will overtake the United States as the world's largest national economy;[55] it will account for more than one-fifth of global economic growth in the coming decade.[56] China will be home to more than one-third of the one billion or so people who will join the global middle class in the next decade.[57] As its consumers see their real incomes rise steadily, its demand for goods and services of all kinds will continue to grow in volumes not offered by any other market.

For Canada specifically and most other countries, China has been the fastest-growing export market for the past fifteen years and more.[58] This includes the period of the pandemic, during which Canadian exports to China grew while exports to almost all other countries shrank.

In addition to these quantitative factors, China is a technology leader and standard setter in several key sectors. The IMF estimates 120 of the world's 190 economies, including every country in the Indo-Pacific except for Bhutan, have China as their number one trading partner.[59] Turning our backs on China risks shutting Canadians out of market opportunities in China and many third countries while also removing options for supply chain sourcing and global distribution partnerships.

## Not Everyone Agrees

China is also unique among the countries treated in this volume for being the only one about which there is serious discussion of dramatically *reducing* Canadian engagement.

This is primarily the result of actions by China's party-state authorities, agencies, and enterprises. This assertion is contested; some observers feel that alarm about China's behaviour is driven mainly by Washington's desire to block China's rise. However, such a view fails to account for the numerous governments, institutions, and individuals whose natural inclination and material interest would be to welcome deeper engagement with China but who find themselves reluctantly—in some cases very reluctantly—driven to take a more China-skeptic position. The Government of Canada falls within this category. It has plenty of company.

The PRC actions in question will also be familiar to readers. The briefest of summaries would include employment of coercive trade measures against Australia, Canada, South Korea, Norway, and other countries; technology theft; militarization of the South China Sea and rejection of the arbitral tribunal ruling on competing claims with the Philippines; moral support for Putin's invasion of Ukraine; harassment, intimidation and co-optation of Chinese citizens and people of Chinese origin resident in western countries; and, for Canadians, the arbitrary detention of Michael Kovrig and Michael Spavor. Relevant domestic actions of China's party-state include large-scale human rights abuses targeting Xinjiang's Uyghur ethnic minority, long-standing persecution of lawyers and human rights advocates of all kinds, political repression in Hong Kong in defiance of explicit international commitments, and worrying new trends in repression of LGBTQ and women's rights advocates.

Such actions abroad and at home have resulted in a steep drop in trust in China as a partner, as has been well documented in the regular opinion-polling on attitudes toward Asia by the Asia Pacific Foundation of Canada[60] and the Pew Research Institute[61], among others.

So, uniquely among major countries in the Indo-Pacific, China presents itself to Canada with a question mark. *Should* Canada engage?

What would it mean for Canada to choose a path of significantly reduced engagement with China?

On the assumption that China would reciprocate Canada's disengagement in such a scenario, a plausible set of outcomes could look like this:

- Many Canadian exporters shut out of the market, delivering the greatest growth opportunities;

- Canadian higher education suffers from a drop in students from China, with a loss of fees (though some would be made up by students from elsewhere, given recent diversification trends);

- Loss of some of the highest-quality graduate students and researchers in the world. It would be harder to offset this loss entirely by intake from elsewhere;

- Loss of foreign direct investment (though with a stock of $20 billion, China stands as only the seventh-largest direct investor in Canada, at less than 5% of the U.S.' investment volume[62]);

- Canadian tech firms could be less competitive in some markets due to the inability to access components from China;

- China could block Canadian accession to regional trade and security bodies;

In such a world, can we confidently assume that having successfully pressured allies such as Canada to reduce their engagement, Washington would not keep open to itself the full range of engagement options—for example, continuing to negotiate bilateral trade deals to guarantee purchase of American products over those of other suppliers? Can Canada count on any reward for forgoing economic and geopolitical opportunities?

In light of such considerations, it is proposed here that it is in Canada's interest to maximize engagement with China, *to the extent compatible with our national security, our ability to express our values, and the constraints that could be unavoidable due to a more aggressive disengagement from and confrontation with China by the United States.*

## How Are We Doing?

By most measures, Canada has underperformed its peers in accessing the China market and in attracting FDI from China. For example, in both categories, Australia stands out as having grown its exports and market share in China consistently over the past 25 years while attracting almost three times Canada's volume of FDI from China.[63]

In terms of building societal capacity to engage effectively with China, where Canada has only a few small-scale programs to support China-focused education and exchanges, the United States and Australia, both federal states like Canada, with education delivered at the state level, have managed to establish robust, well-resourced national programs to fund language training, research, and exchanges. One example (of several) in the United States is the federally funded Chinese Flagship Program,[64] offered at 13 universities and colleges and providing four to five years of accelerated language learning and individualized tutoring customized to the student's field of study/future career.

Under Australia's New Colombo Plan,[65] Canberra supports some 10,000 Australian undergraduate students per year to undertake internships, language study, research trips, and study abroad in Indo-Pacific countries for up to one year. The ambition: "The Australian Government wants study and work-based experiences in the Indo-Pacific to become a rite of passage for young Australian undergraduate students."[66]

Singapore sets the gold standard for official bilateral engagement with China and depth of understanding of China in government. A Deputy PM-led high-level joint annual dialogues since 2002, supported by ongoing working groups in functional areas, has driven year-round collaboration and coherence among ministers and departments. Such mechanisms also exist at the provincial level with several Chinese provinces. Having such a regular high-level exercise over so many years, with demand for and tracking of deliverables on an annual or even more frequent basis, has been a key driver of sustained political and senior public service engagement for Singapore, while also building personal ties with Chinese counterparts at various levels, including notably promising provincial leaders who eventually ascend to national office.

## An Engagement Strategy

Engaging effectively with China will require long-term actions by the Government of Canada at home and abroad.

In the short term, at the time of writing this paper in early 2022, a plan for anything other than disengagement will have to take account of the skepticism of a large majority of Canadians regarding trade and investment ties with China. In such a political climate, even the thought of a major bilateral trade agreement with China is probably a non-starter, a situation that could take years—if ever—to turn around. (That said, our trade does not by any means require an FTA to grow considerably, given China's needs for much of what Canadian exports.)

Having previewed but then shied away from announcing an explicit strategy for China relations for the past few years, the Liberal Government will need, at a minimum, to embed a clearly articulated approach to China within the broader "Indo-Pacific" strategy expected to be launched sometime in late 2022. By treating China within a broader regional perspective, the Government can provide reassurance to skeptical Canadians that it has a serious plan to diversify export markets in Asia beyond China, which should, in theory, have the effect of reducing Canada's vulnerability to any coercive trade measures by China. Along similar lines, while a bilateral trade agreement is not likely, a path forward to mutual trade liberalization—if desired—may eventually be offered through a regional, multi-country agreement such as the CPTPP[67]or global multilateral agreements.

At the same time, the Government needs to have the confidence to make the case—no small matter, in a highly partisan, highly-charged media environment—to support Canadian businesses to pursue opportunities in the country that offer the greatest share of global growth in the coming decade. Those same businesses and their national associations will need to explain to stakeholders and the general public how their activities are beneficial for the Canadian economy and how security, ethical, reputational, and other risks can be mitigated. Other aspects of gaining a social license for China engagement are addressed below.

Five priority Canadian actions to enable effective engagement with China are suggested here:

**1. Remain true to our values:** Canada should continue to speak up consistently and objectively on issues related to human rights and a rules-based international order. We have an obligation to ourselves and humanity to hold to account national governments that do not uphold their obligations on matters such as coercive trade measures, hostage diplomacy, and transparency on public health. While this is a fundamental policy for a society such as Canada's, it is also clearly in our material self-interest to build international solidarity around norms that some state actions are simply not acceptable. This will mean continuing to speak up on specific issues.

We also must resist improper foreign interference in our society and institutions, including harassment of people on Canadian soil. A credible regime for doing so must include measures such as legislation on foreign interference with political parties and public officials and significantly increased human and technical resources for investigating and prosecuting cases of harassment of residents of Canada by foreign agents. Success in this area can be measured by:

- actions are taken together by like-minded countries to respond collect-
ively to coercive diplomacy, including not taking commercial advantage of each other when China imposes arbitrary trade measures;
- indications that international pressure has improved human rights
observance in China (the dramatic decline in executions, from an estimated 12,000 in 2002 to 2,000 in 2018, is one example[68]);
- a decrease in reports of interference and harassment on Canadian soil.

**2. Be mindful of security:** Where business and research collaborations pose
legitimate security threats to our national interest, care should be taken to
define such areas as narrowly as possible, with a presumption toward openness in research partnerships as being of fundamental value to our society
and prosperity. This will require a robust and clearly defined regime for pro-
tecting sensitive technologies from espionage and acquisition attempts for
undesirable purposes by PRC State/Party organs. This includes establishing
clear guidance from federal authorities on what technologies are off-lim-
its. That, in turn, requires those agencies to be well-resourced to manage
assessments in an expert and timely manner. Universities, accelerators, and
other tech organizations & companies need to develop reasonable internal
procedures for identifying and assessing risk.[69]

Success in this area could be measured by:

- Establishment of clear guidelines consulted with stakeholders, and
provision of adequate institutional resources for assessment and
enforcement;
- Successful prosecutions of offenders; and
- Avoiding leakage of sensitive technological and other information
while minimizing the chilling of legitimate research partnerships and
the arbitrary pressure of researchers of Chinese origin.

**3. Support Canadians to access economic opportunities:** offered by
China's growth. China is not monolithic; it is a vast country and complex
society with many private companies, dynamic entrepreneurs, and global
leadership in technologies of the 21st century, including electric vehicles,

e-commerce, clean technologies, and renewable energy. China's growth offers unparalleled opportunities for Canadians in areas such as agri-food, health technologies, educational services, clean technologies, and energy transition. We can pursue business opportunities and support our businesses with information and other resources to help them succeed.

Businesses need to do their due diligence regarding partners in/from the PRC, using information resources from Government and other service providers. Canada's Trade Commissioner Service is one source of support, alongside crown corporations Export Development Canada (EDC), the Business Development Bank of Canada (BDC), and the Canadian Commercial Corporation (CCC). The government will need to ensure that these organizations are fully resourced to fulfil this mandate, which includes helping Canadian businesses to understand risks associated with human-rights abuses in supply chains and with unscrupulous local partners with a track record of leaning on local authorities to squeeze foreign partners.

Maintaining clear, firm Government of Canada positions on the values issues identified in priority action #1 above is critical to gain Canadians' social license for promoting expanded commercial engagement with China. With robust support systems to help Canadian businesses and consumers make well-informed decisions and comply with Canadian laws and ethical standards, the government would be well-positioned to work through official bilateral channels and directly engage with non-state players and the public in China open new market opportunities for Canadian businesses. Promising areas include agri-food, cleantech, healthcare services and technologies, educational services and "healthy lifestyle" consumer goods and experiences, to be supported by promoting Canada's brand as a reliable, ethical supplier of high-quality goods services, and consumer experiences in China and Canada.

On investment, reciprocity of treatment must be a key objective of Canadian policy. At the same time, we are interested in developing and publishing clear guidelines on what types of proposed foreign investments will be subject to review for national security and national benefits reasons. This is needed as much by current owners of assets in Canada (potential sellers) as by would-be acquirers and is especially required by communities living in areas where greenfield, job- and spinoff-creating investments could be attracted.

Beijing's increasing restrictions on the management of data and flows of financial information will present significant challenges for Canadian investors and exporters of services. This will make it all the more important that Canada's trade commissioner service is well-resourced in China and elsewhere to help companies (and those who advise them) to have the best possible understanding of China's opaque and still-unpredictable regulatory regimes. At the same time, this is an area where Canada can benefit by making common cause with other countries whose businesses are active in China to pressure Beijing to reverse recent trends toward less transparency. It may be helpful to invoke reciprocity in some form as part of such discussions. However, it will not be symmetrical, given that transparency standards in free-market economies are general and, unlike tariffs, cannot be lowered or raised in bargaining with individual partner countries.

Finally, and crucially, to realize any ambition for higher trade volumes to Asia, governments in Canada must make or facilitate urgent, large-scale investments in hard and soft infrastructure, including maritime port capacity, air cargo facilities, and logistics zones, as well as information technology infrastructure. Industrial policy is urgently needed to promote the development of higher value-added processing capabilities in agri-food, minerals, energy, and other natural resources. Canadians can capture more of the benefits of supplying growing markets abroad.

Measures of success under priority #3 could include:

- volume and diversity of Canadian exports to China;
- whether exports of new, higher-value products are growing;
- Chinese consumer awareness of Canadian brands;
- Canadian firms able to source ethically with confidence; and
- Investors and local communities have access to clear guidelines on what type of FDI is welcome and what is not.

**4. Invest in China- and Asia competency**: We need to equip ourselves as Canadians to understand and engage with China and the rest of Asia. This means increased public investment in China- and Asia-related curriculum—including language training—in our schools, opportunities for young Canadians to have study and work experiences in China and other places in Asia, and sustained investment in China- and Asia-related research and networks.

Businesses need to equip themselves with Board members, executives and staff who have some Asia competency, with the highest priority for most companies being China competency. Such individuals should be able to provide insights on such matters as the potential China market for the company's products, how to assess the reliability of potential suppliers and partners, and—not the least—how to track potential competition from China-based companies in Canada and third countries.

Fortunately, younger Canadians coming into the labour market are already much more China-savvy than the preceding generation.[70] The labour market in Canada will see an increasing supply of recruits with the requisite technical skills who also possess language and cultural awareness relevant to doing business in China and in a world where China-based firms play an ever-larger role.

Civil society organizations also need to conduct due diligence on engagement with partners in/from the PRC while remaining open to exchange and dialogue. Initiatives that provide exposure to the breadth and diversity of society in the PRC should be encouraged, along with engagement in culture and sports.

The education sector at all levels, from primary to post-secondary, has a vital role in preparing Canadians for a world in which China plays an ever-larger role. There is an urgent need to modernize primary and secondary school curricula across the country to include content on China and Asia and offer Chinese language classes as an option for young learners in the public-school systems. Leaving this task to agencies of the Government of China has proven to be highly problematic, underlining the need for provinces to step up to provide necessary resources. It can be done; working with the British Columbia government, the Asia Pacific Foundation of Canada has established a successful pilot program of curriculum modules on Asia now being used in some BC schools.[71]

We must also follow other countries in facilitating opportunities for young Canadians to have a study or work experience in China, when conditions permit. The Global Skills Opportunity program launched by the federal government in 2021 to support student experiences abroad in "non-traditional" destination countries is a good start.[72]

Success in building China competency can be measured by:

- increasing numbers of Canadian students gaining exposure to China- and Asia-focused curriculum at all levels of the education system across the country;
- increasing numbers of Canadians gaining access to training in Chinese language (Cantonese as well as Mandarin);
- increasing numbers of Canadians having a study or work abroad experience in China; and
- surveys of corporate board composition indicating increasing numbers of directors with China competency.

**5. Seek meaningful bilateral engagement**: Being able to engage with China comprehensively on a government-to-government basis at all levels is in our national interest. While access to high-level official thinking within China's opaque political system is a considerable challenge, Beijing likely sees Canada as:

- a reliable, stable source of natural resources that will be needed in greater amounts as China's economy continues to grow;
- a stable source of agri-food products and technologies, of growing importance due to China's growing domestic challenges with water and soil;
- a destination for foreign investment, to secure access to resources and also a low-risk environment for capital preservation, needed to support China's growing pension needs;
- a partner for technological innovation, through both commercial deals and university research;
- a potential ally on global trade-policy issues; and
- at the same time, generally, subservient to U.S. foreign-, defence- and trade policy interests, and motivated by a U.S.-led intent to constrain China's economic and political rise.

In this context, and to pursue the objectives outlined above on values, commerce, and security, **we should strive to establish productive relationships between our respective policymakers, technical experts and public institutions.** Some of this will necessarily be constrained by our values-based advocacy, but our goal should be to seek such relationships where possible. Not to do so will mean marginalizing ourselves (and effectively giving our proxy to the United States) in regional and global policymaking on issues essential to the health, safety, values, and prosperity of Canadians in areas such as climate change, public health, technology standards, and rules for trade and investment. An excellent first step, as suggested by an informal working group of Canadian experts on China convened by the Asia Pacific Foundation of Canada in June 2021, is to establish a rapid-response bilateral working group to deal with irritants such as standards enforcement, customs inspection issues, labelling and trade remedy actions, with an overall coordinating centre established within each government, requiring an initial response within a set period (say, thirty days).

Success in implementing priority #5 would be measured by:

- examples of effective use of official channels to resolve bilateral trade and investment irritants; and
- examples of Chinese support for Canadian initiatives in multilateral forums and Canadian participation in regional trade and security architecture.

## Practical Considerations

To be effective, a made-in-Canada strategy for China engagement needs to include:

- provision of substantial new budgetary resources, for a range of departments well beyond Global Affairs Canada, including ministries and agencies responsible for health, agriculture, environment, innovation, science and economic development, natural resources, public safety, and northern affairs, and providing for investments beyond core

government to help build China capacity in business, NGOs, and educational institutions;
- specific, aligned provisions in mandate letters for all relevant ministers
over consecutive mandates, with key performance indicators;
- prime ministerial leadership, with buy-in from the finance minister;
- a commitment by the prime minister, ministers and senior officials to
travel regularly to Asia, including China as conditions permit, to build
relationships with counterparts and show Canada's resolve; and
- regular federal-provincial consultation and coordination, with buy-in
from provincial and territorial first ministers.

At the same time, **Canada's overall strategy for the Indo-Pacific region**
should maximize our autonomy to make policy choices based on Canadian
interests. Success in building stronger relationships with middle powers in
the region will strengthen Canada's hand in dealing with China and preserve our ability to make policy choices independent of American priorities
where these do not align with our interests.

A China that recognizes Canada as an independent actor with strong
partnerships in the region may be more likely to heed Canadian positions
on bilateral, regional, and global issues to Canada's benefit.

An approach based on the ideas in this paper will necessarily be highly
conditional on the environmental factors outlined in the opening sections,
including how open China will be to engage in general, how far the United
States and other Western allies go in decoupling or otherwise setting
boundaries on engagement with China, whether Canadian public opinion on engagement with China continues to harden, and ultimately, on the
choices freely made by the Canadian private- and public-sector actors, based
on their weighing of relative opportunities and risks for them in China and
elsewhere. The duty of policymakers will be to ensure that these Canadians
have access to the very best information, tools, and strategic perspectives to
enable them to make well-informed decisions about whether and how to
engage in what will surely be an extremely dynamic environment between
now and 2030.

# 8

# Canada and ASEAN

## The Hon. Jean Charest, Wayne C. Farmer, the Canada-ASEAN Business Council (CABC), with input from the C.D. Howe Institute

T HE ASSOCIATION of Southeast Asian Nations (ASEAN) is a regional organization formed of ten Southeast Asian Member States, including Brunei, Cambodia, Indonesia, Laos, Malaysia, Myanmar, the Philippines, Singapore, Thailand, and Vietnam, to promote regional stability, trade, and economic growth.[73] ASEAN encompasses approximately 622 million people (the majority under the age of 30), has an average annual growth rate of 5%, and is projected to have the fourth-largest economy by 2050.[74] The rising importance of ASEAN, due to its central role in regional affairs, its countries' rapidly growing populations and economies, and its strategic location in global trade routes, positions the organization as the key to the development of Canada's Indo-Pacific strategy. The launch of negotiations for a Canada-ASEAN Free Trade Agreement in the fall of 2021 set the foundation for a robust relationship between Canada and ASEAN with immense future mutual benefit.

The ASEAN region holds many opportunities for Canada, driven by its sizeable and diverse economies, fast-paced growth, and rise of its middle class. In 2020, the estimated total GDP of all ASEAN states increased significantly to approximately US$3.08 trillion.[75] According to data collected by the University of Toronto's Munk School, ASEAN is the second-largest destination (after China) for Canadian companies located in Asia, with 256 companies in 651 locations; it is a growing and important hub for Canadian businesses.[76]

ASEAN is an attractive trade partner with its increasing and active participation in leading multilateral trade agreements, such as the Comprehensive and Progressive Agreement for Trans-Pacific Partnership (CPTPP) (signed in March 2018) and the Regional Comprehensive Economic Partnership (RCEP) agreement (signed in November 2020). Four of the ASEAN Member States (AMS) are signatories of the CPTPP, and six have ratified the RCEP, which came into force on January 1, 2022. RCEP is the world's largest free trade agreement, bringing together the 10 AMS and 5 of ASEAN's existing FTA partners in the Asia-Pacific. It accounts for nearly 30% of global GDP and a third of the world population.[77]

Trade agreements such as these are rapidly opening Asian markets and increasing the ease of trade and doing business, creating enormous potential for Canadian firms.

ASEAN is the Indo-Pacific's geographical trade and consumer centre and represents Canada's sixth-largest trading partner.[78] Recently strained ties with China and the ongoing migration of labour-intensive supply chains from China to emerging ASEAN markets re-emphasize ASEAN's importance.[79] This is demonstrated by Canada's private sector increasingly taking or considering a "China Plus One" strategy.

Historically, Canada's Asian lens has overwhelmingly focused on China and, to a lesser extent, India, Japan, and South Korea. However, changing demographics in the AMS position the region as an optimal destination for increased Canadian investment and business expansion. Consumer spending in developing Asia is likely to reach $32 trillion and comprise approximately 43% of worldwide consumption by 2030, making ASEAN a key driver for worldwide consumption and a lucrative destination for Canadian exporters.[80]

As the fourth-largest market for Canadian agri-food exports, ASEAN is a vital key for Canada.[81] In 2018, Canada–ASEAN trade in agriculture, agri-food, fish, and seafood totalled CAD 4.1 billion, with Canada exporting CAD 2 billion to the region.[82] The top three export destinations were Indonesia, Vietnam, and the Philippines.[83] As Southeast Asian countries develop and populations grow, rising food demand offers vast opportunities for Canada's agri-food commodity exports, such as grains, dairy products, pulses, meats, soybeans, and branded consumer food products.[84] An FTA with ASEAN will maintain Canada's competitiveness and level the playing field vis-à-vis other ASEAN trading partners like Australia and New Zealand.

## The Bilateral Picture

Bilateral merchandise trade between Canada and ASEAN grew by about 6.4% per annum over the past two decades, with Canadian imports from ASEAN rising by approximately 6% per annum.[85] ASEAN is an increasingly significant trading partner, and Canada needs to enter a formal trade agreement to reap the maximum benefit from the relationship.[86] The launch of negotiations for a Canada–ASEAN FTA in 2021, on the heels of the signing of the CPTPP in 2018, marks a key milestone in providing more access to ASEAN's emerging markets for Canadians.

Thus far, Canada's trade relationship with ASEAN has been inconsistent and slow to develop; the full potential of bilateral trade with the growing bloc (See Appendix A for a Canada-ASEAN trade timeline) remains unrealized. While the launch of official FTA negotiations is welcome, more action is needed to ensure robust and resilient trade ties with the region.

According to the C.D. Howe Institute's latest economic analysis, a Canada–ASEAN FTA, based on the RCEP template, would provide economic welfare gains of CAD 1.66 billion by 2035 and boost the value of GDP by 0.051% in the baseline in 2035. A more ambitious tariff elimination could further increase GDP value gains to CAD 2.13 billion and economic welfare gains to CAD 1.6 billion, respectively (see Table 1).[87] In the RCEP scenario, bilateral trade is projected to increase by approximately CAD 3 billion; more ambitious tariff reductions see this rise to CAD 4.5 billion.[88] Services sectors stand to make the most substantial gains, with pork and poultry, oilseeds and vegetable oils, and machinery and equipment also projected to see significant increases in farm/factory-gate shipments (for more information on the sectoral impacts of a Canada-ASEAN FTA, see Appendix B).[89]

Table 1: Macroeconomic Impacts of the ACFTA on Canada[90]

| | RCEP Template | Ambitious Tariff Reduction |
|---|---|---|
| Major Indicators | | |
| Economic Welfare (CAD millions) | 1,165 | 1,605 |
| Economic Welfare (% change) | 0.044 | 0.061 |
| GDP Value Change (CAD millions) | 1,657 | 2,134 |
| GDP Value Change (%) | 0.051 | 0.066 |
| GDP Volume (% change) | 0.021 | 0.031 |
| GDP Deflator (% change) | 0.031 | 0.035 |
| CPI (% change) | 0.017 | 0.014 |
| Terms of Trade (% change) | 0.027 | 0.038 |
| Real GDP Expenditure Components | | |
| Consumption (% change) | 0.054 | 0.069 |
| Government Expenditure (% change) | 0.056 | 0.072 |
| Investment (% change) | 0.032 | 0.047 |
| Total Exports of Goods and Services (% change) | 0.046 | 0.074 |
| Total Imports of Goods and Services (% change) | 0.080 | 0.122 |
| International Trade | | |
| Bilateral Exports of Goods and Services (CAD millions) | 1,387 | 1,981 |
| Bilateral Imports of Goods and Services (CAD millions) | 1,378 | 2,340 |
| Total Exports of Goods and Services (CAD millions) | 609 | 921 |
| Total Imports of Goods and Services (CAD millions) | 804 | 1,205 |
| Trade Balance (CAD millions) | -195 | -284 |
| Factor Markets | | |
| Capital Stock (% change) | 0.016 | 0.024 |
| Real wage Unskilled (% change) | 0.025 | 0.038 |
| Real wage Skilled (% change) | 0.021 | 0.032 |
| Labour (number of jobs) | 1,815 | 2,799 |
| Unskilled | 1,328 | 2,047 |
| Skilled | 487 | 752 |
| Jobs (% change) | 0.008 | 0.013 |
| Labour productivity (% change) | 0.012 | 0.018 |
| Key Ratios | | |
| Real GDP/Real Trade | 0.33 | 0.32 |
| Real Wages/Productivity | 1.92 | 2.03 |

To correct the underperformance of Canada in the ASEAN market, Canada's Indo-Pacific strategy should prioritize a trade agreement with ASEAN. A defining feature of the RCEP is that it integrates all the ASEAN FTA partners, and a Canada–ASEAN FTA would position Canada as an ASEAN Plus One partner, fulfilling a prerequisite for joining RCEP.[91] Beyond these optimistic impact forecasts, a Canada–ASEAN FTA would diversify Canadian trade by providing Canada with a more substantial export base that would act as a catalyst to galvanize more business and economic activities with ASEAN and the rest of the Indo-Pacific.

In addition to a Canada–ASEAN FTA, Canada should pursue complementary bilateral trade agreements, such as the Canada-Indonesia Comprehensive Economic Partnership Agreement (CEPA), the negotiation for which was launched on June 20, 2021. Additional bilateral trade agreements with countries such as the Philippines and Thailand could offer preferential access to key markets in ASEAN.

With access to 15 FTAs, Canada is also an attractive trading partner for ASEAN and an ideal gateway into the major markets of Europe, North and Latin America. Canada's highly skilled workforce, relatively low corporate tax rates, and ease of doing business make the country an excellent location for ASEAN businesses to expand and set up global offices. ASEAN also stands to make substantial gains from an FTA, as demonstrated by the projected export gains in Table 2.

**Table 2:  ASEAN's Leading Bilateral Export Gains, CAD millions[92]**

|                                  | Canada's Bilateral Imports from ASEAN |
| -------------------------------- | ------------------------------------- |
| Textiles and Apparel             | 417                                   |
| Other Manufacturing              | 224                                   |
| Chemicals Rubber and Plastics    | 210                                   |
| Food Products                    | 121                                   |
| Machinery and Equipment          | 107                                   |

# The Role of Canadian Businesses and Civil Society

Southeast Asia hosts many leading Canadian companies that have flourished in the region's diverse and emerging economies, such as Manulife, Bank of Montreal (BMO), Scotiabank, National Bank of Canada, Sun Life Financial, Canpotex, OpenText, Toronto Dominion Bank, Canadian Imperial Bank of Commerce (CIBC), Canadian National Railway, CAE Inc., Shopify, TELUS International, and others. Companies successful in Southeast Asia play an active role in thought leadership and regional development, increasing Canada's business community's visibility and positive perception.

Successful Canadian companies can serve as leading examples and guides for prospective companies seeking to expand into ASEAN. Groups such as the Singapore-based Canada–ASEAN Business Council (CABC) represent Canada's private sector interests in ASEAN and provide necessary policy advocacy, networking, education, and connectivity for expansion into ASEAN. Leading Canada-based think tanks, research institutes, and business councils such as the C.D. Howe Institute, the Asia Pacific Foundation of Canada, and the Business Council of Canada are also strong voices raising awareness for the mutual benefits of increased Canada–ASEAN integration.

## Security and Development

Currently, Canada plays a limited role in providing security support to the ASEAN region. It lacks defence agreements with any ASEAN country and has no multilateral defence agreement with countries from Southeast Asia.[93] While Canada attends regional meetings such as the Shangri-La Dialogue and the ASEAN Defence Ministers' meeting, it is neither a member of the Quadrilateral Security Dialogue (QSD) nor the East Asia Summit the new AUKUS security group between the United States, Australia, and the United Kingdom. Without significant and long-term security investment and participation in the region, Canada should not expect membership in these groups anytime soon.

Non-traditional security challenges, such as climate change, food security, energy security, transnational crime, and pandemics, which all pose significant threats to Southeast Asia, are often neglected by countries outside the region. With its experience and expertise in these areas, Canada is well-positioned to support ASEAN countries dealing with such challenges.

## A Partner in Food Security

Canada's agricultural expertise can help solidify its position as an essential partner and build a deeper relationship with ASEAN. Approximately 60 million people in ASEAN are undernourished, particularly in Laos, Cambodia, and Myanmar.[94] Canadian technology and agri-food commodities are essential in supplying ASEAN with the means to diversify their food sources and produce self-sufficiently using sustainable methods.

Being a leader in researching and developing agri-tech and plant-based protein well positions Canada to help address Southeast Asia's food security challenges. ASEAN governments may also leverage government-to-government buying and procurement from Canada for food staples to ensure a sustainable food supply.

The food supply strain in Southeast Asia will be stretched even further in light of the current geopolitical crisis. The impact of the ongoing Russia–Ukraine War on Southeast Asia's food supply and food prices is projected to be stark, as seen by the 30% rise in global prices for wheat and barley, the 60% increase in rapeseed and sunflower oil prices, and a large hike in fertilizer prices in the first half of 2022.[95]

While Russia and Ukraine combine account for nearly a third of the world's cereal exports,[96] Canada is among the top four largest producers of wheat in the world and a well-recognized stable and high-quality supplier of many food staples. It is time for Canada to be proactive and play an even more instrumental role in supporting Southeast Asia (and the rest of the world) in meeting their food and nutritional demands as well as maximizing this export opportunity.

In additional to food supply, the disruption to global fertilizer supply also presents Canada with an immense opportunity to be a reliable and stable fertilizer supplier to the agricultural industry in Southeast Asia given its role as the world's largest producer and exporter of potash.

## Collaboration on Energy Security and Sustainability

The Russia–Ukraine War has sent shockwaves to the global energy market and exposed the over-reliance on Russian as the world's second-largest natural gas producer and one of the top three crude producers.[97] In contrast, Canada is a country with low political risk and this stability positions Canada as a trusted partner in the global energy supply chain.

As a top energy producer, Canada can provide Southeast Asian countries with the long-term energy security they require. In terms of oil and gas production, Canada is the fourth-largest producer of crude oil and fifth-largest producer of natural gas.[98]

In addition to the abundance of resources, Canada is also at the forefront of clean tech and more sustainable energy alternatives, such as hydrogen, renewables, advanced biofuels, and liquid synthetic fuels. This Canadian expertise can be instrumental in supporting ASEAN countries in their green transition amidst strong energy demand.

According to Canada's 2022 Federal Budget, CAD $9 billion will be allocated to address climate change, including the implementation of mandatory climate disclosures for banks and insurance companies beginning in 2024—in alignment with the Task Force on Climate-related Financial Disclosures (TCFD) framework.[99] These actions demonstrate Canada's willingness to honour its 2050 net-zero commitment, and contribute to its role as a global leader in sustainability. This makes Canada a natural partner for ASEAN to share best practices and knowledge in sustainability and good governance. Knowledge sharing from Canada, in expertise and good governance relating to climate models, such as Emissions Trading Schemes and Carbon Pricing, would help ASEAN in the fight against environmental degradation. Shared expertise is essential to protect against future crises—as demonstrated by the COVID-19 pandemic.

Canadian construction, design, and project management firms can deliver world class services for ASEAN's environmental sustainability initiatives, be they the targeted integration of 23% renewable energy by 2025, major projects such as the ASEAN Power Grid, transportation projects in the pipeline,[100] or other decarbonization efforts and smart city projects. The Toronto Region Board of Trade, for example, has launched the multi-year Smart Cities Initiative held in partnership with the City of Toronto, which highlights Smart City companies, defines a road map of priorities, and develops an inventory of the City's "smart assets."[101] Solutions and models such as these can offer evidence-based blueprints for smart city development and capacity-building in Southeast Asia.

Canadian investment firms leading in sustainability and Environmental, Social, and Corporate Governance (ESG) are contributing to ASEAN's environmental targets by investing into green power generation, transition activities, and other initiatives that help cut emissions. Canadian investor Brookfield Asset Management has raised approximately $7.5 billion for a new ESG/Climate-focused fund, for instance.[102] The Bank of Montreal (BMO) also works with 15 listed banks across ASEAN to strengthen sustainable banking in the region and to improve overall ESG management; its "Financial Institutions and Climate Risk" 2020 engagement project works with ASEAN banks to improve their climate risk and opportunity management.[103]

# Canada as Part of ASEAN's Infrastructure Development

With its long project lifecycles, infrastructure development is another high-potential sector that can nurture long-lasting ties between Canada and ASEAN. It is estimated that developing Asia requires investing 26 trillion dollars from 2016 to 2030 to meet its sustainable infrastructure needs.[104] Canada, as a world-class leader in critical infrastructure—globally renowned airports, mass-transit and railway networks, wastewater facilities and hydropower plants—is exceptionally well-positioned as a partner for ASEAN's sustainable infrastructure development. Canadian firms' solutions, technologies, and expertise can support the successful and efficient development of major infrastructure and smart city projects in ASEAN countries, such as Thailand, the Philippines, and Indonesia.

The Canadian Pension Plan Investment Board (CPPIB), Caisse de dépôt et placement du Québec (CDPQ), Ontario Teachers' Pension Plan (OTPP), and the Ontario Municipal Employees' Retirement System (OMERS) are Canada's leading institutional investors in sustainable infrastructure in Asia. As they pivot to Southeast Asia, many of these funds have recently opened offices in Singapore, with plans to dedicate more extensive portions of their portfolios to ASEAN. For example, in 2019, CPPIB's Indonesian investments included the acquisition of a 45% interest in PT Lintas Marga Sedaya (LMS), the concession holder and operator of the Cikopo-Palimanan (Cipali) toll road.[105]

The Canada Commercial Corporation (CCC), using its Government-to-Government (G2G) contracting model, can act as a critical vehicle for Canada to assist ASEAN's infrastructure development and clean energy transition by offering a mechanism through which governments can buy abroad from Canadian exporters at low risk with an attractive financing mechanism and project guarantees.[106] Export Development Canada (EDC), which has its only standalone global office in Singapore, is also a key organization for Canadian infrastructure players in doing business in ASEAN. FinDev Canada, Canada's nascent government development finance institution, should also open a regional office in Singapore to support development finance initiatives in ASEAN.

## Enhancing Cross-Cultural Ties

The educational sector plays a crucial role in Canada–ASEAN relations, as it lays the necessary social and cultural foundation required for a deeper long-term Canada–ASEAN partnership.

Home to leading universities and research centres, Canada offers the educational expertise required for ASEAN's developing economies to evade the "middle-income trap." Moreover, as a multicultural society ranked third globally in student attraction, Canada is an ideal destination for students from ASEAN.[107] Express Entry, the Atlantic Immigration Pilot, and the Provincial Nominee Program (PNP), also offer pathways for skilled workers to immigrate to Canada. However, students and professionals in Southeast

Asia continue to face mobility issues: the Canada–ASEAN Business Council (CABC)'s 2020 report on business mobility noted that there is no agreement with ASEAN under the International Experience Canada (IEC) Program, which provides the opportunity for foreigners to travel and work abroad.[108] Nor are internships in Canada defined in the Immigration and Refugee Protection Act (IRPA) or its regulations.

## Canada in Relation to Others

Compared to its international peers, Canada's engagement with ASEAN, while improving, can be characterized as an ad hoc series of initiatives without comprehensive objectives or metrics and has been lacklustre. Of all ASEAN's official dialogue partners, Canada is the only nation not to reach strategic partner status.[109] This is consequential. Without the necessary economic and political ties to ensure competitiveness, Canada risks losing its counterparts in key export markets.

The EU, with its much more forward-looking and multifaceted strategies toward ASEAN that span far beyond economic/commercial engagement, offers guidance. For example, despite not having a trade agreement, as of December 2020, the EU has moved from a formal to a strategic partnership with ASEAN. The EU also has an FTA with Singapore, which entered into force in November 2019. The two are working toward a Digital Economy Agreement (DEA), allowing EU businesses to use Singapore as a base to expand operations to the rest of Asia and ASEAN in particular.[110] The EU also collaborates with ASEAN on a range of other initiatives, including the ASEAN COVID-19 response and maritime security, the formation of Green Alliances to fight climate change, and the Horizon Europe Research programme to support healthcare systems and pandemic preparedness.[111]

## Key Recommendations

Despite lacking a distinct strategy and comprehensive set of initiatives for ASEAN, Canada is a global middle power that can be a critical strategic partner and economic asset.

Southeast Asia represents not just an export market with immense potential for Canadian businesses but a way to diversify the economy for long-term economic growth due to its macroeconomic stability and growth trajectory. Canada must define and implement a more targeted and multi-faceted approach to ASEAN as part of Canada's Indo-Pacific strategy, with a clear set of defined goals to spell out success for the future. The following recommendations offer a *three-tiered approach for Canada to engage with ASEAN economically, politically, and socio-culturally.*

**1. Canada to fast-track negotiations for the Canada–ASEAN FTA and provide more post-trade deal coordinated support for businesses.**

In light of the recent initiation of negotiations for a Canada–ASEAN FTA, Canada must maintain its political support for the timely implementation of the agreement. In addition, resources and on-the-ground support must be supplied for Canadian and ASEAN businesses to capitalize on the benefits of eased bilateral trade.

A challenge to maximizing the current and future benefits of FTAs is raising awareness for Canadian companies of the existing agreements. As part of the Indo-Pacific strategy, educating Canadian businesses on ASEAN's benefits and fundamental importance as a group of growing economies should be prioritized. This includes offering Canadian companies more direct information and support to navigate the legal, regulatory, and tax environments of specific markets ripe for Canadian export growth and business expansion.

**2. Canada to achieve strategic partner status with ASEAN.**

While ASEAN and Canada have discussed elevating their status as dialogue partners during various bilateral consultations, this has not materialized. To maintain a strong position with its international counterparts, Canada should actively pursue becoming ASEAN's official strategic partner as rapidly as possible.

**3. Canada to create more education and employment agreements (in both directions) with ASEAN.**

Entering an agreement with ASEAN countries under the International Experience Canada (IEC) Program will help develop deep cross-cultural ties. Canada is already at a disadvantage when it comes to other closer destinations for work and study, such as Australia and Europe, which are often preferred. By promoting Canada as a prime destination for work/study exchanges and implementing the necessary processes to facilitate them, the positive experiences shared by young people participating in the programs will help to promote "Brand Canada" in ASEAN as an ideal place to go abroad to study and work, as well as to raise the awareness and attractiveness of Canada.

Canada may consider launching more specific study programs/exchanges with Canada dedicated to Southeast Asia's labour force demands through the ASEAN Scholarships and Educational Exchanges for Development (SEED) program.

Canada should also implement its updated version of the "Colombo Plan," as Australia has done with ASEAN countries.[112]

**4. Canada to upgrade its presence by appointing senior-level representation in ASEAN, a significant political appointment with a direct link to the Prime Minister's Office (PMO), and more frequent ministerial visits.**

Having a senior political appointment and/or innovatively basing its regional Director-General in ASEAN would also be beneficial from a strategic perspective, selectively elevating key missions to senior appointments. This would optimize engagement with stakeholders in the region and inform Global Affairs Canada, PCO, and PMO of crucial developments to coordinate more timely and effective action plans.

**5. Canada to work jointly with ASEAN on non-traditional security issues.**

Canada and ASEAN should collaborate on tackling specific issues relating to impending challenges that pose a threat to both parties, such as maritime security, piracy, and energy transition/security. As Canada becomes more deeply engaged with ASEAN and holds a more vested interest in its success, a targeted approach to crisis prevention and economic/social development is imperative to maintain stable and robust economic and commercial ties with the region.

This may include more high-level dialogues and joint initiatives on food security and sustainability, such as creating collaborative institutions or research centres dedicated to fighting some of Southeast Asia's most imminent environmental threats. An example can be taken from the EU's Horizon Europe research and funding program, which works jointly with ASEAN to respond to climate change challenges.[113]

Canada may consider becoming a key strategic partner for food security in ASEAN due to its leading expertise and research in agri-food. The Global Institute for Food Security, which just received $3.2M in funding from the Saskatchewan Government, would be well-positioned to work with ASEAN and its institutions toward combating food insecurity.[114]

**6. Canada prioritizes security cooperation with ASEAN to facilitate deeper integration with the region.**

This includes initiating or being part of multilateral defence agreements with ASEAN and countries in the Indo-Pacific region, more engagement with the Shangri-La Dialogue, and actively seeking admission into the East Asia Summit and the ASEAN Defence Ministers' Meeting-Plus.

Canada should seek assistance to accelerate its procurement needs, such as evaluating shipbuilding capacity in the Philippines or utilizing Singapore's home-grown independent military technology and expertise. In particular, supply chain enhancements with the Philippines could tap the influential Filipino diaspora in Canada and increase country-to-country relations with a critical partner while signalling a commitment to becoming a security partner for ASEAN nations.

Additional collaboration on police and security services training, anti-piracy patrols and activity, forward positioning of supplies, and potential training bases would demonstrate Canada's commitment to the ASEAN region.

Canada may also support joint research or events profiling Canada in ASEAN countries to raise its profile and security presence. For example, through working with and supporting initiatives by organizations such as the ISEAS–Yusof Ishak Institute, which focuses on socio-political, security, and economic trends and developments in Southeast Asia.

7. **Continue to support private sector initiatives by industry groups such as the Canada-ASEAN Business Council, the Business Council of Canada, the Asia-Pacific Foundation and the Canadian Chambers of Commerce in ASEAN.**

These groups are essential to facilitating Canada–ASEAN business connectivity and should be empowered to take on a more direct role in bridging the two regions. Stable funding and coordinated action will ensure long-term capacity in programming, networking events, and research in Canada and ASEAN.

8. **ASEAN to set up a Canadian office for trade, investment, and cultural exchanges supported by the Canadian government.**

In addition to an increased Canadian presence in ASEAN, an ASEAN office in Canada would provide a direct link between Canada and ASEAN to more effectively coordinate trade and policy issues.

### Appendix A:  Canada's Trade History with ASEAN[115]

| Year | Milestone |
|------|-----------|
| 1977 | Canada becomes an ASEAN dialogue partner, and the parties increase cooperation on regional integration. |
| 2009 | Canada appointed an ambassador to ASEAN and adopted the Joint Declaration on the ASEAN-Canada Enhanced Partnership. |
| 2011 | Canada and ASEAN become parties to the Canada-ASEAN Joint Declaration on Trade and Investment (JDTI) (2011), which provides a platform for Canada and the AMS to exchange trade and investment opportunities and strengthen commercial engagement. |
| 2015 | Canada and the AMS adopted a new work plan to guide the implementation of the JDTI from 2016 to 2020. Efforts focus on several areas, including Small and medium-sized enterprises, education, innovation, and corporate social responsibility. |
| 2016 | Canada opened its dedicated mission to ASEAN and appointed its first dedicated ambassador to ASEAN. |
| 2017 | Canada and the AMS launched exploratory discussions for a possible Canada-ASEAN free trade agreement (FTA). |

*(continued)*

## Appendix A: Continued

| Year | Milestone |
|---|---|
| 2018 | The Government of Canada conducted public consultations through the Canada Gazette to seek the views of Canadians on a possible FTA with ASEAN. |
| 2019 | Canada and ASEAN announced the conclusion of exploratory discussions for a possible Canada-ASEAN FTA on September 10, 2019. |
| 2021 | Canada and ASEAN announced negotiations for a free trade agreement on November 16, 2021. |

## Appendix B: Predicted Sectoral Impacts of a Canada-ASEAN FTA[116]

### Canada's Gaining Sectors, CAD millions

| | Bilateral Exports | Bilateral Imports | Total Exports | Total Imports | Domestic Shipments | Total Shipments |
|---|---|---|---|---|---|---|
| Trade-driven gaining sectors | | | | | | |
| Pork and Poultry | 292 | 0 | 247 | 20 | 23 | 269 |
| Oil Seeds and Vegetable Oils | 356 | 11 | 201 | 29 | 49 | 249 |
| Machinery and Equipment | 142 | 107 | 79 | 86 | -23 | 56 |
| Income-driven gaining sectors | | | | | | |
| Other Services | 0 | 0 | -9 | 15 | 709 | 700 |
| Trade | 3 | 1 | -4 | 12 | 364 | 360 |
| Construction | 0 | 0 | -1 | 1 | 349 | 349 |
| Business Services | 4 | 13 | -28 | 34 | 272 | 244 |
| Financial Services | 6 | 7 | -11 | 24 | 158 | 147 |

# 9

# Canada and Japan

# Ian Burney

THERE IS no longer any question that the Indo-Pacific region has emerged as the most important economic and political region of the world, and the dominant theatre for great power rivalry. Looking out to 2030, it is equally clear that Japan will continue to occupy a preeminent position within the region, given its size, influence, and centrality both to economic supply chains and to regional security—principally through the anchor of its military alliance with the United States.

The events now unfolding in Europe in the wake of Russia's brutal invasion of Ukraine have further underscored the importance of Japan's role in the Indo-Pacific in promoting stability, democracy, and a rules-based international order. With China actively seeking to undermine support for Western sanctions, Japan—as the G-7's only Asian member—has been working the diplomatic front in an effort to rally support for a stronger response to the invasion from regional actors leery about getting caught in the crossfire. Japan will also be a central player in NATO's longer-term drive to intensify collaboration with the principal democracies of the Indo-Pacific in order to grapple with the now much-worsened global security environment.

In the context of any broad pivot to the Indo-Pacific region, it will be essential for Canada to forge closer ties with Japan. We have a solid foundation to work from in this regard, with the benefit of a longstanding and generally positive bilateral relationship. We also bring potent assets to the table with Japan, not least our abundant natural resources and technological strengths that play directly to Japanese demographic and economic anxieties.

Canada has also now pinned its stripes to the "Free and Open Indo Pacific" (FOIP) vision that is at the heart of Japanese foreign policy, which gives us an opportunity to engage with Japan from a position of greater relevance.[117]

However, as this chapter will argue, Canada's engagement with Japan has typically lacked the sense of purpose and priority that such an important relationship deserves. Despite shared interests and priorities, and ample potential for expanded cooperation, the relationship tends to be taken for granted by both countries, drifting along with relatively sporadic high-level attention. Moreover, on our side the federal Government is decidedly late in laying out a Canadian Indo-Pacific strategy—one that presumably will provide the framework and resources needed to scale up our engagement across the region. Our competitors are now years ahead of us in rolling out their respective variations, and intensifying their collaboration with Japan specifically. We will therefore be playing catch-up in a crowded field, and at time when trans-Atlantic priorities are also once requiring much attention.

If we are to succeed in competing for Japan's attention and persuading it to prioritize its engagement with Canada, we will need to:

- engage at the highest political levels and elevate the relationship to a "strategic partnership";
- fashion our engagement in ways calculated to resonate with Japan's priorities, notably its security preoccupations;
- come to the table with ideas and resources to match our ambitions; and
- mobilize key non-governmental actors to likewise step up their game in Japan.

This chapter will focus on the key elements of such a forward agenda with Japan and why this all matters, but will begin with some observations about the geopolitical context that shapes Japan's international engagement.

## Strategic Environment

Japan lies on the front lines of the Sino-U.S. rivalry, with hostile neighbours to most sides. It faces a rogue, nuclear-armed regime in North Korea that routinely launches missiles in its direction in order to perfect ever-more lethal weapon systems, and it may now be preparing once again to resume nuclear tests. Japan's relations with South Korea have meanwhile degenerated to a post-war low over historical grievances and domestic political pressures in both countries, though the recent election of President Yoon Suk-yeol in South Korea creates at least the opening for a possible rapprochement.

With Russia, relations have long been hobbled by a territorial dispute over four islands north of Hokkaido, a legacy from the World War II that still prevents the two from concluding a peace treaty. Dogged efforts by former Prime Minister Shinzo Abe to try to resolve the issue yielded little of consequence, and Russia has now shut the process down in retaliation for sanctions imposed by Japan over its recent invasion of Ukraine. Japan's reactions to past Russian aggressions, including the annexation of Crimea, had been relatively muted in part to avoid a rupture in these discussions. Its response to the current crisis has been profoundly different, not only because of the magnitude of the carnage and the implications for global security, but because Putin's nuclear brinksmanship strikes a particularly raw nerve in Japan.

Over the long term, however, the greatest strategic challenge facing Japan lies in China's continuing rise and growing assertiveness. Its Belts and Road Initiative (BRI), rapidly expanding military capabilities and persistent encroachments in the East and South China Seas, are all viewed from Tokyo as reflecting hegemonic aspirations that threaten core Japanese interests. Provocations in and around the Japanese-controlled but Chinese-claimed Senkaku Islands in the East China Seas remain a key flashpoint. In the South China Seas, while Japan has no territorial claims, it is deeply concerned by China's sweeping claims and efforts to militarize features in these waters, through which so much of global trade and the vast majority of Japan's imported energy supplies traverse.

Most alarming to Japan is the sabre rattling over Taiwan, given the potentially catastrophic implications for Japanese security of outright Chinese military intervention.[118] The military and economic toll being imposed on Russia and the relative firmness of the Western response to its invasion of

Ukraine will certainly not be lost on China's leadership, notwithstanding its repeated assertions that there are no parallels between the two situations. This may well result in a recalibration of such matters as timing and tactics, but it is highly unlikely to materially alter the PRC's longstanding and publicly avowed aim of bringing about Taiwan's unification with the mainland by any means necessary, including the use of force. This is still widely viewed as a defining legacy issue for Xi Jinping.

Navigating through this complex geopolitical environment requires Japan to maintain a balancing act between its overriding security reliance on the United States and its acute economic interdependence with China—now its most important trade partner and critical to its supply chains. The approach it is taking, first under Abe and continued by his two successors—Prime Ministers Suga and now Kishida—is to double down on the security relationship with the United States, strengthen its own military posture, and pursue a wide-ranging counter-narrative for the region under the FOIP banner.[119]

The FOIP initiative is by design anchored in values—such as the rule of law, open markets, and sustainability—and framed as a "vision" rather than a "strategy," so as to soften the reaction in Beijing and broaden its appeal to ASEAN and other countries in the region loathe to have to choose between the United States and China. The aim is to shore up maritime security and rules-based approaches in the region, and to offer an alternative to BRI to smaller states across the region susceptible to pressure from China.

Japan has actively sought and secured broad international support for this agenda, while simultaneously working to reinvigorate and broaden the role of the Quadrilateral Security Dialogue (Quad) comprising Japan, the United States, India, and Australia. It has also established itself as the flag-bearer for free trade in the region, salvaging the Trans-Pacific Partnership (TPP) in the aftermath of the U.S. exit under President Trump, and subsequently driving the Regional Comprehensive Economic Partnership (RCEP) to a successful conclusion even in the wake of India's withdrawal.

The widespread endorsement of the language and principles behind Japan's approach to the Indo-Pacific is viewed in Tokyo as a signature

Japanese foreign policy success. The salient point for Canada is that this agenda has become, and will remain under Kishida, the centrepiece of Japan's foreign policy and the lens through which it gauges the relevance of its global partners.

## Japan Still Matters

While fashionable in some circles to write-off Japan's future prospects given its demographics and prolonged economic slump in the post-bubble era, Japan is still the world's third-largest economy—nearly a third again larger than fourth-placed Germany.[120] Its market remains one of the world's most lucrative, and its companies sit on vast pools of capital—estimated at over US$6 trillion[121]—and are scouring the globe for investment opportunities. It is a technological powerhouse, an important actor in global institutions, a major aid donor, and a pivotal player in a region that is at the confluence of some of the world's most pressing political and security challenges.

From the standpoint of Canadian interests, Japan is a key partner in advancing shared priorities on the global stage—strengthening security, promoting democracy, human rights and the rule of law, and securing open markets and supply chains. Japan's engagement is essential on common aims like WTO reform, the expansion of the Comprehensive and Progressive Trans-Pacific Partnership (CPTPP) and addressing climate change, and it is a key partner for us in many global institutions. As noted above, Japan will also be NATO's most important de facto ally in the region in pushing back against Russian expansionism and the emerging Sino-Russian marriage of convenience.

Japan is our fourth-largest export market, and while its appetite for our natural resources and agricultural products will remain voracious, higher value industrial products from Canada are also making significant inroads.[122] It is our top source of foreign investment from Asia and third-largest globally,[123] and its investments typically come with a long-term horizon and without political baggage. It is also an increasingly important partner in S&T collaboration and innovation. Canadian capabilities in areas like AI, robotics, quantum computing, and clean tech are all attracting growing attention in

Japan, driven in no small part by the demographic and energy challenges the country faces. Grassroots connections—tourism, student and youth exchanges, academic and cultural interactions—are historically vibrant and will no doubt regain their pre-COVID lustre when travel restrictions ease.

## Overcoming Complacency and Ensuring Relevance

However positive in tone, the Canada–Japan relationship suffers from neglect on both sides, not only from governments but other key stakeholders. Compared to peers, our engagement is episodic and superficial, in part reflecting the overriding preoccupation of both countries with the United States and China and the lack of major conflict that would demand political attention. In the Japanese bureaucracy, Canada is managed from the edges of "North America" desks that focus almost entirely on the United States, whereas Japan comes a distant second to China within the "North Asia" responsibility centres on our side.

As the smaller party in the equation, the onus inevitably lies on Canada to supply the bulk of the energy and initiative to the relationship, but that in itself is subject to misperception. In Canada, particularly in government circles, Japan tends to be seen as a peer—a middle-sized power with which we can engage on an equal footing to address shared priorities. In Tokyo, however, the relationship with Canada is not viewed as one of equals. Japan's economy is more than three times larger than Canada's,[124] and while Japan is one of our top export markets, Canada is barely in the top 20 for Japan.[125] Moreover, Japan views itself as having greater diplomatic, political and military heft globally, and as being *the* most important strategic ally for the United States—the proverbial "unsinkable aircraft carrier" on the front lines of what is now the world's most important geopolitical battleground.

On the Canadian side, this leads to chronic disappointment that Japan is not more fully invested in the bilateral relationship. From a Japanese perspective, apart from perceptions of asymmetry in size and power, there is also at times a sense that Canada's foreign policy priorities are tangential to its own.

Japanese interlocutors frankly struggle to understand what is meant by a "feminist foreign policy," and the heavy emphasis we put on themes such as diversity, inclusion, empowering the disadvantaged, and the like—however laudable—can come across as not directly relevant to what keeps Japanese national security planners awake at night. With North Korean missiles flying overhead, China relentlessly probing at its frontiers and Russia raising the spectre of nuclear war, there will be limited appetite in Tokyo for initiatives from Ottawa that are peripheral to its core concerns.

There is much about Canada and our bilateral relations that Japan does value, however: our diplomatic support for key priorities such as strengthening rules-based approaches to international relations; our contribution—albeit modest—as a force multiplier in supporting security in the Indo-Pacific; the unparalleled insights we have into the U.S. political and policy-making environment; and—topping the list—our role as a politically stable source of supply for the food, energy, and other critical inputs on which Japan's economy is so heavily import-dependent (with the added virtue that shipments from Canada's west coast take only ten days to reach Japan by sea, and travel through open, uncontested waters). These are the key cards we bring to the table with Japan, which we need to play skilfully to advance our economic and political interests.

## Taking the Relationship Off Autopilot

The starting point for stepping up our engagement with Japan is at the political level, where there is no substitute for the direct involvement of leaders. The last bilateral visit to Japan by the Canadian Prime Minister was six years ago, on the margins of the G-7 meeting in Ise Shima in the spring of 2016,[126] while the last visit in the other direction was then Prime Minister Abe's brief stop in Ottawa in April 2019 to consult ahead of the G20 Summit he hosted in Osaka two months later. This is woefully insufficient for such an important relationship. There should be fulsome visits to Japan by the Canadian Prime Minister on a regular basis—at least every two years—and the next one ideally would serve as the launch platform for a Canadian Indo-Pacific strategy. We also need to more effectively lobby for visits to Canada by the Japanese Prime Minister—realistically, on the margins of trips to the United States.

A key initial aim of such high-level interaction, and important metric by which to measure our success, should be to elevate the relationship with Japan to a genuine "strategic partnership." Such a designation matters in Japan in terms of securing government attention and resources, and it would put our relationship on a comparable footing to that already enjoyed by our peers—not just the United States, but Australia, India, the United Kingdom, Germany, a number of ASEAN states, and others. A central feature would entail regularized Ministerial discussions both on political and security matters (usually in a "2+2" format involving Foreign and Defence Ministers on each side) and economic issues. In our case, again unlike most of our peers, the key bilateral dialogue mechanisms are currently at the senior official level and even still experience long gaps between meetings.[127]

Elevating the relationship would give it more profile and structure, and compel the bureaucracy on each side to periodically take it off autopilot. It would also ensure a more regular pattern of engagement by our respective senior ministers—notably foreign, trade, defence, as well as key line ministers (industry, energy, environment, and agriculture). COVID-19 dealt a significant blow to the cadence of Ministerial interactions between our countries; it is high time to get these back on track.

As part of an agreement to forge a "strategic partnership" and as a show of good faith on our side, Canada should be prepared to at least partially reverse past decisions that significantly reduced our diplomatic footprint in Japan—in particular, by reopening our consulate in Osaka (where we are now the only G7 country without a capital-based presence).

## Leveraging Japan's Security Preoccupations

Nothing conveys Canada's relevance to Japan's interests as tangibly as our direct engagement on regional security in the Indo-Pacific. As tensions in the region have mounted in recent years, Canadian military assets and personnel have been deployed more frequently to Japan, not only for port visits but for joint training exercises (which in 2017 included the first visit of a Canadian submarine to Japan in nearly 50 years) and active maritime security operations. Particularly important have been the deployments, since 2018, of naval and air assets as part of a multilateral effort to counter maritime sanctions evasion by North Korea, which have boosted Canada's credibility in the eyes of the Japanese foreign and defence establishments, though regrettably have had limited visibility outside such circles.

Our commitment to defence cooperation with Japan and our military engagement in the region should be significantly enhanced and made more durable. This will necessitate considerably higher defence spending by Canada, given concurrent demands for (long overdue) NORAD modernization and the now urgent necessity of reinforcing our NATO commitments. Budget 2022 was a small step in the right direction, but plainly insufficient, entailing a modest increase in spending over five years from just under 1.4% of GDP to only 1.5%—still well below NATO guidelines. The Government will have another opportunity to rise to the occasion in the context of the Defence Policy Review it has announced, and it should use the opportunity to commit to a more robust military presence in the Indo-Pacific region.

Beyond defence spending, we need to expand our suite of legal instruments to support defence cooperation with Japan, building on the Acquisition and Cross-Servicing Agreement (ACSA) that came into force in 2019. Our peers are moving ahead with alacrity in pursuing ambitious defence cooperation arrangements with Japan,[128] while in our case we have struggled to advance even a limited agreement to exchange classified information. Concluding an Information Security Agreement (ISA) would yield important security and commercial dividends, but the initiative has been languishing and needs a political kick-start.

We would also do well to raise the profile of our military deployments in the region. These are highly valued by Japan, but—whether owing to an exaggerated concern about how Beijing will react or simply to squeamishness when it comes to showcasing the harder instruments of military power—we seem to go out of our way to downplay our efforts in this regard.

At the regional level, Canada is largely absent from the key groupings that are emerging to address security issues, such as the AUKUS alliance bringing together Australia, the United Kingdom, and the United States, and the recently reinvigorated Quad. Canada's exclusion from the latter has become all the more glaring now that this group has broadened its focus beyond traditional security and into areas where Canada is well-placed to add value, including pandemic response, climate change, supply chain resilience, and critical technologies. With others now knocking on the door, including the incoming government in Seoul, Canada should move forthwith to seek membership in this forum.

In the interim, and to strengthen our case for full membership, we should significantly augment our engagement in "Quad Plus" formats, as we did when the CAF joined military forces from the United States, Japan, Australia, and India in the "Sea Dragon" naval exercise near Guam in early 2021. We should also explore taking on a defined role in partnership with Japan in a specific theatre of the Indo-Pacific, along lines of the trilateral partnership struck by Japan, Australia, and the United States on infrastructure investment in Papua New Guinea. In this regard, there may be interest in Japan in a joint initiative of some kind that targets the small island nations in the Pacific, and/or the Indian Ocean. The bottom line is that others will not clamour for "more Canada"; if we want a seat at the important tables, we will have to earn them through actions.

In the area of intelligence sharing, it would be worth exploring how to work more closely with Japan in the context of the Five Eyes alliance. In 2020, then defence minister Taro Kono floated the possibility of Japanese membership as a trial balloon, but the notion failed to get traction. There are practical issues that would have to be worked through from the standpoint of formal intelligence sharing (and for this too an ISA would be a prerequisite), but there could at least be expanded diplomatic collaboration with Japan in a 5+1 format.

In terms of *economic security*, Japan was profoundly shaken by the supply chain disruptions triggered by the pandemic, since compounded by the invasion of Ukraine. It has invested heavily in making its supply chains more resilient, including by subsidizing the reshoring and diversification of targeted areas of its manufacturing base. Canada is a leading global supplier of many goods critical to Japan, and we proved our reliability throughout the pandemic—keeping supplies flowing at a time when others were rushing to impose export restraints. We are ideally placed to be part of the solution as Japan works to overcome the economic security challenges laid bare by the pandemic and now war in Europe.

This is particularly relevant in the *energy sector*. Prime Minister Kishida has affirmed his predecessor's commitment to achieving carbon neutrality by 2050, but this will be a daunting proposition in post-Fukushima Japan given its overwhelming reliance on fossil fuels (including from Russia, which in 2021 supplied just under 10% and about 4% of Japan's natural gas and crude oil imports respectively). The needed energy transition will certainly drive massive public and private investment in Japan over the coming decades, and present compelling commercial opportunities for Canada given our many strengths in areas such as renewables, hydrogen, ammonia, critical minerals, and carbon capture, use and storage.

By any measure, however, Japan will remain one of the world's largest importers of oil and gas for the foreseeable future, and here too Canada is now poised—at long last—to become an important player. Japanese companies have invested heavily in the Canadian oil and gas sector over the years with a view to securing supplies, but until recently there have been no significant Canadian energy exports to Japan, largely because of our inability to build the infrastructure needed to bring the resources to tidewater. By virtue of an AltaGas export facility that opened in Prince Rupert in 2019, Canada has become a significant supplier of liquified petroleum gas (LPG) to Japan, with exports topping $1 billion in 2021. This has helped to alleviate skepticism in Japan about Canada's ability to execute large-scale energy projects, but doubts persist.

The most important energy project on the horizon from a bilateral perspective is LNG Canada (in which Mitsubishi holds a 15% stake), scheduled to begin shipments in 2025. The successful completion of this project will be pivotal to Japanese perceptions about Canada's ability to support its energy security.

We should maximize the opportunity to expand energy exports to Japan, including supporting a second train expansion at LNG Canada, to advance our own economic interests while simultaneously helping to wean Japan off of supplies from Russia.

## Making Common Cause on Trade Policy

Like Canada, Japan has an outsized stake in a stable, rules-based trading system, and was unnerved by the unilateral and coercive trade measures that have proliferated in recent years. Given our shared interests, and the import-ance of our respective bilateral trade relations with the United States, there is considerable scope for more strategic, high-level bilateral engagement between Tokyo and Ottawa on trade priorities.

The Canadian-led Ottawa Group on WTO reform offers one such vehicle, though there is little indication to date from the Biden Administration that its professed enthusiasm for a return to multilateralism extends to the WTO. Canada is also in a privileged position of influence alongside Japan in shaping the CPTPP's future evolution, given that we are its two lar-gest current members. With the U.K. accession process now underway, and others lining up in the queue, the CPTPP stands to become an increasingly important vehicle for economic integration in the region. We should work jointly to sustain the current momentum behind the accession process, while ensuring—with an eye toward China—that the process of broadening the CPTPP does not dilute its level of ambition.

With respect to Taiwan, there is little doubt that it is well qualified to accede from a trade policy standpoint (arguably best placed among suitors in the region), but the current membership is wary of incurring China's wrath. Insisting, however, that Taiwan cannot precede China is tantamount to blocking Taiwan's bid indefinitely, so the question for the membership is whether the implementation of RCEP, with China at its centre, provides sufficient political cover to move forward separately with Taiwan's CPTPP accession process. Canada should coordinate closely with Japan on this.

For geostrategic reasons, Japan continues to harbour a strong interest in having the U.S. return to the TPP fold. While this does not appear to be in the cards any time soon, there may be scope for more limited initiatives involving the United States and Japan that could potentially serve as stepping stones. One area attracting growing interest is the burgeoning field of "digital trade," which was the subject of a bilateral U.S.–Japan agreement in late 2019, and more recently a trilateral agreement amongst New Zealand, Singapore, and Chile (which, along with Brunei, were the "P4" members that initially spawned what became the TPP).[129] The Biden Administration has recently launched consultations on what it calls an "Indo Pacific Economic Framework." Though vague and with unclear prospects (not least since the Administration no longer has "fast track" negotiating authority from Congress), Canada should monitor this closely and ensure that we are involved if it does get legs.

## Reinvesting in Public Diplomacy

In the area of public diplomacy, Canada has much to work with in Japan, including an extensive network of "sister city" relationships and "friendship societies," and in normal times strong tourism, educational, and cultural links.[130] This is a field that covers much ground, and there is never a shortage of ideas on how we can do more, most of which are a function of resources. Let me note three:

- First, with the Tokyo Olympics/Paralympics now in the rear view, the next major global event in Japan of a "cultural" nature is Expo 2025 in Osaka. Canada has signalled its intent to participate, as we have in all four past expos in Japan.[131] We should make the most of this opportunity, and showcase our technological strengths to challenge stereotypical views about Canada that still prevail in Japan.
- Second, past austerity measures virtually eliminated federal support for "Canadian studies" programs abroad, but there are still many academics in Japan who remain committed to the cause and routinely plead for financial support. Canada now lags far behind its peers in this area,

including Japan.[132] This is an area where even a modest restoration of funding would go a long way toward raising our profile in Japan.

- Third, youth exchange programs can offer substantial, long-term returns. One of the most farsighted is the Japan Exchange and Teaching (JET) program, which over three decades has created an enormous pool of Japanese-speaking youth (including 10,000 + from Canada) who generally become life-long champions of Japan and its ties with their home country. A major Canadian program to entice youths from Japan and other Indo-Pacific countries to come to Canada for an extended period would need to be structured in a different way, but if done at scale, could offer significant benefits and serve as a signature deliverable in a new Indo-Pacific strategy.

## Business Engagement

Canada–Japan commercial relations are substantial and have significant future potential, particularly with the benefit now of the CPTPP. Despite that, bilateral opportunities are nowhere near top-of-mind for either of our business communities, for which the United States and China consume most of the bandwidth. This is unfortunate, as recent events have underscored the downsides to excessive reliance on either of the world's top two economies.

Since its launch in 2014, the Japan–Canada Chambers Council has served as the primary forum for bilateral B2B discussions. It has the benefit of influential and committed co-chairs on both sides,[133] but has struggled to broaden its membership, and COVID-19 has compounded the challenge of organizing in-person meetings. The Business Council of Canada has also sought to reinvigorate its ties with Japan's leading business federation—the Keidanren—making two visits to Japan in 2019, and it should return to the charge as soon as travel conditions permit.

Given the importance of personal relationships in Japan, strengthening B2B mechanisms and increasing the frequency of high-level interactions between business leaders in the two countries should be a key priority for Canada.

To that end, the CEOs of Canadian firms with major stakes in Japan need to become more personally invested in bilateral initiatives. As we look ahead to the 100th anniversary of diplomatic relations toward the end of the decade,[134] it may be timely to borrow from the Canada–Japan Forum concept[135] and establish an Eminent Persons Group composed of luminaries from the private sectors of both countries with a mandate to make recommendations on how to inject momentum in bilateral ties, with a focus on our business relations.

## Conclusion

By 2030, Japan's population will have dipped below 120 million, but the country will remain a formidable global power, one of Canada's top commercial partners, and our single most important ally in the region in advancing our global interests. Against the backdrop of China's growing capacity and determination to challenge the post-war world order, Russia's ever more brazen aggressions and a domestically preoccupied U.S. administration, it has arguably never been more important for like-minded, middle-sized powers like Canada and Japan to work together on the global stage.

Our two countries are largely aligned on values and interests, and we have the benefit of a sizeable reservoir of goodwill between our respective citizens, yet each tends to be so preoccupied with more immediate concerns that we often pay scant attention to one another.

If we succeed in elevating the relationship to a genuine strategic partnership, and give it the targeted investments and sustained attention it deserves from governments and key stakeholders, it would undoubtedly generate a far greater contribution than at present to the economic prosperity and wider international interests of both countries.

# 10

# Canada and India
# Nadir Patel

T HE INDO-PACIFIC region is anchored by the world's largest and fastest-growing economies and its most populous nations. More than half of global trade passes through its waters. To succeed, the region requires stability, leadership, and a democratic, rules-based model for development, one that doesn't threaten the sovereignty between neighbours.

In any Indo-Pacific strategy, it is imperative for Canada to establish a partnership with a strong and democratic India. India is already engaged, actively, with Indo-Pacific partners, across South and Southeast Asia, as a core part of its foreign policy framework. Through its security and defence partnerships, India is providing a basis for long-term stability. And through its structural economic reforms, India is emerging as an attractive economic powerhouse.

What's perhaps most remarkable, is that modern India's rise isn't a product of accident, it is emerging as a result of intention. At the 2018 Shangri-La Dialogue, Prime Minister Narendra Modi laid out his direction for India's priorities in the Indo-Pacific. He described a vision defined by openness, inclusiveness, a common pursuit of progress, peace, and prosperity through dialogue and collaboration. The values he described underpin an emerging Indian foreign policy that has begun to set aside the non-alignments of the past, not featuring the imposition of rival models, but rather a basis for what ought to be the norms governing the growth of the region for the next half century and beyond. It presents, in every way, a vision aligned with Canadian interests. In planning for the future, India must become the centrepiece for Canadian Indo-Pacific engagement.

Commensurate with the pace that India has been undertaking structural reforms, Canada's relationship with India has also been transforming over much of the last decade. Record levels of investment and trade have been accomplished, despite occasional political headwinds or more recently, challenges brought about by the global pandemic. Bilateral trade in goods and services combined has reached record highs in recent years, nearing the $15 billion mark, and total two-way investment flows, led principally by Canadian institutional investors, have eclipsed an estimated $70 billion. A stronger economic partnership with India will lead to new jobs and growth in both countries. If Canada can consider India's development as the priority strategic partnership, and a principal gateway to the Indo-Pacific, then the partnership will contribute to broader stability in the Indo-Pacific region as well.

Our people are already leading us in this direction. India is Canada's largest source for permanent residents and foreign students, with over 200,000 Indian students studying at Canadian educational institutions. Nearly 4% of Canada's population is of Indian heritage. English-speaking, multi-talented, profoundly pluralist—Indian immigration to Canada provides a critical artery for Canadian economic growth.

Canadian Indo-Pacific ambitions, nascent as they are today, provide an opportunity to choose priorities judiciously, focusing on quality over quantity. An incapacity to be everywhere provides an opportunity to be focused on what is critical to the Canadian interest. Over the next decade alone, India is expected to grow from a $2.5 trillion economy to a $5 trillion one. It is on the trajectory to rank as the world's third-largest economy, with all of the responsibility that the Indian republic carrier in its international affairs.

The world knows about Indian potential. Ottawa has yet to feature as prominently in New Delhi as Quadrilateral capitals—Washington, Tokyo, and Canberra. Among the G20, Indian diplomacy is more active than most others, from Paris to Riyadh. What our peers have done, is to invest significant time and effort into building ties with India over the past decade, particularly with the Narendra Modi government, primarily driven by foreign, defence, and trade policy interests. These ties are manifest in regular ministerial and Cabinet-level engagements defining clear outcomes, deeper expert level exchanges to generate stronger knowledge about the Indian opportunity, Leader-level government summits to focus cooperation, large-scale, and long-term commercial deals, all well-documented in recent years. Australia has released its comprehensive India engagement strategy, which followed extensive consultations across Australia. Led by their former Foreign Secretary, it may provide a model for future Canadian engagement.

Whatever the modality, this is why Canada needs to amplify its focus on the India imperative. It is a game-changing opportunity. By prominently and effectively partnering with India, Canada's importance across the Indo-Pacific will be immeasurably enhanced. To do this will require a concerted effort and a deliberate strategy—but we're not starting from scratch. In fact, in some ways we would be playing from a position of strength. Take for example, our economic ties with India: as outlined above, in recent years we have established a robust foundation upon which we can build further. A concerted effort should build upon expanding our economic relations and bring new ambition to the security and defence arrangements across the Indo-Pacific region, to influencing a new way in how Canadians view the strategic importance of Canada–India relations—alongside the most important alliances Canadians can forge.

In short, we need a plan for India: not one built out as a construct for Canada in the Indo-Pacific, but one that places India as the natural focus for Canada across the Indo-Pacific.

## The Indian Economy and Indo-Pacific Development as the Priority for Canada

The Canadian economy is fuelled largely by export-led growth, and Canadian companies are increasingly looking for new, stable markets with democratic governance, common interests, a predictable regulatory environment and a commitment to the rule of law.

While the number of Canadian businesses actively engaged in India has grown significantly over the past several years, even more companies are actively exploring India as a place to trade, do business or invest. India is one of Canada's fastest growing trading partners, now ranked in the top 10. It needs to become among the top 5 markets for all Canadian commercial activity.

On the basis of a strong investment-led foundation for trade with India, the partnership demands a truly concerted engagement bilaterally and across the Indo-Pacific. India's expanding economy will continue to be an important driver for all aspects of economic growth in the Indo-Pacific, and Canada's growing trade and investment ties with India, and with other Indo-Pacific nations, will continue to provide impetus for Canadian influence in the region.

Canada continues to underperform relative to the size of our respective economies and relative to the performance of our peers. Growth in bilateral trade and investment has undoubtedly been aided by ambitious, successful economic reform measures undertaken by the Modi government. These measures will continue to make India an attractive economy to engage— reducing red-tape and generating long-term growth. So long as India continues its reforms, especially those on market access restrictions for certain goods, addressing issues of increasing tariffs, and faster resolution of commercial or investor disputes, Canadians will find the Indian market increasingly attractive.

Better yet, Canada can leverage its natural strength as a major investor in India, and as a G20 partner, to accelerate the pace of Indian growth as a principal partner in five key areas.

First, sub-national engagement. While Canada's relationship with India's central government in New Delhi will continue to be paramount, greater engagement with states and cities will open new opportunities for Canadian companies. Over the next decade, India's urbanization trend—17 of the world's top 20 fastest growing cities over the next decade are expected to be in India—will continue to create both opportunities for its people and challenges in need of solutions. These sub-national governments wield extensive influence, provide incentives and hold decision-making authority to attract business. They are all thirsting for Canadian partners.

Across 28 states and 8 Union territories, engaging 1.4 billion Indians as a principal partner will require much more of Canada. Each state holds the potential of entire nations in other parts of the world. And across the Indian federation, like Canada, there are the states that are performing versus the ones that perform less effectively. Indian democracy succeeds because of its decentralized constitution, elevating state leaders who are critical to Canadian engagement. Across India, Canadian leaders in business and government should focus on the highest potential and highest performing subnational governments of India, and support our own provinces in their partnerships with their counterparts.

Second, innovation is leading to commercialization. The Indian start-up ecosystem is the third largest in the world, populated by students from some of the most advanced technical and engineering schools in the world, and backed by a young entrepreneurial population that constitutes the largest emerging middle class in the world. Yet, apart from a handful of moderately funded accelerators and incubators, Canadian and Indian innovation ecosystems are largely unaware of each other, when for Canada, the Indian ecosystem should be a marquee area of our bilateral cooperation, with the potential for co-creating game-changing businesses that will drive growth in both countries.

Canada is well on its way to becoming a significant international player in innovation and start-ups, with success in the Toronto-Waterloo corridor, technology clusters in and around Vancouver, Montreal, Ottawa and other regions. Investors and companies in Silicon Valley are capitalizing on this growth. At the same time, India has emerged as a technology powerhouse, with technology clusters in Delhi/Gurgaon, Mumbai, Pune, Bengaluru, and Hyderabad; with over 80 unicorns created over the past few years, and 41 unicorns in 2021 alone. An Indian entrepreneurial spirit, enabled through support for start-ups in education, business, government, investors and associations, have made India among the world's leaders in innovation leading to commercialization. Building a well-funded, talent-driven Canada-India innovation ecosystem that leverages investment and markets, entrepreneur-ship and innovation, will unlock transformative technologies in the two economies with mutually complementary strengths.

Third, sectoral diversification. While not all sectors are equal in terms of opportunity and potential, particularly those that are protected, there are many sectors that are full of opportunity for growth. Canadian engagement has tapped our traditional strength natural resources, education, and agri-food exports. Diversification into emerging areas such as deep technology and innovation, infrastructure services, biotechnology and healthcare, and agricultural technology can significantly expand the breadth of potential bilateral trade.

Fourth, leveraging Canada's investing success. Canadian institutional and private investors have committed significant capital across India over the past several years, estimated today at over $65 billion. It signals a strong, long-term, and ongoing commitment to the Indian market. This confi-dence in the Indian market has been welcomed and appreciated by India, and places Canada among world leaders in India's business environment. Canadian investment in India is important to both industry and govern-ment, an impact that can and should be leveraged to grow bilateral trade. Canadian investment can play a major role in the development of major Indian infrastructure projects, and offers opportunities for Canadian com-panies active in the infrastructure sector. The development of Indian infra-structure across rail, road, port, and air alone is remarkable. The country is on the path toward a transformation akin to that pursued by China in the last half century. With world-class Canadian investment and infrastructure capabilities, Canadian leadership can play a critical role in participating in this transformation.

And fifth, market access and trade agreements. Without a free trade agreement, bilateral trade can continue to grow modestly, but an agreement can be helpful in spurring greater trade both ways. However, as negotiations for a Comprehensive Economic Partnership Agreement have been going on for more than a decade without conclusion, consideration should be given to first, launching an updated feasibility study, and second, to focus on areas of common ground to lock in an agreement that includes a firm commitment toward more graduated liberalization.

The only feasibility study that was undertaken before the formal launch of negotiations was completed in 2010; since then, much has changed in the global trade landscape, and by extension the bilateral trade landscape, across technology sectors, economic reforms, and a global pandemic. An updated Joint Study would yield clear outcomes for a prospective trade agreement, and inform specific areas to focus on for concluding a near-term agreement that serves mutual interests, given today's reality. And second, rather than a comprehensive agreement, what can be achieved in the short term are agreements on specific areas where cooperation has already been achieved. To build a basis for long-term cooperation, concluding initial agreements alongside timelines for further expansion would help unlock initial agreements providing companies the confidence to engage with the requisite ambition for building the relationship.

## Economic Ties a Gateway for Development in the Indo-Pacific

A strong Canadian focus on Indian economic development provides a natural gateway to Canadian engagement in Indo-Pacific development and growth. As partners for soft power across the region, Canada and India can scale up the benefits of a partnership that succeeds in India, and across ASEAN nations. Together in the region, the success of Canadian and Indian collaboration as economic partners, in such areas as strong economic domestic reforms; scaling innovation to modernize rural regions; environment and climate change policy; sectoral diversification from energy transition to food security; partnerships across infrastructure and investment; and, trade agreements animating movement of services and people, holds tremendous potential.

A Canada-India partnership should be built on a foundation both nations care deeply about: elevating women, addressing climate change, and rules-based security cooperation, to start. Such a partnership can accomplish meaningful results in the day-to-day lives of people who demand infrastructure that works, reliable local electricity, and public transportation and sanitation that is essential to health and dignity.

For Canada to achieve the impact it desires across the Indo-Pacific, it should focus not on the quantity of bilateral engagements, but quality on those it prioritizes. To this end, India as a focus for Canadian economic engagement, and as a gateway to a developing Indo-Pacific, makes eminent sense.

## Mutual Security with India for Canadian Security in the Indo-Pacific

There is no question that Canadian engagement in the Indo-Pacific must be multi-faceted, going beyond trade, investment and economic security, and include a concerted effort as rules-based allies supporting regional security.

Our democracies are confronting similar threats, and with international alliances updating themselves to counter authoritarian regimes and technology-enabled disruptions, so too must the Canadian and Indian security relationship grow.

Security cooperation is essential to confront authoritarian disinformation, transnational crime and terrorism, cybersecurity threats and other destabilization efforts. It rests on a mutual understanding of the post-pandemic world, where vulnerabilities have become more pronounced, where commerce has become weaponized, and where greater engagement, dialogue and collaboration can reinforce mutual objectives toward greater security in the region.

India provides a particular partner for Canadian strategic defense interests across the Indo-Pacific. The existing foundation includes training exercises, liaison officers, and personnel training, but defence technology collaboration, joint training, and defence production stand to be dramatically improved. Canada and India can accomplish shared objectives in border security with high arctic and mountain warfare cooperation, liaisons aimed at strengthened interoperability across the Quadrilateral Security Dialogue partners, and stronger cybersecurity and intelligence cooperation.

India also is in need of trusted partners in scaling its defence production and technologies. While Canadian defence industry has been focused on supplying allied and U.S. security, it has technologies capable of strengthening Indian defence capacity in the Indo-Pacific age of competition. As Indian defence procurement and production capabilities expand, the Canadian national security space should seek to engage with India as indispensable partners in Indo-Pacific security.

Finally, Canada and India must confront a central issue that has at times inhibited needed ambition in mutual security. As countries born of the same political heritage, woven together in modern times by strong interests for deeper collaboration, a clear understanding of how extremism affects security cooperation is required in both strategic communities. Both countries are dynamic democracies, governed by the rule of law, and empowered by freedom of speech and religion. Neither shares the extreme authoritarian tendencies exhibited by others in the region. For our countries to cooperate in national security, it is essential to confront extremism in both countries, and for governments to prioritize mutual security interests in support of security and stability in the region.

## Elevating the Canada India Relationship

### Bridging Governments

The first step toward India emerging as Canada's priority across the Indo-Pacific is by elevating regular government-to-government relations. This builds on a multi-faceted relationship, but one dormant in many areas. Ottawa needs to elevate India to the level of its relationships with its partners in NATO.

This would feature frequent direct contact by Ministers and in-person visits that are followed by meaningful engagement in foreign policy, trade, energy, and finance. With the Indian presence not only at the G20, but now a regular observer at the G7 table, it is incumbent on both governments to ensure a robust strategic dialogue between Finance Ministers, thus far a notable omission. For both democracies, critical conversations on monetary policy, supply chain security, regulatory alignment and international finance are essential, perhaps more now than ever before given the global pandemic coupled with worldwide macroeconomic headwinds.

Trust also needs to be strengthened between foreign ministries, which can only be accomplished by wider, deeper, and more frequent engagements between the two capitals. These engagements require regular working groups, where officials in both countries can come to know each other better, and engage in frank discussions from which all partnerships benefit. There will be issues where interests don't align or perspectives differ. But a strong relationship is one where parties agree to disagree. As others have done, Canada needs to pursue an ambitious partnership with India that doesn't ignore key differences, but also doesn't treat them as fundamental barriers to making the relationship a priority.

In prioritizing India for Canada in the Indo-Pacific, more Canadian personnel are required to animate the relationship across India. Compared to our peers, Canada's diplomatic presence remains significantly understaffed and could stand to benefit from greater ambition—a trade policy and market access team, more investment attraction professionals, for example. Canadian provinces should be more engaged by federal officials to enhance coverage across more Indian states, particularly those with promising governance and aligned economic priorities. More Canadian trade offices should be established in second tier cities emerging as regional economic hubs such as Surat, Pune, and Gurgaon.

Internationally, from the G20, World Bank ,and the United Nations, from India's observer status at the G7 and Canada's potential as an observer at the Quad, from the World Health Organization to forums spanning the Arctic, the oceans and outer space, Canadian and Indian experts should be convened by their governments toward closer multi- and pluri-lateral cooperation. Canada must strive to attain a seat at the table in key regional groupings and forums, the Quad being the most notable example. Others are actively working to enmesh India as a key ally/partner in the context of these regional groupings, and India's voice is carrying a growing regional influence, and a say in future groupings. A stronger and closer partnership with India will bolster Canada's influence in the region.

## Reframing How Canadians Perceive India

There is no doubt that Canada, a country of 40 million, can easily be eclipsed by India, with its a population of 1.4 billion. Not only does there need to be a better understanding of India's importance in Canada, there also needs to be a great deal of teamwork by Canada and India. Nearly 1.5 million Canadians of Indian origin are both a domestic constituency and a cultural bridge between two vibrant democracies. In many ways, a strong, thriving, active Indian diaspora in Canada helps ensure relations continue to thrive and grow.

The Indian diaspora is important to India too. India has had a ministry dedicated to serving overseas Indians. It features prominently for the Modi government, which prioritizes large scale outreach to diaspora communities across the world. Business, academic, spiritual, and cultural communities across Canada, can enhance greater engagement.

Canadian private philanthropy could be engaged to invest in thought leadership and in elevating knowledge about India, and India's importance to Canada in the Indo-Pacific, across wider Canadian public opinion. The Canadian government's upcoming Indo-Pacific strategy also provides an opportunity to support businesses, associations, think tanks, and universities in defining India's importance to Canadian ambitions in the Indo-Pacific.

Much of this can be accomplished by establishing a centre of excellence in Canada focused on the Canada-India relationship and its importance to Canadian interests in Indo-Pacific stability and security. Properly constituted, such as a centre can be an indispensable resource for deep knowledge, forward-leaning thought leadership, relevant policy research collaboration, and leveraging talent in both countries.

## Conclusion

We need a plan if we are to succeed, a plan that makes the most of long-standing, multi-faceted ties. A plan for a transformational economic relationship. A plan reflecting our mutual security interests. And a plan for the long-term engagement of our strategic communities. Approaching the relationship with persistence, patience and a long view is critical, and will pay dividends on both sides.

The competitive nature of diplomatic engagement with India should not be underestimated, and anything short of an all-in approach to engagement will set Canada apart from its competitors, to its disadvantage.

In the Indo-Pacific age now upon us, Canadians will need to make critical choices around our most important partnerships.

India presents this opportunity. With India at the center for Canadian priorities across the Indo-Pacific, Canadian strengths can be leveraged and realized across the region, assuring our place as much as a Pacific power as Canada has been an Atlantic one.

# 11

# Canada and Indonesia
# Leonard J. Edwards

LOCATED FAR from Canadian shores and in line of sight seemingly tucked away behind most of Southeast Asia, Indonesia remains a largely unknown country to most Canadians. Indonesia's modest exports to Canada get little recognition. The personal ties that are so important for building familiarity are few. There are only about 21,400 Canadians of Indonesian descent, according to the 2016 Census, and very little in the way of the educational, cultural, or touristic interaction common with many other Asian countries. Accordingly, awareness remains low. To the extent Canadians think of Indonesia, it is often coloured by the memory of Indonesia as an autocratic state under presidents Sukarno and Suharto from 1966 to 1998, and of Jakarta's brutal suppression of East Timorese independence from 1976 to 1999. The demonstrations against President Suharto during the Vancouver APEC Summit in 1997 and the public inquiry that followed provided news coverage well into 2001.

The lack of familiarity has not been helped by Canada's general reluctance for the past two decades to embrace Asia as a national priority in foreign policy, economic and security terms, and our "come and go" pattern of engagement generally with the region. Among the larger Asian countries, Indonesia has been the most consistent recipient of Canadian neglect.

## Why Indonesia Matters?

Today's Indonesia is far from the dated image just described. It is already a country of consequence, dominant in Southeast Asia and a rising global player by most measures.

Indonesia currently has the world's eighth-largest economy measured in GDP based on purchasing power parity (PPP). It has been predicted to rise to seventh place in 2030 and fourth place by 2050.[136] In contrast, Canada is ahead in nominal GDP (9th place to Indonesia's 16th), but in PPP terms is already behind Indonesia in 17th place, falling possibly to 22nd spot by 2050.[137]

At 277 million persons in 2020, Indonesia is the fourth most populous country globally and the largest predominantly Muslim state.[138] It is projected to grow to 300 million in 2050.[139] Unlike most other Asian countries where ageing is underway, Indonesia is relatively young, with 50% of its population under 30, guaranteeing a robust labour force and consumer market for years to come. Despite its multitude of rural towns and villages, Indonesia is urbanising in remote locations. According to Statista, over 56% of Indonesia's population resided in urban settings in 2020, up from just under 50% in 2010. Indonesia is also digitally "well connected" with almost 200 million smartphone users and the fourth-largest smartphone market in the world.[140] While poverty still exists, the Asian Development Bank has estimated that Indonesia's middle class, with its attendant purchasing power, will grow to 220 million persons by 2030.

These are remarkable facts and prognostications. They bolster Indonesia's growing political influence outside its borders, harkening back to its post-independence leadership in the Non-Aligned Movement and the Group of 77 bloc of developing countries within the United Nations. Indonesia (with Canada) was among the founding members of the G20, where it sees itself as a continuing voice for developing countries. Regionally, Indonesia was very active in creating the Asia Pacific Economic Cooperation group (APEC) in 1989 and hosted the most important of its earliest meetings in Bogor in 1994. Representing around 40% of economic activity within the Association of Southeast Asian Nations (ASEAN), Indonesia is its leading player, and the home of ASEAN's Secretariat since 2013.

Indonesia also matters because it has become, since the end of the Suharto period in 1998, the world's third-largest democracy after India and the United States. This remarkable turnabout—though still imperfect—provides

a vital kinship opportunity for Canada and other democracies with a growing Asian power at a time when democratic institutions and democracies
themselves are being tested almost everywhere.

Finally, Indonesia matters for reasons of regional and global security.
Challenged with a make-up of 4 large islands and almost 17,500 smaller
ones across a maritime area wider than all of Canada, Indonesia is a maritime "giant" with a massive exclusive economic zone (EEZ). It sits astride
the most critical shipping lanes in the world. The Strait of Malacca between
Indonesia, Singapore, and Malaysia, plus the Lombok and Sunda Straits
through the Indonesian archipelago, account for almost half of the world's
total annual seaborne trade tonnage.[141] According to ESCAP, 42% of the
world's exports and 38% of global imports in 2021 were expected to pass
through the Indo-Pacific.[142] While hostilities could have catastrophic
impacts, lesser events such as acts of piracy and terrorism or environmental
and natural disasters threaten lives, sea lanes, and livelihoods.

Indonesia is also caught up in China's claim to sovereignty over a large
area of the South China Sea within its self-proclaimed "nine-dash line"
(a claim not supported by a ruling by the Hague Tribunal in 2016), which
has raised tensions with ASEAN countries wishing to exercise the right
to develop the resources within their EEZ's. This includes areas around
Indonesia's Natuna Islands Group, where China conducted seismic surveys
in the second half of 2021 as a way of asserting its claim.

## Taking Stock: Good Beginnings but Poor Results Since 2000

Canada's relationship with Indonesia has a firm political foundation, going
back to Canada's support for Indonesia's independence in the late 1950s and
1960s, and Jakarta's effort to acquire UN membership. Many Indonesians
positively remember the innovative Canada/Indonesia South China Sea
workshop process in the 1990s, a non-governmental initiative that explored
the difficult maritime issues now in the headlines due to China's aggressive
claims. Much goodwill is also present from Canada's role as a provider of

Official Development Assistance over many years, evolving in recent years into such areas as capacity building and poverty reduction, governance and regulatory reform.

The political relationship was much tested during Indonesia's three-decade shift to autocratic rule and Jakarta's occupation of East Timor. Nonetheless, official, ministerial, and other occasions (such as the major Team Canada visit to Jakarta in 1996 led by then Prime Minister Jean Chrétien) provided avenues for frank political dialogue, accompanied by good trade and business relations growth. With the end of the Suharto period in 1998, the political environment improved, only to be countered by the dampening effects of the Asian financial crisis post-1997 and Canada's lower engagement generally in Asia during the first decade of the 21st century.

Since 2010 there has been an effort to rekindle the official relationship. In 2014 foreign ministers agreed to an "Indonesia–Canada Plan of Action 2014–2019" of largely conventional steps to reinvigorate bilateral links. However, the wrongful arrest and conviction in 2014 of a Canadian teacher in Indonesia led almost immediately to the suspension of all high-level official contacts and initiatives by the Canadian government, a situation not resolved until the teacher's release in 2019.

In business and trade, the pattern is repeated by several strong historical performances. In 1968 Inco Canada Ltd. signed an agreement with the Government of Indonesia to establish nickel mining and smelting in Sulawesi. Brazil's Vale took over Inco Canada in 2006. In the financial sector, Canada's Manulife has been offering insurance and wealth management services since the 1980s. Sun Life is also present. Recently, major exporters have included Canpotex in providing fertilizer potash, and Cargill Canada and AGT Foods of Regina in the agri-food sector. Blackberry and Bombardier, and environmental service firms have also been active.

In trade terms, however, the 2000s have been years of stagnation. exports to Indonesia slumped between 1996 and 2010, and while they climbed afterwards, Canada's overall share of the Indonesian import market fell from 2% in the 1970s and '80s to about 1% in 2015.[143]

A report published in 2016 by Canada's Centre for International Governance Innovation (CIG) following a major bilateral symposium in Jakarta on the future of Canada–Indonesian relations and co-organized by Indonesia's prestigious Centre for Strategic and International Studies, came to this conclusion:

> *"The scope and record of Canadian engagement in Indonesia have been uneven. While our development efforts continue to shine and our "brand" is broadly positive, Canadians are seen to be inclined to short-term transactional approaches to commerce and as seldom staying long on the brief in terms of regional security. Partly as a consequence, Indonesians underestimate the advantages of working with Canada as a potentially valuable partner on the North American platform."*[144]

## A New Foundation and a Fresh Start

It is clear that Indonesia increasingly matters in today's world. It is also clear that Canada, after a strong start, has not taken full advantage of the opportunities available through its relationship with a growing Indonesia.

In comparison, and while proximity dictates the importance Australia attaches to Indonesia, the cluster of major bilateral initiatives between those two countries since 2017 is striking: a Comprehensive Strategic Partnership (CSP) (2018), a Comprehensive Economic Partnership (2018), a Maritime Cooperation Plan (2018), a CSP Plan of Action (2020), and a Blueprint for Trade and Investment (2021). New Zealand has followed suit with its Comprehensive Partnership agreement with Indonesia in 2018 and a Plan of Action (2020).

Canadians have a decision to make. Do we continue to treat this future economic giant, a key regional and growing global player, as a lesser interest in the Indo-Pacific? Or do we raise Indonesia to the level of other "First Tier" relationships in Asia—with India, Japan, Korea, and Australia—setting aside the unique challenge of China?

If we choose the latter path, we have much work to do.

While there is a lingering fondness for Canada among older Indonesian elites who remember Canada's past profile in Asian affairs and our active bilateral presence in the '80s and '90s, they also wonder why we backed away. At the same time, today's leadership in government and business have far less knowledge about Canada. Therefore, we must ensure that our Indonesia "strategy" includes efforts not only to re-convince still influential older Indonesians that Canada is back to stay but to persuade younger decision makers that we have as much or more to offer than many of the new competitors now courting Indonesia.

This calls for a fresh start rather than an adjustment in today's outdated approach, a re-build, not a renovation. We need a new foundation for a 21st-century relationship.

The 2016 CIGI report "Innovation and Change: Forging the New Canada Indonesia Partnership" suggests some "commonalities" that could form such a foundation and serve as "drivers" in our relationship:

- Our roles and responsibilities as major economies, G20 members, and supporters of a prosperous and peaceful international order;
- Our commitment to democracy and democratic systems of governance;
- Our responsibilities as major "maritime states";
- Our challenges as large countries: for example, overcoming distance, infrastructure needs, internal cohesion, needs of rural and remote communities, adapting to and fighting climate change; and
- Our positions as major resource-rich commodity producers.

This new Canada–Indonesia relationship must be strategically managed and integrated into a coherent whole. It will require engaged leadership from the top on both sides and managed under a ministerial-level oversight mechanism. It should have a regularly reviewed action plan. It must weather differences of view and short-term crises (including difficult consular cases).

Long-term success will also depend on a deliberate effort to strengthen the weak underpinnings of mutual awareness that now exists in both countries by encouraging more travel, cultural, educational, and more people-to-people exchanges generally.

To quote the "Innovation and Change" Report:

*One overarching conclusion is clear: an integrated and interdisciplinary approach, pursued in an innovative, pragmatic and results-oriented manner, would serve Canada best.*[145]

## Going Forward: Partners in Opportunity

Through a strategic approach and taking advantage of the opportunities opened up by the "commonalities" we share, we have a good chance of establishing by 2030 the beginnings of the durable "Tier One" partnership we need to have with Indonesia this century. Here are four areas where we should move forward quickly.

**1. Expanding trade, business, and economic cooperation**

An essential step in this direction was the announcement on June 20, 2021, that Canada and Indonesia have launched negotiations on a "Comprehensive Economic Partnership Agreement" or CEPA. If successful, it will cut or reduce tariffs and non-tariff barriers in areas of importance to growth in two-way trade and greatly facilitate growth in trade in goods and services. While the level of ambition is not set out in the public announcement, it is hoped to be high.

In parallel with this initiative, Canada should seek to institutionalize regular exchanges with Indonesia on economic policy, development priorities, regulatory systems, and other areas, especially where Canadian experience might be helpful to Indonesian policymakers. This could, in turn, create a more receptive environment for Canadian business. The Canadian government should enhance its in-country support to business ahead of the conclusion of the CEPA, both as a sign of serious intent to the Indonesians and to give businesses a head start in exposure to the opportunities expected to flow from it.

More Canadian companies must be physically present in Indonesia to track possible opportunities and market their products and services. As many international companies do, dealing with Indonesia from an offshore base such as Singapore will increasingly be regarded in Jakarta as indicating a lack of seriousness and even respect.

The establishment in 2012 of the Canada ASEAN Business Council has helped Canadian companies expand trade and investment opportunities in ASEAN, including in Indonesia. With the CETA talks underway, it could be time to establish a specific Indonesia–Canada CEO Dialogue between the Business Council of Canada and an Indonesian counterpart to provide impetus and input.

The 2016 "Innovation and Change" study cited above identified four areas of exceptionally high potential for Canadian businesses:

• Infrastructure Development[146]
• Agriculture and Food Security[147]
• Services, especially Financial Services[148]
• Education and Technical Training[149]

Indonesia's infrastructure needs are enormous, and the opportunities available are widely known. Canadian firms in various fields are world-class, including project management, engineering, transit systems, aerospace, telecommunications, and environmental services. The Canadian Government has provided funding to Indonesia in the past to help develop the county's P3 (public-private partnership) model. Canada's long association with Indonesian resource development should help open the door to our engineering and project management expertise, and environmental services, among others.

Canada and Indonesia are also natural partners in agriculture and agri-food security. The opportunity lies in developing food security partnerships that combine the supply of high-quality Canadian food products with elements that improve the productivity and nutritional value of Indonesia's own food production. For instance, Saskatchewan provides grains and pulses plus significant potash shipments for agricultural use in Indonesia. Other examples include technical assistance and training by Canadian institutions and agri-food companies that maximize the nutritional benefits in Canadian products, the teaching of agriculture and aquaculture sciences, the supply of Canadian genetic materials, and the improvement of Indonesia's food chain infrastructure. These initiatives could make this sector a major people-to-people "highway" between Indonesia and Canada, engaging producers, agri-businesses and rural communities.

Canada could facilitate Indonesia's efforts to market their agri-food products in Canada by removing technical barriers to trade often raised by the Indonesian side.

The services sector represents another partnership opportunity, starting with financial services. Manulife and Sunlife have established Canada's solid reputation. Working with the University of Waterloo, the Canadian government has contributed to a project to build regulatory capacity in Indonesia's financial, insurance, and pension sectors. Therefore, the environment is suitable for other financial firms, including Canada's banks hitherto largely absent in the rapidly growing Indonesian economy.

Other areas of opportunity include engineering and oil and gas project management services. With its young digitally connected population, there is also a market for services in information technology and "creative industries."

An exciting opportunity lies in education and training. World Bank and other studies conclude that without a significant expansion in the supply of skilled workers and able managers, Indonesia will be hard-pressed to maintain annual GDP growth of 5 to 6% as projected, and could fall short of needs by as many as 9 million persons educated to secondary or tertiary levels by 2030.[150] Opportunities thus exist for Canadian educational institutions and businesses in both the vocational and university fields.

Historically, Indonesians have not gone abroad in large numbers to study. If they go, they prefer Asian destinations for proximity and cost reasons. While Australia gets around 16,000–17,000 students annually as an English-speaking destination, Canada's modest numbers rose 65% between 2014 and 2018 to almost 2000 students. They could increase further depending on scholarships and cost considerations, plus the availability of welcoming communities and social environments, which are important factors.[151] Demand for international university education, particularly in English, is likely to grow as Indonesia's integration into the global economy increases.

Education and training services will have a long-term payback in enhanced awareness of Canada in Indonesia especially if some of Indonesia's future leaders in business and government can trace their education back to Canada.

## 2. Advancing regional security

The relative peace and stability have been fundamental to East Asia's dynamism and growth in the past four decades. Economics and security are also intertwined in the future of the Indo-Pacific.If Canada wishes to achieve a deeper economic partnership with Indonesia, we must also demonstrate a deeper interest in Indonesian and ASEAN security. In doing so, we will also enhance Canada's security in both regional and global terms.

Our shared experience as maritime nations provides a unique platform and a set of opportunities for collaboration with Indonesia. Canada has the longest coastline of any country in the world, with Indonesia the second longest. We both have substantial maritime spaces and exclusive economic zones, with the same challenges: oversight of sea lanes and ports, the exercise of sovereignty in the exploration, regulation and use of marine resources (including oil and gas) in our exclusive economic zones and over the continental shelf, management of offshore fisheries, and environmental protection. We both face the need constantly to demonstrate "domain awareness."

There is no shortage of exciting options for cooperation with Indonesia under the maritime security theme. We only have to convince them that engaging with Canada on such matters has benefits. Informal conversations might be a place to start.

Memories are still positive in Jakarta from the non-governmental Workshop that Canada and Indonesia co-chaired during the 1990s on "Managing Potential Conflicts in the South China Sea." While the threat of conflict has reached a level that requires initiatives by governments themselves, such as confidence-building and other measures, there may still be potential in using the Workshop mechanism to explore ideas in functional cooperation in the South China Sea, thus lowering tensions and perhaps restoring some semblance of regular activity pending formal resolution of the dispute, which could take many years. One useful initiative could be a Workshop on developing cooperation in the management of fisheries in the contested areas. Fisheries have been seriously disrupted by the dispute affecting the livelihoods and safety of fishers from all affected states.

While these and other possible initiatives with Indonesia would help build a stronger relationship, contribute to Indo-Pacific security and demonstrate Canadian commitment, they should be accompanied by a greater presence by Canada's Armed Forces and closer ties with Indonesia's military.

Indonesia's military is the largest in ASEAN, the 6th largest in Asia and the 14th largest globally. These rankings justify Canada making Indonesia a priority country for an enhanced defence relationship and cooperation between Canadian and Indonesian militaries. Under the envisaged new strategic relationship between Canada and Indonesia, this could take the form of an agreement for regular in-depth discussions and cooperation on security and defence issues, particularly in the maritime context, enhanced military-to-military visits and personnel exchanges, especially between navies, and increased participation in regional exercises.

### 3. Supporting good governance and democracy

Canada already has a long history of working with Indonesians in developing their country through the provision of resources and expertise. Many Canadian individuals and institutions, led by Canada's Development Cooperation programs, and involving the International Development Research Centre (IDRC), the Conference Board of Canada, the Canadian International Grains Institute, and universities such as McGill and Waterloo have established relationships and shared experiences and advice with Indonesian counterparts.

The broad area of governance stands out in terms of major potential. As democracies, we have similar governance challenges. We can learn from each other in such areas as making economic success accessible to everyone in society, involving marginalized groups in the political process, and engaging more youth. Canada could learn from Indonesia—unencumbered by historical political practices and systems—how digital tools are being used to reach remote communities and voters, organize politically at the grassroots level, and vote and compile election results.

These kinds of exchanges and debates featuring Indonesian and Canadian democracies—one relatively new and adaptable, the other older and more fixed in its ways—one Asian the other "Western"—could be beneficial during these times when democratic forms of government are under siege around the world. Perhaps our countries can help make democracy work better globally and adapt to the times.

### 4. Cooperating on global affairs

Canada has long prided itself on a global vocation, engaging positively on major political, security, and economic affairs. As our relative position in the world's power rankings declines, we will need "alliances" with some rising powers to ensure Canada's voice, the collective voice of Canadians, still carries weight at the world's decision-making tables in the decades ahead.

This is another reason to make Indonesia, a leading "emerging" nation, a "strategic partner" and one of our most important relationships this century. This transcends the Indo-Pacific context, although it is relevant to it since Asia will be wielding ever-greater influence over global affairs as the years pass.

Canada should look hard where Indonesia can become a close partner in global affairs and begin building a stronger working relationship with Jakarta. Regular high-level "strategic" consultations on global matters should become the norm. The future of the rules-based trading system and the WTO could be a common area. We face similar challenges on climate change arising from our exploitation of natural resources, agricultural production, and transportation challenges over long distances. Shoring up the nuclear non-proliferation system at a time of rising international tensions could be another.

# Conclusion

The 2016 Report quoted earlier entitled "Innovation and Change: Forging the New Canada–Indonesia Partnership" concluded as follows:

*"Canada has a choice to make: either continue to deal with Indonesia as one of a number of Canada's 'second-tier relationships' in the Asia-Pacific, with episodic incremental activity and a responsive approach to developments, or to move decisively and deliberately to place Indonesia among its first tier of priority countries both regionally and globally."*[153]

Among the recommendations contained in the Report were the following[154]:

* Upgrade Canada's relations with Indonesia to a "Strategic Partnership" by 2020;
* Create an annual Multi-Ministerial Dialogue of Foreign, Defense and Trade Ministers to provide overall direction to this new partnership;
* Initiate regular high-level political-military talks and enhance defence and military diplomacy, visits, and exercises, emphasizing navy-to-navy;
* Launch a Trade and Investment Policy Agenda to open up trade in both directions;
* Establish a Canada-Indonesia Bilateral Business Dialogue;
* Designate Indonesia as a priority country in Canada's International Education Strategy;
* Organize a major Maritime Nations Conference, and set up an informal track 1.5 workshops on fisheries management issues in the South China Sea chaired by Canada and Indonesia;
* Establish a Canada-Indonesia Citizens Network on Governance; and
* Hold a "Year of Canada" in Indonesia.

Of these ambitious recommendations, only the proposal on a Trade Agenda has been taken up, improved to include the negotiation of a Comprehensive Economic Partnership Agreement mentioned in this chapter. This is a significant step for which the governments of Canada and Indonesia should be applauded.

The remaining proposals for significant initiatives are more urgent six years after their writing in 2016, for the reasons set out in this chapter. If Canada is to have anything like the kind of sturdy and beneficial *long-term* partnership it needs with this coming Asian giant and fully functioning in 2030, we must move now.

# 12

# Canada and Republic of Korea

# Tina J. Park

O NCE CALLED "A land of morning calm," the Korean peninsula, located at the centre of Northeast Asia, holds an essential key for peace and prosperity in the Indo-Pacific region and the global market at large.[155] During its more than 5,000 years of history, Korea has survived frequent invasion by powerful neighbours, including Mongolia and China; it has fought to preserve national unity and has found its own identity amidst various waves of imperialism. The 20th century brought new challenges: the Japanese occupation and the Korean War, which continues to leave its mark with the division across the 38th parallel. Geopolitically, the Korean peninsula is one of the only remnants of the Cold War as the south remains preoccupied with security threats posed by North Korea (backed by Beijing and Moscow), China's growing assertiveness, as well as an ongoing presence of the UN Command and the Combined Forces with the United States. Today, some 28,000 U.S. Forces are stationed in South Korea, and South Korea's defence strategies are closely aligned with American priorities. Yet, China is also the country's biggest trading partner, with exports of over USD 13.4 billion in 2021; Chinese support is essential for containing North Korea's nuclear ambitions. For the last South Korean President Moon Jae-in, whose term ended this spring and whose top priority has been reconciliation with North Korea[156] (including a formal end to the Korean War), these realities necessitated a delicate balancing of the relationship between Beijing and Washington.

From the Canadian perspective, Korea first gained Ottawa's attention after Canada's participation in the Korean War, and more significantly after the sale of CANDU reactors in the 1970s, when it was clear that the South Korean economy had quickly transformed from a former aid recipient to a viable trading partner. Canada and South Korea's bilateral history has been overwhelmingly positive. Still, it has often been taken for granted by both countries, their respective foreign policies preoccupied with the United States and, more recently, China. While Ottawa and Seoul share many everyday concerns, values, and priorities, there is room for a more substantive political and economic partnership.

## Historical Context: Canada–Korea Relations in a Nutshell

Canadian engagement on the Korean peninsula began with early missionaries in the 1880s, pioneers who served as human bridges linking the two countries until official diplomatic relations were established in 1963. This unofficial missionary contact formed the backbone of Canadian involvement on the Korean peninsula until the outbreak of the Korean War. Europe, rather than Asia, was Ottawa's preoccupation, although Ottawa did establish a legation in Japan in 1929 and opened an embassy in Nationalist China in 1943. The Canadian embassy in Seoul did not open until 1973.

When the UN Command Military Armistice Commission was established to supervise the implementation of the armistice agreement ending hostilities on the Korean peninsula, Canada, in full support of the then-newly created United Nations and its ally, the United States, deployed 26,791 soldiers between 1950 and the summer of 1953. In total, 516 Canadians died in Korea, and 378 of those soldiers were buried in the UN Memorial Cemetery in Busan.[157] Commonly referred to as a "friendship sealed in blood," Canada's participation in the Korean War, coupled with its missionaries' earlier cultural and intellectual work, significantly contributed to Canadians' positive perception of the Korean public. More recently, there have been efforts to commemorate the Korean War and to better recognize Korean War veterans in Canada, most notably through the Korean War Veterans Act (S-213).[158]

Having been introduced to the peninsula as part of the United Nations forces, and guided by the influence of church boards and the offspring of former missionaries, Ottawa's strategic interest and humanitarian impulses continued to guide Canadian–Korean relations well into the 1960s. Ultimately, South Korea's rapid industrialization and the sale of the CANDU reactor in the 1970s elevated Seoul's importance for Canadian policymakers. Since then, political relationships between the two countries have remained cordial and without any notable friction; Canada and Korea see each other as like-minded allies in multilateral forums such as the UN and the G20.

Through trade, immigration and defence cooperation, Canadian–Korean relations continued to blossom from the 1980s onwards. These relations have more recently borne fruit with the establishment of the Canada and Korea "Strategic Partnership" in 2014 and the implementation of the Canada–Korea Free Trade Agreement in 2015—Canada's first FTA in the Asia-Pacific region. As the two Koreas technically remain at war, Canada has continued to maintain its presence in the UN Command. It participates in various exercises with the United States and other allies to help keep peace and security on the Korean peninsula.

# A Snapshot of the South Korean Economy & Society Today

Today, South Korea boasts the tenth-largest economy globally, with a Gross Domestic Product (GDP) of USD 1.6 trillion in 2020 and a population size of 51.8 million people (as of July 2021). South Korea's growth from the 1960s, when its GDP per capita was comparable to the levels of poorest African countries, to its emergence as a highly developed and globally connected economy today, is a story of remarkable economic success. South Korea's GDP is concentrated almost entirely in industry and services (97.6%), notably in semiconductors, electronics, telecommunications, automobile production, chemicals, shipbuilding, and steel.[159] Tech giants like Naver, Coupang, and Kakao, gaming companies and K-Pop and *Hallyu* (The Korean Wave) cultural products have become ace players for the South Korean economy. For instance, BTS, a seven-member South Korean K-Pop group, generated

USD $4.9 billion for the South Korean economy and the movie *Parasite* generated USD $258 million in revenue.[160] Even K-Dramas, South Korean TV shows like Squid Game and Single's Inferno, which Netflix produced, have enjoyed global popularity, especially during the COVID-19 pandemic. These successes are generating ripple effects in job creation, related sales of Korean products, attracting tourism and expanding South Korea's soft power. Generally referred to as the "content industry," South Korea's export of cultural products generated USD 10.8 billion in 2020. As the chart below from Bloomberg indicates, the value of the content industry is still only one-tenth of semiconductor exports. Still, it is fast-growing and well ahead of household appliances.[161]

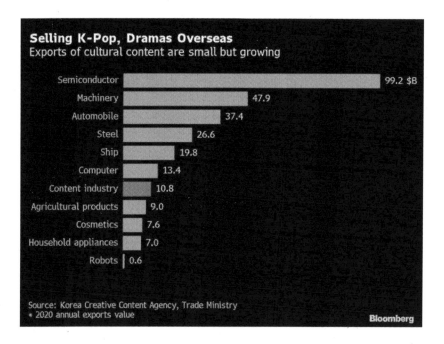

**Selling K-Pop, Dramas Overseas**
Exports of cultural content are small but growing

| | |
|---|---|
| Semiconductor | 99.2 $B |
| Machinery | 47.9 |
| Automobile | 37.4 |
| Steel | 26.6 |
| Ship | 19.8 |
| Computer | 13.4 |
| Content industry | 10.8 |
| Agricultural products | 9.0 |
| Cosmetics | 7.6 |
| Household appliances | 7.0 |
| Robots | 0.6 |

Source: Korea Creative Content Agency, Trade Ministry
* 2020 annual exports value                                    Bloomberg

To put things into perspective, South Korea's land size is about 1/100th that of Canada's. Approximately 70% of the country is considered mountainous, which has resulted in a high population density, especially in metropolitan areas such as Seoul, Gyeonggi, and Busan. With most minerals on the Korean peninsula being concentrated in areas north of the 38th parallel, South Korea's economic growth since the Korean War has not been driven by natural resources but by its highly educated workforce, high productivity levels, and a cultural penchant for efficiency.

In light of its dependency on high-performing human capital, it is a bit concerning that South Korea's demographics point to a rapidly shrinking population. According to the CIA's estimate, it has one of the world's lowest birth rates (0.26% population growth rate) and an aging population.[162] The fertility rate in Seoul is at about 0.84, far below the replacement rate of 2.1 to sustain a population. According to *The Economist*, changing roles for women and extended hours of South Korean businesses, combined with rigid social hierarchies and the high costs of affordable housing and raising a family, are all contributing factors to this decline.[163] Moreover, many young people in South Korea find marriage, which they perceive as getting in the way of professional success, to be unappealing—meaning that the average annual consumer expenditure in South Korea has been growing steadily over the last decade at about 5.0% per year. A rising middle-class population has also led to the rapid growth of the consumer food service industry (due to an increase in disposable income), with an expected total sales value of USD $104.6 billion by 2025 and some USD $31.1 billion for packaged food sales.[164]

Throughout the COVID-19 pandemic, South Korea was very successful at limiting infections through the use of a Triple C approach (Test, Trace, and Treat). It did not impose lock-down measures found in Canada or other parts of the world. Fuelled by stronger demand for exports, South Korea's economy remained resilient throughout the pandemic, shrinking by just 1% in 2020 compared to global output, which fell by 3.5%.[165] The Bank of Korea noted that South Korea's economic resilience during the pandemic could be attributed to its large manufacturing industry, effective pandemic response measures, and a strong base and culture for online shopping (South Korea is the world's third-largest e-commerce market).[166] According to an IPSOS report in 2021, the South Korean economy was the least impacted OECD country during the pandemic, again thanks to e-commerce and online/mobile shopping prevalence.[167] The OECD projects a 3% growth rate per year for the South Korean economy in 2022 and 2023, a solid projection of growth well ahead of many Western countries.

# Canada–Korea Free Trade Agreement

The Canada–Korea Free Trade Agreement, entered into force on January 1, 2015, represents a significant milestone for both countries.[168] Before the CKFTA, efforts to strengthen Canada's trade with South Korea included Team Canada missions and sectoral agreements.[169] None compared to the access that the CKFTA provides for both economies, particularly considering South Korea is the fourth-largest economy in Asia. The CKFTA is expected to increase Canadian exports to the ROK by 32%. Today, South Korea is Canada's seventh-largest merchandise trading partner, and two-way merchandise trade is valued at CAD 14.3 billion in 2020. Canada's exports to Korea totalled $4.7 billion, and Canadian imports from Korea totalled nearly $9.6 billion in 2020. Korean exports to Canada include passenger cars, wireless phones, automobile parts, tires, and steel. Key items for Canadian exports to Korea include mineral ores, mineral fuels, oils, copper ore, iron ore, meat, machinery, uranium, and pulp.[170] Upon full implementation of the CKFTA on January 1, 2032, it is expected that Korean tariffs will be eliminated on 99.75% of Canada's current exports and that the CKFTA will continue to foster collaboration and co-prosperity between the two countries in fields such as medicine, rail, steel, aerospace, artificial intelligence, and defence procurement.[171]

# People to People Ties

As well, South Korean immigration to Canada has been growing steadily since the 1966 reform of federal immigration regulations, which allowed for a merit-based points system. By 1969, there were only about 2,000 Koreans in Canada. That figure grew to nearly 20,000 by 1980. In the late 1990s, the ROK was the fifth-largest source of immigrants to Canada, according to Statistics Canada. There are over 220,000 individuals of Korean origin living in Canada at the moment, with an additional 25,000 international students from South Korea. As noted by Global Affairs Canada, the Indo-Pacific region represents the biggest source of international students in Canada, with South Korea ranking as the top third source country after India and China.[172] There are robust Korean–Canadian communities within Canada, most concentrated in Ontario, British Columbia, Quebec, and Alberta. There are also growing numbers of Canadians who live and work in the ROK; the latest figures include some 27,000 Canadians living in Korea, about ⅛ of them working as English teachers. Through immigration, tourism, education, investment, and cultural exchanges, people-to-people exchanges now form the foundation of the relationship between Canada and the ROK.

## Regional & Global Security

The security situation on the Korean peninsula has direct implications on market stability and global security well beyond the Indo-Pacific region. Geographically, the Korean peninsula is located in the strategic centre of Northeast Asia. This region includes China, Mongolia, Japan, and Russia, with the world's highest concentration of military and economic capabilities. Since the end of the Korean War in 1953, which resulted in a stalemate rather than a peace treaty, the demilitarized zone (DMZ) along the 38th parallel remains the most heavily fortified conflict zone in the post-Cold War era. The very existence of North Korea, led by successive dictators, is a cause for concern for the international community. From its nuclear weapons programme to inter-continental ballistic missiles to cyber operations, North Korea continually defies international norms and threatens peace and security on the Korean peninsula. Successive Kim regimes in the DPRK have used a façade of "*juche*" (self-reliance) to justify their excessive military spending, despite starving their 25 million people and committing crimes against humanity.

While the UN Security Council has imposed a series of sanctions over the past decade to tame North Korea's nuclear ambitions, it has not deterred the Kim regime. North Korea is actively engaged in illicit arms trade with Iran, Syria, and non-state terror groups like Hezbollah and Hamas to generate revenue. The regime has developed more sophisticated schemes to evade sanctions. Moreover, China's relationship with North Korea, often characterized as "close as lips to teeth," has been necessary for North Korea's survival. Beijing supplied North Korea with 200,000 tons of food aid and 500,000 tons of fuel to help with the DPRK's natural disasters in 2020; two-way trade between North Korea and China has been steadily growing in the past two decades.[173] Chinese companies have been conducting business with North Korea for a wide range of UN-prohibited goods, such as seafood, textiles, iron and steel, and machinery and vehicles while hosting a few dozen North Korean officials connected to the DPRK's weapons programmes or banks.[174] China has also been home to illegal human trafficking from North Korea, especially of young North Korean women, a practice that generates revenues for the DPRK regime in the range of USD 105 million annually.[175] Until the outbreak of COVID-19, trade with China—both official and unofficial—was the sustaining lifeline of the DPRK regime. Although North Korea shut down its borders completely during the pandemic, it has resumed launching missiles. North Korea's bilateral trade with China continued as of January 17, 2022.[176]

## Looking Ahead: Prospects for a Closer Partnership

There is a solid and compelling business case for a closer partnership and collaboration between Canada and South Korea, especially given the anticipated full implementation of the Canada–Korea Free Trade Agreement. Compared to other Korean allies, such as Australia or the United States, Canada has yet to reap the full benefits of its special relationship with South Korea. Moreover, South Korea now has free trade agreements with some 57 countries, many of whom are courting South Korean businesses far more actively than Canada. This section highlights sectors of notably high potential for future collaboration between Canadian and South Korean companies.

## Artificial Intelligence

Canada has a vast AI ecosystem, well supported by the public and private sectors and academia. Three notable AI centres of excellence—Amii in Edmonton, Mila in Montreal and the Vector Institute in Toronto—represent truly world-class expertise in deep and reinforced learning. The Pan-Canadian AI strategy announced by the Canadian government in 2017 marked the first national AI strategy in the world. South Korea followed suit two years later and released its first national AI strategy. Both countries have shared objectives and focus areas, such as developing an AI ecosystem and promoting human-centred AI principles. Canada and Korea are ranked fourth and seventh in Tortoise Media's Global AI Index Rankings, with each country receiving high scores in terms of the depth of government commitment to AI.

Interestingly, their respective scores suggest a high degree of complementarity between the two economies. Canada ranks well in terms of the talent pool, environment (regulation and public opinion), and the level of start-up and investment activities. In contrast, South Korea is a leader in infrastructure distribution and the level of global involvement in establishing standards. As countries rush to gain dominance in AI, Canada and South Korea's comparative strengths mean they are well-suited partners rather than competitors. Canada's R&D capabilities, for example, would benefit from Korea's strong manufacturing base, especially the production of memory chips. AI systems require advanced chips, and Canadian businesses can leverage South Korea's dominance in this area because Korea strives to become a leader in smart chips by 2030.[177] Likewise, Canada's strength in R&D can be pivoted toward the Indo-Pacific market through South Korean companies seeking to apply AI technologies to their products and services. Such partnerships are already underway: Canadian universities are forging ties with Korean organizations and are providing opportunities to Small Medium Enterprises (SMEs). For example, South Korea Electrotechnology Research Institute (KERI), Changwon, and the University of Waterloo have established a joint AI laboratory to innovate manufacturing technologies for SMEs.[178] For Korean businesses, Canada is an attractive hub for AI research. Already, Korean conglomerates are investing in hiring leading AI researchers in Canada. Two of seven international AI research centres run by Samsung are located in Toronto and Montreal.[179] LG also has an AI research centre in Toronto. With Canada ranking first in terms of talent in the Global AI Index, more Korean companies, whether big or small, are expected to look to Canada for a highly-trained talent pool.[180]

Developing international standards and codes for the use of AI is another area where Korea and Canada can lead. Canada and South Korea are actively participating in multilateral efforts, and both countries are members of the OECD Global Partnership on AI (GPAI). In October 2020, for instance, the Asia Pacific Foundation of Canada and the Korea Artificial Intelligence Ethics Association signed a Memorandum of Understanding to cooperate on artificial intelligence ethics projects.[181] Through this partnership, Canada and Korea will promote bilateral and multilateral cooperation on AI governance, and they will work on joint projects and research on AI ethics.

## COVID-19 & Bio-Healthcare Cooperation

Bio-healthcare, along with semi-conductors and future mobility, is one of the South Korean government's three strategic industries.[182] Since May 2019, Seoul has developed a series of national strategies and policy directives to further innovate in the field; the Moon Jae-in administration also repeatedly expressed support for biotech R&D capabilities, increasing South Korea's national budget for R&D in biotechnology by 30% in 2021.[183] Considering Korea's focus on reinvigorating R&D, exchanges between the two countries' talents in academia will be critical to further developing a Canada–Korea partnership.[184] Although Korea's bio-industry boasts strong generic manufacturing capabilities, its R&D capability and export power lag behind Canada and other leaders in the field. Few global pharmaceutical companies are based in Korea, leading Seoul to introduce tax benefits to lure foreign bio companies to the region.[185] While major global companies are building new pipeline models to reduce R&D costs through outsourcing, Korean bio firms are also actively outsourcing R&D functions to minimise burdens and expand R&D capabilities.[186]

Vaccine production is one possible area for Canada–Korea cooperation. When COVID-19 hit the global economy in 2020, South Korea had the lowest GDP decline among the 37 leading economies of the OECD.[187] However, in August 2021, the country had the lowest vaccination rates among all members of OECD.[188] South Korea is currently procuring vaccines overseas, but seven Korean companies are developing COVID-19 vaccines, most of which have reached phase two clinical trials.

To encourage South Korea's potential as a global player in such production, President Moon Jae-in announced the Global Vaccine Hub strategy, which aims to make Korea a top-five vaccine producing powerhouse by 2025.[189] Over the next five years, South Korea plans to invest 2.2 trillion Korean won (approximately CAD 2.37 billion) in vaccine production technologies and support local bio-health industries with tax incentives for R&D and facility investments.[190] The Global Vaccine Hub Strategy is exclusively designed to gain vaccine self-sufficiency through multiple global partnerships. Notably, the plan lists Canada as one of four potential partners with the United Kingdom, Germany, and Australia.[191]

Plant-based vaccines present an exciting opportunity for the Canada-Korea partnership. The ROK government has already pledged to invest $13.5 billion toward plant-based vaccine research.[192] Medicago, a biotech firm, is developing the world's first plant-based COVID-19 vaccine in Canada. The ROK government has also promised to invest USD 13.5 billion toward plant-based vaccine research.[193] For a meaningful long-term partnership, it is imperative to establish regular bilateral channels in the bio-health industry and encourage collaborations in raw materials development and R&D.

International cooperation in the biotechnology sector will be necessary as governments and companies look to accelerate the biopharmaceutical pipeline to meet the current challenges posed by COVID-19 and prepare for future pandemics. Cooperation among business, academia, and the government will be critical to expanding Canada's presence in Korea. As South Korea looks to innovate its local biotechnology sectors through rigorous investment and government incentives, promising Canadian bio-health companies may find an opportunity to become a significant market player in the Indo-Pacific.

# Transition to Low-Carbon Economies: Clean-Tech & Renewable Energy

Clean technology and the renewable energy sector represent a new area of significant potential for expanded Canadian–Korean partnerships. Clean technology, as defined by Natural Resources Canada, is any product, service or process that reduces environmental effects. This means innovative technologies to harness the sun, wind, and oceans to reduce carbon emissions for the energy sector. Clean-tech also encompasses industry; in the mining sector, for instance, there is a need to supply nickel, copper and lithium for electric vehicle (EV) batteries, uranium for nuclear energy, and iron and neodymium for wind turbines.[194] In 2019, the value of Canada's environmental and clean technology products sector was estimated at CAD 70.5 billion, representing 3% of Canadian GDP. Three provinces were the top contributors in 2019 to the total value of clean-tech products: Ontario (36.1%), Quebec (28.6%), and British Columbia (14.4%).[195] Canada is also one of the world's top 10 hydrogen energy producers.[196]

South Korea, by contrast, is the world's fourth-largest importer of coal and the third-largest investor in overseas coal projects.[197] The country currently relies on energy imports to meet 97% of its domestic needs; reducing its dependency on energy imports has long been a priority for the ROK government. By 2035, the South Korean government will use renewable energy to make up 11% of the country's total primary energy consumption by 2035.[198] It aims to achieve carbon neutrality by 2050, and this inevitably means phasing out all coal-fired power plants or converting them to liquefied natural gas.[199] South Korea needs to accelerate its clean technologies drastically, and Seoul has developed a plan to achieve its goals. On 14 July 2021, the government announced the Korean New Deal 2.0, which encompasses the Digital New Deal, the Green New Deal, the Human New Deal, and the Local New Deal. This ambitious plan, which has increased funding initially set for 42.7 trillion won (CAD 46 trillion) to 61 trillion won (CAD 66 trillion)[200] to promote a low-carbon and eco-friendly economy by encouraging collaboration with eco-friendly industries including EVs, electricity generation, and other clean technologies.

One of Korea's interests in low-carbon power that is particularly important for Canada is nuclear power, which currently provides some 10% of the world's electricity and will play a key role in combating global climate change. Unlike other energy sources such as coal or natural gas, nuclear power displaces more than 50 megatonnes of greenhouse gas emissions each year in Canada.[201] Nuclear power generates 15% of Canada's electricity, 60% in Ontario, and about 36% in New Brunswick and Canada's nuclear waste management framework is considered the gold standard internationally.[202] While the federal government spearheaded the first significant advance in Canadian nuclear power (CANDU), the provinces have taken the lead of late. In December 2019, Saskatchewan and New Brunswick agreed to work with Ontario to promote small modular reactors (SMRs). This initiative aligns with the National SMRs Roadmap, which aims to unleash the technology's economic potential across Canada, including rural and remote areas.[203] The compact design of the SMRs allows them to be factory-built and transported to where they are needed. As such, SMRs can leverage economies of scale to provide a lower cost and more flexible energy stream. South Korea has already shown interest in such technology; a recent Memorandum of Understanding between the Canadian Nuclear Laboratories and Korea Hydro & Nuclear Power aims to promote joint research efforts and share knowledge on the storage, transportation and disposal of used fuel, as well as collaboration on nuclear waste management initiatives.[204] As well, SNC Lavalin is very active in the South Korean market—it won four contracts with Korea Hydro and Nuclear Power Ltd. in 2020, valued at CAD 22 million, to assess fuel channels and components for Wolsong CANDU nuclear power plants.[205] Considering the access that the Canada–Korea Free Trade Agreement provides for Canadian companies, the South Korean market represents significant opportunities for Canadian exporters in clean-tech ecosystems, most notably carbon capture and storage, waste to energy and waste management, water treatment, hydrogen and fuel cell electricity generation, energy storage, and smart grid technologies in the decade to come.[206]

# Conclusion & Key Recommendations

In light of the historical relationship between Canada and South Korea and the economic and strategic importance of the South Korean market, this chapter has called for a re-conceptualization of Canadian–Korean relationship to fully reap the benefits of the CKFTA. As an export-based country with high human capital and a growing economy, South Korea presents an incredible set of opportunities for Canadian businesses. To capitalize on these opportunities, this chapter offers six recommendations for Canadian policymakers and senior business leaders to consider as they look ahead to the next decade of Canadian–Korean relations.

## Revitalizing High-Level Political Engagement & Sustained Leadership

The Canadian–Korean relationship needs a reset. For far too long, this bilateral relationship has been handled by limited resources at the bureaucratic level (the Canada desk occupies a tiny percentage of the North America division at the ROK Ministry of Foreign Affairs and, in Canada, the Korea desk has seen a lot of turn-over in the Asia Pacific division at Global Affairs Canada). To rekindle excitement and political leadership between the two countries, the Canadian government should promote high-level diplomatic engagement, ideally preparing for a state visit by the Prime Minister to Seoul or the new South Korean President's visit to Ottawa. Investment in high-level political engagement between heads of government/state would signal that Canada is back.

### 1. Investing & fostering institutional linkages

The Canadian government and businesses must continue investing in Korea's institutional connections and civil society to foster regular dialogue and cooperation. Recent positive developments include a joint report commissioned by the Federation of Korean Industries and the Canadian Business Council of Canada. The Canada–Korea Forum, which will celebrate its 19th anniversary in 2022, has long served as the premier policy forum for bringing together top civil servants, academics, and political leaders for candid and constructive collaboration. Other notable civil society initiatives include the Canada–Korea Society, the Canada–Korea Dialogue on the Hill, various reports and meetings organized by the Asia Pacific Foundation of Canada, and a very strong group of Canadian companies that belong to the Canadian Chamber of Commerce in Korea. The Canadian government should actively engage with these groups and allocate more funding to promote track 1.5 and track 2.0 diplomacy for strengthening the bilateral relationship.

**2. Investing in Canada's long-term situational awareness on the Korean Peninsula**

Canada lags behind countries like Australia when it comes to its capacity to collect intelligence about Korea's markets and to develop relationships with Korean business leaders, a deficit that hinders Ottawa's ability to cultivate a long-term strategy of engagement on the peninsula. While Australia reaped the benefits of South Korea's emerging food processing industry, Canada did not, despite possessing excellent agricultural sectors. Canada also lacks the human capital, such as Korean-speaking experts and professionals, necessary to provide real-time intelligence to build the long-term relationships required for completing solid business deals. For far too long, Canada's foreign ministry has been occupied with China and the United States. The Canadian government needs to invest more in human capital and dedicate more resources toward the Korea desk and its embassy in South Korea.

**3. Collaboration with provincial actors in South Korea**

Quebec has been very active in the Korean market (and it expanding), and other provinces such as Alberta, British Columbia, and Ontario maintain a presence in South Korea. While small in size, these provincial offices serve as an excellent gateway for the Canadian companies interested in doing business in Korea, along with the Trade Commissioner Services. That said, more efforts should be made by the federal government in Ottawa to actively liaise and collaborate with these provincial offices to maximize this potential and eventually amplify Team Canada's efforts.

### 4. Strengthening marketing efforts for Canada's competitiveness

Being Canadian should not equate to being humble about our global competitiveness. Canada and Canadian businesses are leading the world in artificial intelligence research, bio-health, and clean technologies, but Canada has not marketed its competitive edge properly. The South Korean market is fast-paced, highly competitive and very aggressive; a complementary approach is required for Canadian businesses. Thanks to the early involvement of Canadian missionaries in Korea and Canada's contributions during the Korean War, South Koreans retain Canada's overwhelmingly positive public image. But, lest it be seen as a faraway land of beautiful nature and polite people, Canada needs to do more to capitalize on this goodwill. At the federal level, more resources should be allocated toward re-branding and actively marketing Canada's competitiveness, which sets Canada distinctly apart from the United States and Australia, with clear incentives for Korean businesses.

### 5. Improving talent retention & management

Over the past few decades, Koreans have sent their most precious resources to Canada—their children and family members—because they value and trust Canada's education system. As mentioned earlier, Canada attracts a substantive pool of international students from South Korea at all levels, many performing very well academically. These students develop a very positive personal experience of Canada. Considering that education is a top priority for Koreans across all socio-economic spectrums, Koreans have long chosen Canada as a destination that speaks highly of Canada's Korean families. That said, Canada must do more to retain or remain connected to these talented students, many of whom tend to return to their home country after graduation. Currently, the Canadian government has made almost no effort to nurture this expansive alumni network many former international students pursue very successful careers in law, government and business.

The Canadian embassy or another civil society organization should create a database and actively manage this alumni network to build Canada's long-term human intelligence.

**6. Re-establishing credibility on the Korean Peninsula on security matters**

Finally, there is no doubt that stability on the Korean peninsula is in Canada's national interest, both politically and economically. Having fought in the Korean War, Canada is firmly committed to promoting the rule of law and democracy on the Korean peninsula. Containing North Korea also contains China's spheres of influence.

Despite a long-term commitment to promoting a peaceful, democratic system in the Indo-Pacific, Canada's policy on North Korea badly needs an update. The last official policy dates back to 2010 when the Canadian government introduced a Controlled Engagement Policy toward North Korea to restrict any government-level engagement with the DPRK except for humanitarian assistance, human rights or regional security reasons. Canada still applies economic sanctions to the DPRK regime, and aside from co-hosting the Vancouver Foreign Ministers' Meeting in 2018, Canada has been largely missing in action. In the meantime, the humanitarian situation on the ground in North Korea has deteriorated (some 17 million people in North Korea suffer from hunger and malnutrition), which has been further exacerbated by the COVID-19 pandemic.

In light of the disruptions we have seen lately with the Trump and Biden administrations in the United States, Canada can no longer afford to follow the status-quo of American leadership on the Korean peninsula. Canada's passive approach must be replaced by an engagement strategy, drawing from our balanced view and track record of success in promoting global humanitarianism. Canada has a very positive reputation in both Koreas and has an excellent pool of civil servants (both current and retired) with world-class expertise in negotiations. Looking ahead to the next decade, Canada must re-establish its credibility on the Korean peninsula with a long-term strategy, uniquely Canadian, aimed at promoting peace and stability in the Indo-Pacific region at large.

# 13

# Energy and Climate Change
# Martha Hall Findlay

B EFORE ENGAGING in a discussion of what the energy-related opportunities are for Canada in the Indo Pacific region, a few energy facts are needed. First, about what Canada produces and where it goes, and then about the energy needs in countries of the Indo Pacific.

Writing in the summer of 2022, a global energy crisis that started during the pandemic has been exacerbated by the Russian invasion of Ukraine, forcing a global reconsideration of the importance not only of accessible, affordable, and easily used energy, but also security of supply and the importance of supply from dependable and responsible countries. Environmental, Social. and Governance (ESG) issues are all factors but the S and the G have taken on more critical importance than before. This should be a major opportunity for Canada, which ranks among the top countries in the world for ESG, although we continue to be hampered by political and regulatory challenges to building the infrastructure needed to provide more of our energy globally.

## Canada's Energy Mix

Canada is a major producer, consumer, and exporter of energy. Energy makes up 10% of gross domestic product and is a major source of capital investment, export revenue and jobs.[207] Our wealth of energy comes in various forms, including (i) electricity (generated from dammed water, nuclear, natural gas, wind, solar; and (for a while longer) coal); (ii) oil (including crude, upgraded, and refined); (iii) natural gas; (iv) biofuels (ethanol, and increasingly other types of renewable biofuels); and (v) biomass (i.e., wood pellets). We also produce and export materials that help others in the energy ecosystem, including uranium rare earth metals. We also have extensive, often world-leading—and exportable—human expertise in these areas.

We produce more energy than we need ourselves, so we export—although because of regional differences, we also have to import energy. The production, use, export, and import activities are driven not by specific policies such as domestic energy security but by historical economic opportunities, combined with historical (primarily political) challenges in building infrastructure. As with many commodities and trade generally, the United States is our biggest market. But there is a growing opportunity in the Indo-Pacific region as countries work to find the prosperity that energy is required for and the increasing desire to meet global climate challenges. For this region, the UN Sustainable Development Goals provide an important reminder that *"ending poverty and other deprivations must go hand-in-hand with strategies that improve health and education, reduce inequality, and spur economic growth—all while tackling climate change and working to preserve our oceans and forests."*[208]

Particularly for energy products, however, Canada's ability to take advantage of developing Indo-Pacific markets is constrained due to insufficient infrastructure. Some constraints are due to the type of energy (i.e. electricity and natural gas and their respective transportation limitations), but some constraints are of our own making, often tied to anti-oil and gas sentiment or NIMBY-ism that feeds political opposition.) This is quite different from other countries, better poised and more politically oriented to building on already strong exports of resources and energy to the region (Australia is a good example.)

**Oil:** Even domestically, because we do not have sufficient pipeline infrastructure from the oil-producing regions in the West to the eastern parts of the country, oil is imported into those areas.[209] Thanks to pipeline protests in the last decade and more, virtually no new infrastructure has been built, leaving Canada with very little access for oil to the Pacific. Although this will improve somewhat with the completion of the Trans Mountain expansion, Canada will still be unable to significantly increase oil exports anywhere in Asia—where demand is expected to continue to grow for decades. Not only is this a lost opportunity for Canada, our inability to meet that demand simply provides more opportunity to other producers around the world, in particular OPEC+. This lost opportunity is even more frustrating with the much greater focus now on securing supply from stable and reliable (and high ESG-rated) countries.

**Natural gas:** Canada has extensive natural gas reserves, which, thanks to existing pipeline infrastructure, supply large parts of Canada[210] (although we still export and import into some areas.) But while natural gas is in rapidly increasing demand worldwide,[211] pipelines can't move gas to other continents—the gas needs to be liquified and then transported by ship. The production and sale worldwide of liquified natural gas (LNG) is rapidly increasing,[212] but Canada is being left behind because of our almost complete inability to build LNG capacity. Despite massive reserves, Canada has only one major LNG export project in construction, Shell-led LNG Canada. It is not expected to be running until at least 2025. Of over 20 LNG projects proposed in Canada in recent years, only four remain active, all with uncertain production dates. Most cancellations have been due to climate-related opposition or political challenges rendering them either impossible or uneconomic—more constraints of our own making.[213] Although we rank sixth in the world in natural gas production (after the United States, Russia, Iran, Qatar, and China), our ability to export beyond the United States is negligible. At the same time, due to significant increases in LNG capacity in the United States, the United States will soon become the world's largest natural gas exporter.[214] Qatar and Australia are both major exporters as well.

**Electricity:** As a country, we produce a great deal of hydroelectricity, mainly in Quebec, Newfoundland and Labrador, Manitoba and British Columbia. Alberta, Saskatchewan and Nova Scotia have historically relied on coal-generated electricity, more recently moving to natural gas generation. Ontario produces a significant amount of its electricity mix from nuclear power.[215] We do export electricity, but only to the United States. Electricity cannot go beyond the continent with natural gas (unless liquefied to form LNG). Even then, distances are limiting. And transmission lines are often opposed by local interests (not unlike pipelines) even if they transmit "clean" electricity.[216]

**Hydrogen:** Hydrogen is likely to play a key role as a low emissions energy source in areas otherwise difficult to decarbonize. These could include fuel for large, long-haul vehicles—buses, trucks, trains, and ships where battery storage is not practical. Demonstration examples include California's fuel cell bus fleet and the Alberta Zero-Emissions Truck Electrification Collaboration (AZETEC).[217] Blended diesel/H2 fuelled trucks are a good bridge technology option with lower implementation costs. Hydrogen can also be used for heat by burning pure or blended H2 in industrial processes or blending into existing natural gas distribution grids—a near-term opportunity already being pursued in Canada and others worldwide. With Canada's water, electricity, fossil fuels, and biomass, plus our energy-related skills and expertise, Canada is well-positioned to supply clean hydrogen globally, including the Indo Pacific region. *"With worldwide demand for hydrogen increasing, the global market could reach over $11 trillion by 2050. Each region of Canada can utilize their unique resources to produce and deploy hydrogen domestically as well as to supply a growing export market. Based on their existing country strategies, demand potential, and proximity, Europe, Asia, and the United States have been identified as potential export markets for Canadian clean hydrogen."*[218]

**Biofuels:** Biofuels are increasing in importance due to their ability to "drop-in" to the existing fossil fuel pool to reduce emissions for, in particular, transportation, without requiring major changes in existing vehicles or infrastructure, as is the case with electrification. Canada has significant comparative advantages in this area, given our wealth of natural agricultural and forestry resources.

**Nuclear technology:** Canada was a global leader in nuclear power for many years, exporting our Candu reactors and technology. Unfortunately, that global leadership has all but disappeared with the global move away from large-scale nuclear plants. However, Canadian development of various small modular nuclear reactor (SMR) technologies is happening at pace—again, the global opportunity is not in the electricity or heat produced, but in the sale of SMRs and related technology and expertise—and uranium. Canada is the world's leading producer of uranium, and we export by far the majority (85%).[219]

**Other technology and expertise:** Canada is also busy developing and enhancing emissions-reducing technologies, which in themselves provide an opportunity for export and engagement. The Canadian oil and gas industry has been reducing emissions intensity dramatically (by 30% in the oil sands) and is now focused on getting to net-zero production by 2050—one part of that will be one of the world's largest CCUS projects, building on existing Canadian knowledge and experience from earlier projects at Weyburn,[220] Boundary Dam,[221] and Quest.[222] Canada is indeed a world leader and could be more active in selling that knowledge and expertise—CCUS is increasingly recognized as a critical part of our global emissions reduction efforts.[223] This includes countries of the Indo-Pacific region where combusting fossil fuels will continue and thus being able to capture and store the resulting CO2 will be necessary.[224] This is an area where Canada has tremendous—and growing—expertise that can be exported.

**Climate change:** One barrier that Canada is addressing, which is being increasingly recognized, is the reputation we have for high emissions per capita and the inability for Canada to, historically, meet our emissions-reduction targets. This has led to some calls to shut down the Canadian oil (and gas) industry, despite continued long-term global demand. Thanks to significant emissions reduction efforts by the government[225] and industry, this is changing.[226] The more Canada succeeds in reducing production emissions, the more attractive Canadian oil and gas will be—and the more support there should be within Canada to build the necessary infrastructure to capitalize on that production. (The alternative will simply drive that production to others, such as OPEC+ for oil, or countries like Russia and Qatar for natural gas.) A recent IEA report focused on Canada[227] recognized the opportunity for our country even as oil demand is poised to decline globally. While worldwide oil consumption will decrease, it will not fall to zero. Fatih Birol, Executive Director of the International Energy Agency (IEA) pointed out specifically that "I would like to get this oil from good partners, like Canada, who want to reduce emissions from oil and gas." This opportunity for Canada is now far greater since the Russian invasion of Ukraine, but we can't take advantage of it due to the lack of export infrastructure.

## Indo-Pacific Energy Needs

Any detailed analysis of the energy needs of all of the different countries in the Indo Pacific region—or even a few of them—is far beyond the scope of this chapter. But we can discuss the energy needs of, in particular, developing economies, particularly those without significant sources of energy of their own—true for not all, but certainly some of the countries in the region.

First is to recognize a few facts about global energy demand. In 1980, over 80% of the world's energy needs were met by fossil fuels. This included fuels for transportation, energy for heat and cooking, and fossil fuels to generate electricity. (Electricity is not an energy *source* of its own—it has to be developed from other primary energy sources, whether that be the stored water behind a dam, capturing energy from the sun or wind, burning of coal or gas, geothermal heat, or nuclear.)Despite forty years of significantly increasing calls for climate action; significant increases in global commitments; notable successes in mobilizing sustainable finance opportunities globally; and (relatively) significant increases (and decreases in cost) of renewables such as wind and solar—despite all of that progress, *in 2019, over 80% of the world's energy needs were still being met by fossil fuels.* The fact that the proportion has not changed is not a question of ideology—it is reality.

This fact may be shocking to many, particularly those in affluent countries with more energy choices, because of the headlines about the increases in renewables. But those headlines ignore the context of total energy demand, caused by two things: Continued growth in the world population as a whole, people all needing some energy for, at minimum, food and shelter; and significant numbers of people reaching levels of income that permit acquiring more goods and services that in turn require energy—precisely what is happening in large parts of the Indo-Pacific region. The most conservative projections still show the need for significant oil and gas well into and beyond 2050.[228] This is the reason for the concept of "net zero." It is recognized that not everything or every country will cease GHG emissions. There will still be some combustion of fossil fuels. Hence the need to globally remove emissions from the atmosphere using things like nature-based solutions and technologies like direct air capture of $CO_2$.[229] There simply will not be nearly enough GHG-free energy to supply the entire world's needs even by 2050. To be clear, this is not a preference—everywhere around the world, all things being equal, most people would prefer low or no emissions energy. However, all things are not equal, particularly for developing countries. Affluent, developed countries have already developed prosperous economies, in great measure thanks to the historical use of coal, gas and oil, and geographies that have permitted local hydro-generated electricity. Coal and then oil and gas became globally ubiquitous because they have been affordable, easily accessible, easily transported and easily used for people's needs.

Returning to the importance of the overall UN Sustainable Development Goals. Many developing countries have still not been able to afford those energy sources; despite global desires to reduce emissions, these countries are even less likely to afford the expense of lower-emitting alternatives. Millions of people in India, a vast and growing economy, still use cow dung or coal for cooking (and the country relies heavily on coal for electricity generation), creating lethal air pollution, let alone significant contributions to GHG emissions.

*India's government has announced a net-zero target by 2070, with a major push to electrification. Still, the details of how electricity will be generated with fewer emissions than the current coal generation, plus transmission over thousands of km, plus the required infrastructure needed for residential and commercial use—and the total costs thereof—are not clear.*

The global push for renewable electricity production is much easier (and cheaper) for countries that already have transmission grids; already have the back-up to cover for the intermittency of wind and solar; already have a population with the infrastructure needed in their homes and commercial buildings to electrify; and the wherewithal and infrastructure too, for example, switch to electric vehicles (EVs). Even with the decreasing costs of solar and wind on their own, one cannot develop policies or strategies without including the total cost of building the required back-up (increasingly natural gas as the "cleaner" option), plus building the transmission lines, plus building the infrastructure needed for residences and commercial activity to be able to use it (last mile from transmission to buildings and local wiring) the cost remains beyond the capacity of most developing countries. It may not be ideal for the climate, but the reality is that many of the countries in the Indo Pacific region will still need oil, particularly for transportation; gas, for heat and cooking, and mainly to replace coal-fired electricity generation. Indeed, both, particularly natural gas, would provide significant emissions reductions by replacing existing coal and bio waste combustion. As the world navigates the energy transition toward a net-zero economy by the middle of this century, the emission reductions represented by switching from higher emitting forms of energy like coal to lower-emitting forms like natural gas is progress. It means that the world realizes greater emissions reductions sooner than they otherwise would.

There are, therefore, significant energy-related opportunities for Canada in the Indo Pacific region. Some we cannot take advantage of (yet) because of (our sometimes self-imposed) limits to our energy infrastructure. But others are more possible, including energy and energy-related technologies and expertise. These opportunities should be particularly strong in those countries which significantly increase their levels of prosperity—and therefore energy needs—over the next decade.

**Oil:** All of the countries in the Indo Pacific region will continue to need oil and refined oil products such as gasoline, diesel and jet fuel, particularly for transportation well through 2050 and beyond. Given Canada's acknowledged strength in all aspects of the environment, social and governance (ESG) behaviours, as Canada reduces emissions from producing its oil—its last remaining ESG challenge—it should become a globally preferred source of oil. But we will need to encourage the infrastructure required to sell it.

**Natural gas:** increasing our capacity to liquefy our natural gas would allow us to participate in the expected continued major growth in demand for natural gas, needed in particular to replace coal-fired electricity generation and to provide resiliency for renewables;

**Hydrogen:** because Canada has expertise with hydrogen, the resources and ability to produce it; because it has significant potential for lower-emitting energy; and because its production and transport are not subject to the same types of physical or political constraints as natural gas or electricity, this is an area of significant opportunity.

**Biofuels:** Canada has distinct advantages over most countries in this area due, again, to our resources (agricultural and forest) and our expertise.

**Nuclear:** For the reasons described, we can't supply electricity itself to the region—but we can provide the technology needed for electricity. Canada has a limited comparative advantage in renewable technology, as so much has been developed in other countries, often more inexpensively. However, Canada does have a comparative advantage with respect to nuclear, thanks to our long history of nuclear expertise and an unparalleled reputation for strong nuclear regulation and safety. Few, if any, countries can match that reputation. And with several promising Canadian-based SMR technologies, this is an area of significant opportunity that deserves more focus by government decision makers.

**CCUS:** A significant opportunity for Canada on the technology and expertise side is carbon capture, use and storage (CCUS). Canada was a pioneer in CCUS with the Weyburn, Boundary Dam, and more recently Quest projects. The foundational project of the Oil Sands Pathways to Net Zero initiative will be one of the biggest CCUS projects in the world. Other global CCUS projects are already using some Canadian expertise, which will only be enhanced with the Pathways project. As CCUS is increasingly seen as a key abatement technology to reduce emissions from the use of fossil fuels into the atmosphere (including for the production of clean hydrogen), this expertise should be a key export for Canada.

**Direct air capture (DAC):** A Canadian company is one of the world's leading players in the nascent direct air capture technology.[230] If DAC can prove economical at scale, it could provide an excellent opportunity for Canada to export both technology and expertise, particularly to countries that remain dependent on GHG-emitting combustion of fossil fuels.

**Nature-based solutions:** Canada has vast forests and natural ecosystems, which play an essential role in meeting climate change objectives. Nature-based solutions are actions to conserve, sustainably manage, and restore ecosystems helping to store and capture carbon and mitigating the impacts of climate change. Canada's expertise in these areas could also be applied to capture opportunities in the Indo-Pacific region.

**Other technologies:** As a country producing all manner of energy, it's not surprising that Canada has a vibrant energy-tech/cleantech sector. Many of these technologies have found their way abroad. The work of organizations such as Sustainable Development Technology Canada (STDC), Clean Resource Innovation Network (CRIN), and Canadian Oil Sands Innovation Alliance (COSIA)[231] are funding, developing, and commercializing more technologies, processes and expertise that other countries could benefit from.

*"Canada is actively advancing innovation in a number of key fields... with a view to serving as a supplier of energy and climate solutions to the world."*[232] There will continue to be significant opportunities for Canada in the Indo Pacific region related to energy—whether in exporting various forms of energy itself (particularly when and where we can build the infrastructure needed to do so); or in the form of energy-producing technologies (i.e., SMRs) or emissions-reducing technologies (i.e., CCUS and DAC); energy-related products such as uranium and rare earth metals; and a range of energy-related expertise.

# 14

# The Digital Economy in Asia
# Deanna Horton

A S WE progress through the second decade of the 21st century, to understand the economic growth potential of Asia, a snapshot of the current digital economy can shed some light on opportunities for Canada.

This chapter looks at elements of the digital economy across a number of markets in Asia—there is no "Asia market" per se, but rather a series of markets connected by trade and investment including e-commerce. For the purposes of this chapter, "digital economy" is characterized by "connectivity between users and devices, as well as the convergence of formerly distinct parts of communication ecosystems such as fixed and wireless networks, voice and data, and telecommunications and broadcasting." [233]

The growing importance of the digital economy has also spurred the development of agreements and frameworks to support digital commerce, and Asian economies are willing participants through both plurilateral and bilateral agreements. Canadian policymakers should take advantage of the type of digital economy partnership agreements that are designed to promote and protect digital commerce.

Even at the turn of the 21st Century, Asia was considered for the most part a manufacturing hub for American and European markets. However, with growth in Asian economies, intra-Asian commercial connections and economic interdependence have flourished and more countries now count China as their number one trade partner. With the focus on the Indo-Pacific and agreements such as the Regional Comprehensive Economic Partnership, Southeast Asia is gaining in importance.

There is no doubt that Asia plays a significant role in global digital value chains and as such offers opportunities for Canadian companies to participate, from selling food products via e-commerce to providing software and analytics. Whilst different countries and organizations are aiming by 2030 to define and characterize the future of 6G communication networks, China with Huawei and South Korea with Samsung are undoubtedly the two leaders in 6G development.[234] Advances in digital technologies have revolutionized a vast array of manufacturing industries as well, and as research for the CanAsia Footprint map has shown, Canadian companies have been adding to their tech sector locations in Asia and, reflecting Asia's advanced digital economy, Canadian software and services and analytics firms represent the largest segment of Canadian tech services companies.[235]

While there is familiarity with the largest tech services firms in China (such as Alibaba and Tencent), their activities in the rest of Asia are also of note, as are the growth of homegrown companies in Asian markets. This chapter gives a brief overview of these Asian firms.

## Summary of Recommendations

- Canadian companies, including SMEs, should take advantage of Asia's highly developed e-commerce platforms to offer goods and services
- Canadian software companies should investigate opportunities in education, health care, and other sectors where Canada has demonstrated expertise
- The Canadian government should participate in Asia-based digital economy agreements to foster greater connectiveness and interoperability
- The Canadian government, including through collaboration with the private sector, should offer capacity-building to Asian emerging economies with cybersecurity and data protection as part of its official development assistance portfolio

# Digital Demographics

Global Internet usage has grown significantly in the past five years and Asia is no exception. As might be expected, the more developed countries in Asia show the highest levels of Internet utilization, topping out at 97% for Korea.[236] According to GSMA, mobile phone ownership in 2019 ranged from 58% in Myanmar to 99% in Hong Kong.[237] Korea now tops the list in Asia in terms of the population with fixed broadband subscriptions (2020 data) at 43.55 per 100 people.[238] For the rest of Asia, Singapore leads in Southeast Asia with 25.94/100.[239] In terms of total number of mobile broadband, however, International Telecommunications Union (ITU) 2020 data shows China in the lead with almost 1.4 billion subscriptions. India follows with 725 million, then Indonesia with 243 million. Combining the number of subscriptions in Asia as a whole (China, India, Japan, Korea, Taiwan, Hong Kong plus ASEAN) gives us a total online consumer market of over 4 billion people.[240]

| Individuals' Internet Usage (%) | | |
|---|---|---|
| Region/Country | 2019 | 2015-19 Increase Rate |
| United States | 89 | 20 |
| Canada | 97 | 7 |
| China | 65 | 28 |
| India | 41 | 175 |
| East Asia | 92 | 7 |
| Korea (Rep. of) | 97 | 7 |
| Japan | 93 | 2 |
| Hong Kong, China | 92 | 8 |
| Southeast Asia | 68 | 64 |
| Singapore | 89 | 13 |
| Malaysia | 84 | 18 |
| Cambodia | 78 | 335 |
| Viet Nam | 69 | 53 |
| Thailand | 67 | 70 |
| Indonesia | 48 | 116 |

*Source:* The World Bank Data

Looking at digital inclusivity, according to the ITU data, men, urban residents and young people are more likely to be online than women, rural dwellers and older people.[241] Canadian data analytics firm RIWI utilizes its random intercept survey technology to gain insights on the gender divide among Internet users. Overall, and perhaps surprisingly, the sub-region with the smallest gender digital divide in Asia is Southeast Asia–countries like Vietnam, the Philippines, and Thailand see on average a 60/40 male/female split, compared to East Asia where the average is approximately 70/30 male/female (with China being a major outlier here at approximately 80/20 male/female). South Asia also has 75–85% of the internet population self-identifying as male.[242]

The development of 5G has been a focus of many governments in the Asia-Pacific. According to OpenSignal, South Korea and Taiwan are currently vying for the fastest 5G experience in Asia.[243] Further inroads in 5G will be essential to further utilization of the Internet of Things, including automotive applications.

## E-Commerce and Trade

Asia is a large market for e-commerce, with both international and local firms commanding a share. Looking at the top consumer-facing e-commerce firms in 2020, ranked by gross merchandise volume, Alibaba ranks highest, more than double that of the second-ranked, Amazon (Canada's Shopify jumped to 5th place).[244] Not surprisingly the pandemic led to an increase in e-commerce sales 2019-2020. China tops the list with 2020 online retail sales at an eye-popping US$1.4+ trillion, representing one-quarter of all retail sales.[245] E-commerce also represents a significant percentage of sales in South Korea at 26% (Canada is at 6%).[246] According to survey conducted in Japan in May 2020, over 50% of households were shopping online.[247]

Asian economies play a substantial role in global value chains in the digital marketplace. A measure of the importance of digital economy-related elements in Asian economies is the international trade in digitally-deliverable services, where China, Singapore, and Japan take the lead on the import side, with the addition of India leading on exports, a reflection of its strength in administrative and other managerial services.[248] Reviewing the share of information and communications technologies (ICT) *goods* as percentage of trade by Asia countries, the list demonstrates the investments by major global manufacturers: Philippines at 49%, followed by Vietnam at 35%, Malaysia at 33%.[249] In 2019 ICT *services exports*, India tops the list with US$ 64+ billion, followed closely by China and then Singapore.[250] Conversely, looking at ICT *services imports*, China leads at US$ 26+ billion, followed by Japan at US$ 19+ billion and Singapore at US$ 15+ billion.[251] When calculating total (import and export) ICT services value, major countries in Asia are skewed towards exports, with totals led by China (US $80+ billion), India (US$ 73+ billion), and Singapore (US$30+ billion)—compare this to the United States at US$ 84+ billion and Canada at US$ 14+ billion.[252]

In terms of trade in ICT goods with Canada, China is by far our largest bilateral trading partner in this foundational sector of the digital economy, at US$6+ billion.[253] Vietnam's numbers are large (US$946 million) due to Samsung's use of Vietnam as a manufacturing hub.[254]

The success of Shopify demonstrates only one sliver of the opportunity for Canadian firms in this large and growing e-commerce market. There is little doubt that the market will continue to grow in the post-COVID economy.

## Asian platforms and Chinese investments

In 2021, 45 of the top 100 global digital platforms (by market capitalization) were based in Asia, compared to 41 in North America and 12 in Europe. However, when doing the comparison by value, North America far outstrips Asia with 67% compared to Asia at 29%, demonstrating the global reach of the US-based tech giants, as well as underscoring the potential for growth among Asia's many domestic platforms.[255]

Of the largest platforms in Asia, many are unsurprisingly based in China and South Korea. The three largest platforms in Asia, as of May 2021, were Tencent, Alibaba, and Samsung, with market capitalization values of US\$699.8 billion, US\$672.8 billion, and \$405 billion, respectively.[256] In recent years, these companies, as well as companies such as Bytedance, PingAn, JD.com, and Kakao have not only dominated their respective domestic markets but have also continued to expand overseas. For example, in 2021, during the 11-day shopping event known as "Singles Day," Alibaba's gross merchandise value across its domestic platforms reached US\$84.5 billion—an 8% jump from 2020—while JD.com's transaction volume increased 28% from last year to reach US\$54.6 billion.[257] At the same time, both Chinese tech giants have made plans compete with established brands such as Amazon by increasing overseas investments in regions as diverse as Eastern Europe and Southeast Asia.[258]

Indeed, while Chinese platforms dominate in China, these companies are also investing in other Asian markets. Many Canadians might not have made note of the **Philippines**' first "unicorn" (tech companies valued at over US\$1 billion), Mynt, receiving \$300 million in its latest funding round. This fintech company is backed by China's tech giant Ant Group and is valued at \$2 billion.[259] This series of transactions is illustrative of China's increasing presence in Asia's digital economy and its strength in the digital financial services market.

On the other hand, according to DealStreetAsia, Southeast Asia seems to be establishing itself as a major ecosystem for startup growth, side by side with India, as China loses some of its luster as an investment destination following its crackdowns on internet giants.[260] According to figures compiled through October 12, 2021, the total number of Southeast Asia's venture capital-backed unicorns has reached 27. India, which added 30 unicorns in this year alone to make its total count over 50, is not far ahead. Overall investment in Indian and Southeast Asian startups are on the rise.

The following table shows unicorns based in Southeast Asia, along with some of the latest unicorns from China, Japan, and South Korea:

| Country | Unicorns (And Year of Unicorn Status) | Sectors |
|---------|----------------------------------------|---------|
| Indonesia | Ajaib (2021), Bukalapak (2018), GoTo (2016, 2018), J&T Express (2021), OVO (2019), Tiket (2021), Traveloka (2018), Xendit (2021) | Financial Technology; Marketplace; Logistics; Travel |
| Malaysia | Carsome (2021) | Marketplace |
| Philippines | Mynt (2021), Revolution Precrafted (2017) | Financial Technology; Architecture |
| Singapore | Carousell (2021), Carro (2021), Lazada (2016), NinjaVan , Nium (2020), Patsnap (2021), Sea (2014), Trax (2019), Grab (2015), Razer (2014) | Marketplace; Logistics; Financial Technology; Intellectual Property; Gaming; Financial Services |
| Thailand | Ascend Money (2021), Bitkub (2021), Flashgroup (2021) | Financial Technology; Logistics |
| Vietnam | VNG (2014), VNPay (2020) | Gaming; Financial Services |
| China | Bytedance (2017), SouChe (2017), SHEIN (2018) | Technology; Marketplace; E-commerce |
| Japan | Playco (2020), Preferred Networks (2018), SmartHR (2021) | Gaming; Artificial Intelligence; Financial Technology |
| S. Korea | Socar (2020), Wemakeprice (2015), Yanolja (2019) | Technology; E-commerce; Travel |

*Sources:* CBInsights,[261] E27 (2021),[262] OECD (2019)[263]

**Singapore** is an established digital hub in Southeast Asia that has not only attracted capital from Chinese internet giants, but also cultivated its own tech unicorns and startups in the past decade, for example Sea Group and Lazada.[264] Chinese firms Tencent, Alibaba, and Bytedance all have regional headquarters in Singapore.[265] Bytedance has been particularly active in recent years, purchasing more cloud-computing servers to backup U.S. data for contingency purposes, leasing space in One Raffles Quay, and hiring hundreds of new personnel.[266]

Alibaba acquired an interest in Lazada in 2016 with an initial $1 billion investment, subsequently becoming the first major international player to enter Southeast Asia when it bought a majority stake (83%) in 2017 with an additional billion-dollar investment. Alibaba then arranged for Lazada Singapore to boost its catalog of five million products with the addition of 400,000 listings selected from Taobao.[267] However, the *Wall Street Journal* noted that Lazada's revenue growth rate has since lagged behind Alibaba's growth in Chinese retail markets, and it has fallen behind local and regional rivals in important markets—most notably Shopee.[268]

Tencent held a 22.9% stake in Sea as of March 5, 2021 according to Sea's annual report.[269] In September 2021, Sea announced that it had raised about $6 billion in a sale of U.S. shares and convertible bonds, in the biggest ever equity offering by a Southeast Asian company, according to Bloomberg.[270] Tencent said that it had priced the deal, which includes both new shares and convertible bonds.[271]

**Indonesia** is an up-and-coming digital hub that in 2020 captured more than 70% of the capital invested in Southeast Asian startups, which include rising companies such as the recently merged Gojek-Tokopedia (GoTo), Bukalapak, and Traveloka. Indonesia also has seen an increase in Chinese investments. In October 2018, Tencent, Chinese e-commerce company JD.com and several other investors poured in USD$1.2 billion into Gojek.[272] Alibaba continued its push into Southeast Asia by leading a $1.1 billion investment into another Indonesian platform, Tokopedia, becoming a minority stakeholder. Tokopedia and Gojek subsequently merged, with Alibaba scored the second-largest single shareholding in the merged company at 13%, behind Softbank's 16%.[273]

In 2017, **Malaysia's** government partnered with Alibaba — and its affiliates Cainiao (logistics), Ant Financial (fintech) and Lazada — to launch a series of initiatives aimed at easing red tape and barriers around cross-border e-commerce in the country.[274] Alibaba stressed that the planned e-fulfillment hub, a physical location to handle inbound and outbound deliveries, and other aspects of the initiative — which it calls eWTP or Electronic World Trade Platform — will benefit anyone who sells online in Malaysia, not just Alibaba. Malaysia's zone will be linked to an existing zone in Hangzhou, Alibaba's headquarters, to enable freer exchange of goods between Malaysia and China and open up economic and social opportunities, according to Alibaba. On November 3, 2020, Alibaba commenced operations at the newly-built e-fulfillment hub, the "Cainiao Aeropolis eWTP Hub, Malaysia."[275]

Another Alibaba initiative, announced at its Alibaba Cloud Summit 2021 in June, is to expand its cloud computing arm in Southeast Asia through a US$1 billion project aimed at supporting local talent and start-ups. The initiative, named Project AsiaForward, will seek to upskill local developers, small-to-medium-sized companies, and connect businesses with venture capital and opportunities.[276]

The developments outlined above portray the variegated marketplaces that characterize Asian economies. Canadian expertise in education software, telehealth, cybersecurity, and logistics services could find a home among the many platforms of these growing digital economies.

## Governments and the Digital Economy

Asian governments have launched a range of policies and initiatives to improve their position in the digital economy, including creating strategies for the promotion of e-commerce. There is the "Korean New Deal"[277]; "Myanmar has released a "Digital Economy Roadmap"[278]; Malaysia its "Digital Economy Blueprint"[279]—these are just a few of many examples. And ASEAN has its "Digital Master Plan."[280] The development of 5G and even 6G is also a priority.

On the regulatory side, there are a growing number of bilateral and plurilateral agreements covering the digital economy. Singapore is the clear leader with membership in the Digital Economy Partnership Agreement (DEPA) with Chile and New Zealand (South Korea and China have indicated an interest in joining), in the 21 member state APEC Internet and Digital Economy Roadmap, and in the Singapore-Australia Digital Economy Agreement (SADEA), and having launched bilateral talks with the UK, South Korea and Vietnam.[281] These agreements will contribute to greater interoperability and data/privacy protection among signatories. As of 2019, Asian countries vary greatly in their standing on the Cybersecurity Index (from 16.10 in Cambodia to 89.8 in Singapore) although there have been notable improvements 2014–2019.[282]

Collaboration in the digital sphere is also directed at the creation of common digital standards. China has been active, as has the United States—
other Asian countries wish to avoid any bifurcation of the digital space.
Canada could also take the lead in supporting the kind of capacity building
that will be critical. For example, to allow for the highest standards available
in free market economies for digital privacy and protection from cyber sur-
veillance by bad actors of all kinds, including governments.

Controversy surrounds Asian governments' policies requiring data on citizens to be held locally, imposing additional costs to foreign investors. While
investors from American and Canadian marketplaces tend to oppose data
localization requirements (although some firms prefer to work behind the
scenes or through associations and governments), Chinese firms are ambiva-
lent, likely due to the situation in China.[283] China is reportedly exploring
cross-border data flows in limited spheres such as free-trade zones. This
arises out of the government's efforts to promote economic recovery and
Chinese firms' need for unrestricted data flows in the markets in which they
operate to remain competitive. However, there is at least one example of a
Chinese company, Alibaba, which has invested in Paytm, supporting data
localization requirements in India to "build trust" in the Chinese firm.[284]

At least some of the data localization requirements can be viewed as protectionist in that they support local and international firms who have already
established a presence in the market. As a result, local data center industries
have flourished, and international firms have established partnerships. For
example, AWS has partnered with two companies in Beijing and Ningxia,
Apple is working with a company in Guizhou, and Microsoft Azure is
working with Beijing-based 21Vianet.[285]

## Canada in the Digital Economy in Asia

Canadian technology-related companies have been establishing locations
and pursuing opportunities in Asian marketplaces since the early 2000's.
The most recent data update to the CanAsia Footprint map which is housed
at the Munk School of Global Affairs and Public Policy at the University of
Toronto shows that there are 317 Canadian technology-related companies

with 1239 locations across 16 countries in Asia (China, India, Japan, Korea, Taiwan, Hong Kong plus the ASEAN 10).

Total number of locations by market

*Source:* CanAsia Footprint Map, Munk School of Global Affairs and Public Policy.

There are three sectors of note where, judging by location numbers, Canadian companies appear to have an edge: advanced manufacturing, which incorporates the automotive sector, and electronics OEM where a good percentage of the firms are large; then software, energy & cleantech, and services and analytics where the companies tend to be small.

| Canadian Tech Companies by Sector Classification and Location | | |
|---|---|---|
| Techmap class | Number of companies | Number of locations |
| Advanced Manufacturing | 73 | 354 |
| Digital and Media | 17 | 89 |
| Electronics and Peripherals | 20 | 101 |
| Energy and Clean Technology | 46 | 115 |
| Life Sciences | 19 | 44 |
| Mobile, Web, and Cloud Integration | 17 | 55 |
| Services and Analytics | 42 | 175 |
| Software | 65 | 255 |
| Telecommunications and Wireless Technology | 19 | 47 |
| Grand Total | 317 | 1235 |

*Source:* CanAsia Footprint Map, Munk School of Global Affairs and Public Policy

Overall, Canadian tech companies with locations abroad are more likely to be SMEs (defined as 499 employees or less) than large firms. This research project has shown, however, that it is often the case that larger firms are the market pioneers.

## Conclusion

The Asian digital economy takes up a 60% share of the estimated $3.8 trillion USD in global digital platforms revenue.[286] In Southeast Asia, the gross merchandise value of the digital economy is expected to surpass 8% of its GDP by 2025, projected after the 2015–2019 growth from 1.3% to 3.7%.[287] Access to this economy will be critical for Canada's economic future in order to diversify and expand commerce and partnerships. Canadian companies should gear up their exploration of its opportunities, including through some of the Asian platforms mentioned above. In addition, perhaps both government and industry could support digital economy agreements that will bolster investment in digital infrastructure and facilitate digital trade.

*The author wishes to acknowledge research assistance from students Yuna Ban and Angus Lam.*

# 15

# The Way Forward
# Jim Mitchell

T HE INDO-PACIFIC contains 60% of the world's population, and by 2050 will be home to three of the world's four largest economies—China, India, and Indonesia (the United States will fall to third place). In the words of former Canadian diplomat Ian Burney, the Indo-Pacific region has become "the world's most important economic and political region and dominant theatre for geostrategic rivalry." Goldy Hyder of the Business Council of Canada says, "We have entered the Indo-Pacific Century. The region is home to a large and growing middle class, one that will dominate global consumer demand for decades to come. There are significant opportunities for Canada within the Indo-Pacific region and many challenges—not least to Canada's long-term competitiveness."

For good reason, then, the Government of Canada has undertaken a thorough review of Canada's relationship with the region, the results of which are to be published in the fall of 2022. The present volume has been written in anticipation of that forthcoming statement of government policy.

## A New World

We are in a period of great change and uncertainty in the world, and the Russian invasion of Ukraine in February 2022 is but the latest evidence of how unpredictable are world affairs. But regardless of the outcome of that conflict, there can be no doubt, as Derek Burney and Fen Hampson put it, "In the third decade of the 21st century, Canada must begin to think and act geostrategically." Their perceptive take on this new international environment speaks of "a new strategic imperative ... to shift Canada's economic interests and military commitments away from the Atlantic and North America towards the Indo-Pacific region."

While Ukraine reminds us that Europe cannot be ignored, the arguments in favour of a major shift in Canadian foreign and trade policy toward the Indo-Pacific region are compelling. That is the key message from the dozen chapters in this volume, touching on every aspect of Canada's multi-faceted relationship with the region.

The core message of the contributors to this volume is that *Canada has no choice but to shift the focus of its international attention and engagement to the Indo-Pacific*. Our future prosperity and, indeed, our security depend on it. Moreover, the urgency of this shift in strategic direction is underscored by the events of the past decade: the rise of China as a global superpower; the realization that the United States is now a less reliable economic partner and guarantor of our security in the world; the uncertainty of the security situation in Europe; the dynamism of India and a dozen other economies in the Indo-Pacific region and the comparatively slower growth in our traditional markets; and the 21st-century opportunities now open to Canadian exporters and investors—these are compelling reasons to support much closer engagement by Canada with the Indo-Pacific.

Despite the obvious size and potential of the region, the reality is that, after a burst of activity in the 1980s and 1990s, Canada has been present but generally quiescent in the Indo-Pacific since the turn of the century. At best, our diplomatic engagement with individual countries and regional organizations has been intermittent and transactional; our efforts at strengthening relationships at the political level have been sporadic at best; and Canadian companies have generally been reluctant to explore the opportunities offered by these dynamic, rapidly growing economies.

The facts are clear. The opportunities are there if we seize them. The real question is, do the Government of Canada and the Canadian business community have the vision and the determination to do what so clearly needs to be done to situate Canada properly for prosperity—and security—in the 21st century?

This chapter pulls together the complementary strands of fact and argument found in the preceding chapters, each of which examines the different dimensions of a diverse region that requires a tailored approach for each country. After briefly touching on key themes and theses from the various chapters, I will set out some broader conclusions to inform Canadian policy and its operationalization, together with several questions that would have to be answered in any substantial reorientation of Canadian policy and practice.

## The Geostrategic Context

Burney and Hampson see three core elements of what they call "a new strategic imperative" to shift Canada's focus toward the Indo-Pacific. The first is to reduce Canada's economic dependence on the United States with a clear diversification strategy. Recent years have taken the shine off what Canadians might once have thought was a special relationship with the United States. This is not just because of the actions of the Trump Administration, but also those of Presidents Bush and Obama before him and Biden more recently. All of them have paid little heed to Canadian interests or even the constraints of NAFTA/CUSMA in advancing the cause of American business. Our traditional status as America's largest trading partner and a preferred energy supplier has been eroded by U.S. environmentalism and protectionism and supplanted by China. Witness the Keystone pipeline decision, the uncertainty over Enbridge's Line 5, softwood lumber (once again), potatoes, and the proposed subsidy for electric vehicles. The message is clear—Canadians must start looking farther afield for new markets with open eyes to both opportunity and risk. And they must do this without forgetting our broader security obligations to the rest of the world.

A pivot toward the Indo-Pacific is the obvious response to these new features of the international environment. This is not only in terms of trade and investment but also of our security, where Canada shares many interests and concerns with the countries of that region. This, too, will require a change in mindset in this country and a re-positioning of scarce military resources, chiefly the Navy. The challenge will be to visibly increase Canada's security presence and engagement in the Pacific without being perceived to abandon our traditional commitments in Europe, particularly when the conflict in that region imposes new demands on Canada's military capacity and commitments.[iv]

This kind of shift in strategic interest and orientation is something Canada's competitors—Australia, the United States, Europe, and the United Kingdom—are all doing. If we do not act quickly, we will fall further behind our competitors.

## The Perspective of Canadian Business

Goldy Hyder rests his argument for an expanded role for Canadian business in the Indo-Pacific because, whether or not Canadians realize it, Canada is an Indo-Pacific nation. This is where the growth and the opportunities will be in the future.

Canadian business traditionally has looked to the United States as our principal export market and the top destination for Canadian investment. But manifest U.S. protectionism and the prospect of only modest projected growth in the United States (perhaps 2% over the coming decade vs 5% in the Indo-Pacific) have created "a much less certain trade and investment environment." There is a growing awareness in the Canadian business community of the need to diversify markets for Canadian resources, services and products, especially those connected to the shift to the "green economy."

But where are those new markets? The rise of Xi Jinping in China and well-known bilateral problems such as the Two Michaels have sputtered and stalled Canada's hopes for a stronger trade and investment relationship with China. The countries of the Indo-Pacific—not only existing partners such as Japan and Korea but also the rapidly growing economies of ASEAN and, of course, India—are the markets of the future for Canadian business.

---

[iv] It is worth remembering that ever since the 1950s, Canada has been gradually reducing its military commitments to NATO, starting with a reduction in the size of Canadian Forces in Germany, the closure of Canada's army and air force bases, the end of the commitment to reinforce Norway, withdrawal from the NATO AWACs program, etc.

The government of Canada cannot tell Canadian companies where to put their efforts or their money. But it can point the way, laying a foundation for increased trade through bilateral and regional trade agreements. It can strengthen political relationships that, in turn, open opportunities for Canadian exporters. Most importantly, it can include the business community as a partner in developing a comprehensive regional strategy for the Indo-Pacific.

Hyder notes that some Canadian companies (Manulife, Sun Life, BMO, and others) have been active in the region. We are now seeing new business partnerships in the auto parts and artificial intelligence sectors. The emergence of a sizeable middle class in the region will only improve markets for Canadian products and services over the coming decades.

The key message from the business perspective is that Canada cannot afford to place all its eggs in the American basket. For Canada, resilience means "becoming more, not less, global." As Hyder says, "If Canada hopes to maintain a strong global presence, more companies will need a meaningful presence where the growth is, in the Indo-Pacific."

## The Major Players: China, India, Japan

## China

Our government has recognized that a strategy for the Indo-Pacific is not the same thing as a China strategy. But China looms large in any geostrategic calculation. It is now both an economic and a military superpower; its global ambitions are apparent in the Indo-Pacific and globally. But as the years pass, China has become more, not less, difficult to deal with. Indeed, Canadians have discovered that we cannot purport to dictate terms to China in any new trade arrangements. Instead, China is a country, a market and a source of supply that will always be hugely important to Canada, as it is to every country. Yet the now-obvious rivalry between the United States and China puts Canada in an awkward position. Those two countries count for roughly 80% of Canada's exports. Our goal should be not to sell less into those two markets but rather to diversify the global reach of Canadian business so that we are not as vulnerable to the ups and downs of the U.S.–China relationship.

Jeff Nankivell sets out the elements of an effective engagement strategy with China as part of a larger strategy for the Indo-Pacific. For him, this means starting with a commitment to our values in dealing with a superpower and taking clear-eyed advantage of economic opportunities while being aware of the risks. As other authors in this volume have urged, it also means investing in the human skills and regional presence that are essential to longer-term success in the region. Finally, he recommends seeking bilateral engagement with China that recognizes what each country needs from the other and is prepared to build on areas of shared interest (such as climate change) while acknowledging the areas where interests and values diverge.

## India

In a chapter titled "The India Imperative," former High Commissioner Nadir Patel argues for putting India at the centre of Canada's Indo-Pacific strategy. The case for closer engagement with India is almost incontestable: one starts with Canada's already substantial trade and investment relationship with India, one that can only be expected to grow in the coming years; the already significant human connection (India is Canada's largest source for both permanent residents and international students); and the natural synergies between the two countries in technological innovation—all these considerations weigh heavily in favour of a more substantial political and economic investment by Canada in India. India is indeed a "great power in waiting."

Strengthening bilateral ties in every dimension of the relationship requires a strategic plan (not necessarily a separate "strategy") for building the relationship. Patel argues for greater effort in engagement with Indian states and cities, in the innovation ecosystem, in new areas of opportunity such as infrastructure services and biotech, and then leveraging Canada's already substantial commercial investments into new areas such as transportation infrastructure. All these dimensions of a closer economic relationship would benefit from improved market access underpinned by trade agreements. While a comprehensive trade agreement has proved difficult to date, there may be opportunities for agreements in specific areas.

Finally, despite the immense differences in population and future strategic "weight" between Canada and India, there is considerable room for improved cooperation in the defence and security area.

## Japan

Ian Burney notes that "in any conceivable forecast for the Indo-Pacific region ... Japan will continue to occupy a preeminent position." It is the world's third-largest economy, a technological and manufacturing powerhouse, Canada's fourth-largest export market, and our top source of foreign investment from the region. Japan will always matter to Canada; it deserves a prominent place in a new strategy for the Indo-Pacific. The challenge for Canada here is to revive a relationship that has suffered from neglect over the past 20 years or so. Our goal should be to elevate the relationship to one of "strategic partnership" at the political level, which would be based in part on a greater security engagement by Canada in the Indo-Pacific, both bilaterally and in multilateral groupings as the Quad. On the economic front, cooperation with Japan in the CPTPP and business-to-business forums would pay dividends to the political relationship.

## Regional Powers: Australia, South Korea, Indonesia

Australia is a traditional and generally predictable partner with which Canada has enjoyed an excellent bilateral relationship. In the words of Michael Small, "both countries regard the other as their closest natural comparator," sharing everything from similar histories to social values to federalism. Collaboration in multilateral forums such as the UN and the WTO has long been evident.

The degree of importance each has attached to the Indo-Pacific region is where the two countries differ. For Australia, the Indo-Pacific *is* its region, the market for 80% of its exports and the locus of its national security preoccupations and presence. This is not the case for Canada. Instead, says Small, "where Australia matters to us is as a trendsetter and a competitor for a Canadian Indo-Pacific strategy." And it is the security dimension of the

Canadian interest in the region that looms largest in terms of strengthening our future relationship with Australia.

Canada's relationship with South Korea is a partnership forged during the Korean War and nourished by people-to-people ties that began with the Canadian missionaries of the 19th century. It now includes the tens of thousands of Korean immigrants and students attending universities in Canada. Business connections have grown with the substantial increase in two-way trade resulting from the Canada-Korea Free Trade Agreement of 2015. Today, Korea is the fourth-largest economy in Asia and Canada's seventh-largest trading partner. Korean business sees Canada as a market for its industrial and high-tech products and as a secure place to invest in 21st-century industries such as artificial intelligence (where Canada is a world leader), green technology, and bio-health. There are no bilateral irritants.

Korea has close economic ties to both the United States and China, and in security terms, it lies squarely at the nexus of the U.S.–China rivalry. It has a natural connection to Canada as middle powers caught between the two superpowers, which was recognized when Canada and Korea formalized a strategic partnership in 2014. *In short, all of the ingredients for a stronger relationship in political, economic, and terms are there. The task is to build on what is already a solid foundation, starting with a revitalized relationship at the most senior political levels.*

Len Edwards opens his chapter on Indonesia by observing that "among the larger Indo-Pacific countries, Indonesia has been the most consistent recipient of Canadian neglect." This is unfortunate because Indonesia is the world's largest Muslim country and the world's eighth-largest economy. By 2050 it will be the world's fourth largest, with roughly 300 million people. It is also a democracy, a G20 country that wields considerable regional weight and a leader in regional groupings such as ASEAN and new trade agreements such as RCEP. In short, *Indonesia is a country that Canada cannot ignore if it wishes to pursue a larger role in the Indo-Pacific.* Indeed, Canada recognized this by opening negotiations on a bilateral Free Trade Agreement in 2021.

Our goal should be a multi-faceted, integrated strategy vis-à-vis Indonesia that focuses on areas of common interest and Canadian strengths, notably infrastructure, agriculture, services and education. There is also an opportunity for enhanced defence cooperation between the Canadian and Indonesian armed forces and prospects for applying Canadian expertise in governance that the Indonesians would find attractive. Finally, there is ample opportunity for cooperation on the future of the rules-based trading system and the WTO, climate change, maritime law, and nuclear non-proliferation. The possibilities are there; the challenge is to make the most of them.

## ASEAN

The Association of South-East Asian Nations (ASEAN) and its ten member states comprise a market of over 600 million people, with an average annual growth rate of over 5%. Recognizing the importance of this regional political grouping, both today and in the future, Canada opened free trade negotiations with ASEAN in 2021. While an agreement may take some years, there can be little doubt about the importance of strengthening Canada's ties to the ASEAN member states, which together constitute Canada's sixth largest trading partner.

Strengthening Canada's relationship with ASEAN will require overcoming a legacy of perceived indifference from successive Canadian governments. This means a considerable increase in diplomatic presence and activity by the government, a more significant and sustained presence by Canadian business in these new markets, and a readiness by Canada to partner with ASEAN and its members on security arrangements in the region.

## *Looking Ahead*

The Indo-Pacific region demands our attention. The considerations and arguments set out in the preceding chapters make this clear. But if we want the countries of the Indo-Pacific to take us seriously—and surely we must—we will have to increase our engagement with them, both economically and on a political level, and we will have to do that on a continuing basis. The "here today, gone tomorrow" behaviour that too often has characterized Canada's relationship with the countries of the Indo-Pacific simply won't do if we are to enjoy future success in the region.

What would an increased engagement with the region mean in practice? What would it entail in terms of diplomatic effort, trade and investment policy, business investment and presence, and the human dimension of this large set of complex bilateral relationships?

We should start from the premise that a deeper engagement with the region cannot be seen as simply a policy choice by the current Government of Canada, just a matter of publishing a "strategy" and a new list of "priority countries" to guide currently modest federal spending on international affairs. This will not be enough; the stakes are too high for empty, symbolic gestures. Instead, a strategic pivot to the Indo-Pacific should be based on a broader recognition that if we are to succeed as a country, if we are to maintain our standard of living and our place in the world, *we must be more closely engaged with the Indo-Pacific in virtually every dimension of our national life.*

Ideally, and as the Australians did, the Government of Canada will engage the Opposition parties in a collective effort to appreciate the importance of the region, today and tomorrow, and the implications of a deeper engagement with those countries. This could be done, for example, by looking to a House or Senate committee for a timely study on Canada and the Indo-Pacific.

Ideally, provincial governments and civil society would be included in a broader process aimed at building awareness and expanding educational and employment opportunities for young Canadians in the Indo-Pacific through programs of language instruction, international exchanges, and increasing the numbers of students from the Indo-Pacific in Canadian universities.

The human dimension of Canada's relationship with the region, especially in terms of immigration and resulting family ties, has been growing over the past 50 years, as is made clear by the authors in this volume. The countries of the Indo-Pacific, and specifically China and India, are the principal source of top talent for the 21st-century digital economy in Canada. But there is much more to be done to strengthen the human connection between Canada and the Indo-Pacific.

The general point is that if Canadians are to do justice to the opportunities presented by the Indo-Pacific, this will require a continuing *national* effort which engages the federal government, the provinces, the business community, the educational sector, and civil society.

# Questions for Policymakers

It is evident that shifting the focus of our external relations toward the world's largest and most dynamic region will not be easily done, nor is it something that could be done by government alone. No government can do everything, still less do everything all at once. But incrementalism is not an option. Complacency by government or business about when and how to move forward will mean Canada will soon be left behind. If we do not move urgently to seize the opportunities of the Indo-Pacific, we will be condemning ourselves to second-class status in the new global economy and irrelevancy in the forums where world affairs are decided.

If the government of Canada is to operationalize a strategy for the Indo-Pacific, it will have to come up with compelling answers to some strategic questions.

*1) What is the role of federal government in a strategic pivot toward the Indo-Pacific?*

Primary responsibility for recognizing the opportunities and leading this shift in strategic direction—the essential "pivot" in the title of this volume—rests first and foremost with the federal government. At a minimum, this leadership role will require a significant investment of political effort, including prime ministerial attention and ministerial visits to the region. It will require a readiness to enter into new bilateral and multilateral agreements, both economic and security, with the countries in the region and give effect to those agreements in political and security terms. And it will mean developing and deploying deep expertise on Indo-Pacific affairs within our diplomatic and trade services and our business communities. The complexity of Indo-Pacific makes it no place for amateurs or the poorly prepared.

A strategic shift to the Indo-Pacific will not be easy. As noted by several authors in this volume, Canada's cultural and historical ties have been with Europe and, for the past hundred years or so, the United States. Just six years ago, the Government of Canada spent considerable effort to negotiate successfully a comprehensive trade agreement (CETA) with the European Union, and then nearly as much effort to salvage a renewed North American free trade agreement (CUSMA) with the United States and Mexico. There can be little political appetite to be seen to be leaving those markets and partners behind. The Russian invasion of Ukraine has only accentuated the significance of European affairs.

We therefore start from the premise that recognizing the increasing economic and political weight of the Indo-Pacific region does not mean abandoning Canada's traditional political and cultural ties with the United States and Europe or longstanding security relationships such as NORAD and NATO. Nor does it mean pulling out of the markets where Canadian exporters and investors have been successful over many years. *Rather, it is a matter of recognizing where the future lies and being prepared to widen the focus of our national attention accordingly.* It also means being ready to make necessary *investments* in the future in the form of diplomatic and military presence and a corresponding effort by Canadian business.

*2) What are the most important points of genuine strategic engagement for Canada with the Indo-Pacific over the next decade or so?*

From the essays in this volume, it would seem evident that the government of Canada should do what it can do quickly, most efficiently and at the lowest immediate cost. It *should start the process of political engagement with key countries in the region.* That enhanced political engagement with key countries should be formalized in the conclusion of Strategic Partnerships, with all their attendant activity at the political and military levels, along the lines of that concluded with Korea in 2015.

This would begin with announcing a well-grounded strategy[v] for the Indo-Pacific, one that has at least the implicit backing of the House of Commons and the Canadian business community. On that basis, the prime minister and key ministers (Foreign Affairs, National Defence, Industry, and Agriculture) should reach out to their counterparts in the Indo-Pacific to begin dialogues and visits aimed at opening the door to increasing trade and strengthening trade agreements in what could be described a super-charged Team Canada approach. Similar outreach to provincial counterparts

---

[v] At the time of writing, such a strategy is expected to be announced within a few months at most.

would be critically important. Unless the provinces see the Indo-Pacific as a region of opportunity for the businesses and people in their communities, no national strategy can hope to succeed.

Concerted efforts at trade diplomacy, including bilateral arrangements, new free trade agreements and access by Canada to regional trade arrangements such as the RCEP would build on these political overtures. Concluding new agreements will take time, but the process should start as soon as a new strategy is announced.

Just as important is a dramatically increased effort to tap those markets by the Canadian business and investment community. This will call for vision and courage on the part of Boards and CEOs who, for understandable reasons of proximity, common language and history, have been comfortable with a focus on the American market. Export Development Canada and the Business Development Bank of Canada will have critical roles to play in this process, especially for small and medium-sized Canadian enterprises.

*3) Which countries should be our priorities for greater bilateral engagement?*
While experts will always disagree, a strong case could be made for starting with the countries with which Canada already has the closest economic ties—namely, Japan and India—as well as those where there is the most obvious potential for growing the trade relationship, namely Korea, Indonesia and Vietnam. Australia will remain a friend in the region, but it is unlikely to be a significant market for our goods and services. However, it will remain a key destination for Canadian investment, and there may well be opportunities for closer cooperation in IT, the gig economy, bioengineering, AI, genomics, and supporting technological innovation to address climate change, where both countries as medium-sized economies face similar challenges in commercialization and building small businesses to scale.

The critical point to remember in building these bilateral relationships is that the expression of good intentions is not enough. *Closer economic and military engagement with selected countries in the Indo-Pacific, based on clear objectives in each case, is the key*. This will require dedicated resources and certainly *additional* resources. This means more money for trade negotiators, investment counsellors, diplomats on site, naval visits and the like.

And if serious engagement by the business community does not follow these expressions of government interest, much of this path-breaking will be of little longer-term benefit to Canada.

*4) What can the Government of Canada do, specifically, to enable and support increased activity by the Canadian business community in the Indo-Pacific?*

The starting point here should be awareness-raising in the business community, both by Ministers and business leaders such as the Business Council and by Canadian officials working closely with provincial counterparts.

The goal should be to make Canadian exporters aware of the opportunities in the Indo-Pacific and the federal government's commitment to greater engagement by Canada in the region. One might describe this as the domestic side of a trade commissioner's job which is to help Canadian businesses by providing information about opportunities and then facilitating contacts and relationship-building.

The second dimension of this increased effort is to increase the trade-related capacity of Canadian embassies in the region, which means more skilled staff and more money for business-related programming. Again, this is to help businesses succeed in areas where they see opportunities.

*5) In a practical sense, what would an increased security commitment and presence in the Indo-Pacific look like, and what would it cost?*

If Canada is to call itself an Indo-Pacific nation, then the government must recognize that what happens in the region in security terms matters to us and it must be prepared to act accordingly. The war in Ukraine has occasioned a strong Canadian response; recognition that an increase in defence spending is essential.

What does this mean in practice? What is the best way for Canada to demonstrate to its allies and the world that it takes the new security environment seriously? In addition to increasing the defence budget, it means showing our friends in the region—notably India, Japan, Korea, and Australia—that we care about threats to regional security and that we are prepared to commit resources to cooperate with them in addressing those threats.

In purely military terms, this will mean:

- a willingness on the part of the federal government to commit increased resources to the Canadian military, notably through a significant increase in Canada's capacity to project power through such means as increased diesel submarine capability;
- an increased naval presence in the Pacific and the Arctic, which would mean repositioning warships from Halifax to Esquimalt and adding support capacity (tankers/supply ships);
- more naval visits to the countries of the Indo-Pacific;
- regular discussions between defence Ministers and between senior military leaders/senior officials and their counterparts in the region;
- readiness to explore technology transfer and facilitate business relationships in the defence sector;
- willingness to contribute to what Michael Small describes as the "non-submarine defence technology priorities identified as part of AUKUS, that is, cyber capabilities, artificial intelligence, quantum technologies and additional undersea capabilities";
- and what is in some ways the most difficult challenge, adjusting our military's strategic doctrine to shift the emphasis from the defence of Europe to strategic engagement (and presence) in the Pacific.

In "civilian" terms, this enhanced security engagement could include such things as assistance to civil authorities in managing crises/natural disasters, offering our expertise on fisheries management both in national and shared waters, training in handling refugee flows, and other areas where Canada has demonstrated expertise.

A shift in emphasis does not mean abandoning NATO or our allies in Europe. Nor does it mean insensitivity to America's strategic priorities because the United States has already announced a shift in focus toward the Indo-Pacific. But it does mean doing things differently, if only because the strategic situation has changed since the Cold War.

A pivot in our defence posture toward the Indo-Pacific would not be cost-free, but neither would it break the bank; it's the shift in focus that's important. To take but one example, we currently have two frigates on patrol off the coast of Africa and another doing drug interdiction in the Caribbean. Shifting

those vessels to new missions in the Pacific would require a shift in strategic
orientation and tasking, not new resources. And the payoff in political terms
through increased military visibility in the region would be substantial.

The government has already signalled a willingness to increase defence
spending, over time, to the NATO standard of 2% of GDP. Precise estimates
of the dollar costs of an increased military presence and engagement in the
Indo-Pacific are beyond the scope of this paper, but if the current budget of the
Royal Canadian Navy, both operating and capital, is roughly $9 billion, then,
say, a 10% increase in that budget would mean an increase of approximately
$900 million per year. Not a small change but not impossible and certainly an
important signal of the government's commitment to the region.

*6) What kinds of efforts by Canadian provinces are required to give substance to
a strategic shift by Canada toward the Indo-Pacific?*

A national pivot toward the Indo-Pacific will require direct engagement
and participation by the provinces. They are where Canadian business and
agriculture are located; they own the natural resources in demand by the
countries of the Indo-Pacific; they are responsible for the institutions of
higher education that educate young Canadians and attract students from
abroad; they are responsible for the urban areas to which new immigrants
are drawn. And, of course, they have as significant a stake as the federal government in Canada's future prosperity, jobs and security.

The challenge for the federal government, working with the interested
Canadian business community, will be to help provincial governments
appreciate the potential for export growth to the region in advanced manufacturing, agri-food, the digital sector and financial services. And the current
crisis in Ukraine has only reinforced the importance of Canadian strengths
in energy and agricultural products. The provinces can then take appropriate
steps to support their business and export community in taking advantage
of new opportunities in these sectors.

*7) What are the implications for Canadian security policy (and existing relation-
ships) of a shift to the Indo-Pacific? For example, what would this mean for our
membership in NATO? Our security commitments to Europe and the United States?*

In political terms, both bilateral and multilateral, there would be no per-
ceptible change in Canada's relationships with its traditional partners. Our
relationship with the United States will remain of paramount concern for
any Canadian government, and our bilateral relationships with the countries
of the EU, for example, are relatively quiescent. The fact that Canada was
paying more attention to the countries of the Indo-Pacific would hardly
register on their radar. Their immediate concern is European security, and
there Canada is making a small but significant contribution.

Canada's relationships with NORAD and NATO would require careful
management in the event of a significant shift in Canada's security orientation. In each case, Canada's partners would want assurance that our existing
commitments of forces would not be diminished by increased attention to
the Indo-Pacific. Even in the face of war in Ukraine, this is not an insur-
mountable challenge.

*8) Finally, what would be required to engage Canada's people, particularly the
younger generation, in this strategic shift of focus for Canada?*

A pivot toward the Indo-Pacific cannot succeed without the engagement of Canadians, particularly the younger Canadians who are the business people, educators, creators and skilled workers of the 21st century.
After all, it is their future that is at stake. How does one shift their perspective on the world toward a greater awareness of the opportunities that lie in
closer engagement with the region?

Here, demography is an ally. An increasing percentage of the Canadian
population has family ties to the Indo-Pacific, not only to India and China
but also to Korea, the Philippines, Vietnam, and other countries in the
region. Many younger Canadians have the language skills, notably Hindi,
Mandarin, Cantonese and Vietnamese, required for success in those markets. Their cultural and linguistic orientation is already directed toward the
Indo-Pacific rather than Europe, which is a good thing for Canada. These
diaspora communities will play a critical and constructive role in the Indo-
Pacific pivot.

But this country's outreach to the Indo-Pacific cannot rest solely on
the shoulders of Canadians of Indo-Pacific ancestry. What is needed is a

broader awareness of Canada's place in the region, of the opportunities that lie with the acquisition of foreign language skills, and generally a readiness on the part of younger Canadians to reach out to the broader world for the opportunities that will build Canada's prosperity in the future.

Here Canada's provinces and cities—not just British Columbia and Vancouver but also across the nation—have an essential role. It is provincial Departments of Education and local school boards that shape curricula and learning opportunities. The provinces have a critical role in welcoming (or not) investment from the growing Indo-Pacific region. If they do not see their place in this larger world of the Indo-Pacific, then no larger strategy of outreach and engagement can succeed.

## The Bottom Line

All this is to say that a pivot toward the Indo-Pacific must be a collect- ive, multi-stakeholder, *national* endeavour based on a sober appreciation of where the world is headed and a sense of urgency about advancing our national interest. To rest comfortably in North America would be to sur- render to complacency when the world is changing dramatically. Shifting Canada's strategic orientation toward the Indo-Pacific must be led by the federal government, but that will require the active engagement of Canadian business, the provinces, and the larger Canadian community.

This shift in strategic orientation will mean a significant increase in activ- ity in our relations with key partners in the Indo-Pacific and in Canada's engagement in regional forums such as the critical East Asia Summit, the CPTPP and RCEP trade groupings, and the region's key security partner- ships: the ASEAN Defence Ministers Plus group, the QUAD, and (in an appropriate way) the new AUKUS.

In short, the Indo-Pacific is both an urgent, multifaceted opportunity and an equally multifaceted challenge for Canada. It is our collective future that is at stake. We have today a chance to build that future together. It's up to us.

# Notes

**1** The report was co-authored by Derek H. Burney, Thomas d'Aquino, Len Edwards, and Fen Osler Hampson.

**2** See Mike Blanchfield and Fen Osler Hampson, *The Two Michaels: Innocent Canadian Captives, High Stakes Espionage, and the US-China Cyber War* (Toronto: Sutherland House Books, 2021).

**3** China has reportedly carried out a number of hypersonic weapons tests, including a space-based, orbiting hypersonic weapon capable of carrying a nuclear payload, as reported by the *Financial Times*. China denied the reports and claimed it had simply launched a reusable space vehicle. China has also tested medium-range ballistic missile which could carry so-called "hypersonic glide vehicles" equipped with conventional or nuclear warheads.

**4** Derek H. Burney and Fen Osler Hampson, Braver Canada: Shaping Our Destiny in a Previous World (Montreal and Kingston: Qubic-Queen's University Press, 2020), ix.

**5** PwC, "The Long View: How Will the Global Economic Order Change by 2050?" *The World in 2050*, February 2017. https://www.pwc.com/gx/en/research-insights/economy/the-world-in-2050.html.

**6** PwC.

**7** Global Affairs Canada, "Canadian Statement on South China Sea Arbitration," July 21, 2016. https://www.canada.ca/en/global-affairs/news/2016/07/canadian-statement-on-south-china-sea-arbitration.html.

**8** Harriet Moynihan, "China's Evolving Approach to International Dispute Settlement," *International Law Programme* (Chatham House, March 2017). https://www.chathamhouse.org/2017/03/chinas-evolving-approach-international-dispute-settlement.

**9** Allan Gotlieb, "The United States in Canadian Foreign Policy" (Lecture Series, The O. D. Skelton Memorial Lecture, Toronto, December 10, 1991). https://www.international.gc.ca/gac-amc/programs-programmes/od_skelton/allan_gotlieb_lecture-conference.aspx?lang=eng.

**10** David S. Jacks, "Defying Gravity: The 1932 Imperial Economic Conference and the Reorientation of Canadian Trade," *Explorations in Economic History* 53 (2014): 19–39.

**11** Office of the United States Trade Representative, "U.S.-Canada Trade Facts," 2019. https://ustr.gov/countries-regions/americas/canada.

**12** Global Affairs Canada, "Statement by Minister Ng on U.S. Final Duty Rates on Canadian Softwood Lumber," November 24, 2021. https://www.canada.ca/en/global-affairs/news/2021/11/statement-by-minister-ng-on-us-final-duty-rates-on-canadian-softwood-lumber.html.

**13** Build Back Better Act, H.R.5376, 117th Congress, 1st session (2021). https://www.congress.gov/bill/117th-congress/house-bill/5376.

**14** The White House, President Biden Hosts the North American Leaders' Summit, 2021. https://www.youtube.com/watch?v=8im0RwfwUV4.

**15** Meredith Lilly, "Chapter 6: The Trudeau Government's Progressive Trade Agenda: Rhetoric or Reality?" in Justin Trudeau and Canadian Foreign Policy, ed. Philippe Lagassé and Norman Hillmer, *Canada Among Nations* (New York: Palgrave Macmillan, 2018).

**16** Chris Hall, "With No Formal Trade Talks, Trudeau Leaves International Trade Minister in Beijing," *CBC News*, December 5, 2017. https://www.cbc.ca/news/politics/justin-trudeau-china-trade-talks-1.4432975.

**17** Fen Hampson and Mike Blanchfield, *The Two Michaels: Innocent Canadian Captives, High Stakes Espionage, and the US-China Cyber War* (Sutherland House Incorporated, 2021).

**18** Meredith Lilly, "A Canadian Perspective on the Future of North America's Economic Relationship," in The Future of North America's Economic Relationship: From NAFTA to the New Canada-United States-Mexico Agreement and Beyond (*Centre for International Governance Innovation (CIGI) Special Report*, 2019), 15–21. https://www.cigionline.org/publications/future-north-americas-economic-relationship-nafta-new-canada-united-states-mexico/.

19 World Bank World Integrated Trade Solution (WITS), "Top Exporters and Importers by Country and Region 2019," 2019. https://wits.worldbank.org/CountryProfile/en/Country/WLD/Year/2019/TradeFlow/EXPIMP.

20 Meredith Lilly, "Advancing Trade with the Indo-Pacific: Canada's Role in Welcoming New Members to the CPTPP," *Canadian Global Affairs Institute* (CGAI), 2021 Taiwan Series, June 2021. https://www.cgai.ca/advancing_trade_with_the_indo_pacific_canadas_role_in_welcoming_new_members_to_the_cptpp.

21 Kati Suominen, "CPTPP as a Global 'Docking Station' for Free Traders? Prospective Members and Potential Gains" *(Center for Strategic & International Studies (CSIS)*, September 2021). https://www.csis.org/analysis/cptpp-global-docking-station-free-traders.

22 Global Affairs Canada, "Comprehensive and Progressive Agreement for Trans-Pacific Partnership (CPTPP) – Accession Process," January 19, 2019. https://www.international.gc.ca/trade-commerce/trade-agreements-accords-commerciaux/agr-acc/cptpp-ptpgp/accession_process-processus_adhesion.aspx?lang=eng.

23 David Webster, "Canada–Indonesia Relations, Past and Present," *International Journal* 74, no. 3 (2019): 473.

24 Global Affairs Canada, "Joint Feasibility Study on a Potential Canada-ASEAN Free Trade Agreement," n.d. https://www.international.gc.ca/trade-commerce/trade-agreements-accords-commerciaux/agr-acc/asean-anase/joint_feasibility-faisabilite_conjointe.aspx?lang=eng.

25 Asia Pacific Foundation of Canada, "Asian Views on Economic Engagement with Canada: Perspectives from Business Leaders and Policy Experts in Asia," May 2020. https://www.asiapacific.ca/publication/asian-views-economic-engagement-canada.

26 Statistics Canada, "Ethnic Origin (279), Single and Multiple Ethnic Origin Responses (3), Generation Status (4), Age (12) and Sex (3) for the Population in Private Households of Canada, Provinces and Territories, Census Metropolitan Areas and Census Agglomerations, 2016 Census - 25% Sample Data," Data tables, 2016 Census, 2016. https://www12.statcan.gc.ca/census-recensement/2016/dp-pd/dt-td/Rp-eng.cfm?TABID=2&Lang=E&APATH=3&DETAIL=0&DIM=0&FL=A&FREE=0&GC=0&GID=1341679&GK=0&GRP=1&PID=110528&PRID=10&PTYPE=109445&S=0&SHOWALL=0&SUB=0&Temporal=2017&THEME=120&VID=0&VNAMEE=&VNAMEF=&D1=0&D2=0&D3=0&D4=0&D5=0&D6=0.

27 Masud Chand and Rosalie L. Tung, "Bicultural Identity and Economic Engagement: An Exploratory Study of the Indian Diaspora in North America," *Asia Pacific Journal of Management* 31, no. 3 (2014): 763–88.

28 Meredith Lilly, "Chapter 7: Reforming High-Skilled Temporary Worker Programs in Canada and the United States: Sticks and Carrots," in Navigating a Changing World: Canada's International Policies in an Age of Uncertainties., ed. Geoffrey Hale and Greg Anderson, 2021. Meredith Lilly, "Chapter 7: Reforming High-Skilled Temporary Worker Programs in Canada and the United States: Sticks and Carrots," in *Navigating a Changing World: Canada's International Policies in an Age of Uncertainties.*, ed. Geoffrey Hale and Greg Anderson, 2021.

29 Ibid, 165.

30 Government of Canada, "Temporary Foreign Worker Program (TFWP) Work Permit Holders on December 31st by Country of Citizenship," Dataset, Temporary Residents: Temporary Foreign Worker Program (TFWP) and International Mobility Program (IMP) Work Permit Holders – Monthly IRCC Updates – Canada, February 11, 2021. https://open.canada.ca/data/en/dataset/360024f2-17e9-4558-bfc1-3616485d65b9/resource/bed6c44f-1cc7-47c2-9483-9b467c3c0f97; and Government of Canada, "International Mobility Program (IMP) Work Permit Holders on December 31st by Country of Citizenship," Dataset, Temporary Residents: Temporary Foreign Worker Program (TFWP) and International Mobility Program (IMP) Work Permit Holders – Monthly IRCC Updates – Canada, February 11, 2021. https://open.canada.ca/data/en/dataset/360024f2-17e9-4558-bfc1-3616485d65b9/resource/4ebf160a-f40d-4372-98b5-d3f9499c1125.

31 Meredith Lilly, "Chapter 7: Stumbling or Striving? Canada's Pursuit of Reciprocity in Negotiating Temporary Entry in Trade Agreements," in *Canada's Fluid Borders: Trade, Investment, Travel, Migration, ed. Geoffrey Hale and Greg Anderson* (University of Ottawa Press, 2021), 143–63.

32 Louis Cornelissen, "Insights on Canadian Society: Profile of immigrants in nursing and health care support occupations," *Statistics Canada*, May 28, 2021. https://www150.statcan.gc.ca/n1/pub/75-006-x/2021001/article/00004-eng.htm.

33 Statista Research Department, "Cash remittances to the Philippines by Filipinos based in Canada 2014-2020," June 24, 2021. https://www.statista.com/statistics/1071078/philippines-value-cash-remittances-overseas-filipino-workers-canada/.

34 Colleges and Institutes Canada, "The Role of Newcomers and International Students in Driving Canadian Economic Growth," October 2021. https://www.collegesinstitutes.ca/news-centre/news-release/colleges-and-institutes-support-immigrant-integration-for-canadian-prosperity/.

35 Office of the Chief Economist, Global Affairs Canada, "State of Trade 2021 - A Closer Look at Foreign Direct Investment (FDI)," 2021. https://www.international.gc.ca/transparency-transparence/state-trade-commerce-international/2021.aspx?lang=eng#a2.Office of the Chief Economist, Global Affairs Canada.

36 Ministry of Economy, Trade and Industry (Japan), "Minister Kajiyama Announced the Asia Energy Transition Initiative (AETI)," May 28, 2021. https://www.meti.go.jp/english/press/2021/0528_002.html.

37 Innovation, Science and Economic Development Canada, "Guidelines on the National Security Review of Investments," December 20, 2016. https://www.ic.gc.ca/eic/site/ica-lic.nsf/eng/lk81190.html.

38 Claudia Cattaneo, "'A Tragedy for Canada': Petronas Cancels $36B LNG Project as B.C. Jacks up Demands," *Financial Post*, July 25, 2017. https://financialpost.com/commodities/energy/a-tragedy-for-canada-petronas-cancels-36b-lng-project-as-b-c-jacks-up-demands.

39 Meredith Lilly, "Hewers of Wood and Drawers of Water 2.0: How American and Chinese Economic Nationalism Influence Canadian Trade Policy in the Twenty-First Century," *Canadian Foreign Policy Journal* 26, no. 2 (May 2020): 167–81.

40 K. Katsaliaki, P. Galesti, and S. Kumar, "Supply Chain Disruptions and Resilience: A Major Review and Future Research Agenda" *Annals of Operations Research* (2021).

41 PwC Global, "The World in 2050," February, 2017. https://www.pwc.com/gx/en/research-insights/economy/the-world-in-2050.html.

42 ESCAP75. Asia-Pacific Trade and Investment Trends 2020/2021, "Trade in Goods Outlook in the Asia and the Pacific."

43 "2021 National Opinion Poll: Canada's Generational Perspectives on Asia," Asia Pacific Foundation of Canada, December 2021.

44 For examples of this family metaphor see Francine McKenzie and Margaret MacMillan, *Introduction to Parties Long Estranged: Canada and Australia in the Twentieth Century*, (Vancouver: UBC Press, 2003), pp. 3–10 and Gareth J. Evans and Bruce Grant, *Australia's foreign relations: in the world of the 1990s* (Carlton, Victoria: Melbourne University Press, 1995), p. 333.

45 See The Glasgow-Burchill Declaration issued by Australian Minister of Foreign Affairs, the Hon. Julie Bishop and the Canadian Minister of Foreign Affairs, the Hon. Rob Nicholson, in Vancouver on July 7, 2015.

46 Canada - Australia Relations factsheet, dated June 2021, on the Global Affairs Canada website; and the Canada country brief on the Department of Foreign Affairs and Trade website, as of December 2021.

47 Quote from Peter Jennings, Director of the Australia Security Policy Institute (ASPI) in a webinar on "Australia - China Relations" hosted by the CIC Victoria Branch, November 29, 2021. https://youtu.be/6lSmRD-3HNY.

48 Calculated for both countries from the COMTRADE database. https://tradingeconomics.com.

49 "A Tale of Two Tories" blog post by Peter Jennings on The Strategist website, May 23, 2014. https://www.aspistrategist.org.au/australia-and-canada-a-tale-of-two-tories/.

50 Allan Gyngell, *Fear of Abandonment: Australia in the World since 1942*, (Carlton: La Trobe University Press, 2017).

51 See the National Press Club Address given in Canberra on November 26, 2021, by the Hon. Peter Dutton, Minister of Defence, and "Expanding Australia's Power and Influence: Speech to the Australian National

Security College" given in Canberra on November 23, 202, by Senator Penny Wong, Australian Labor Party Shadow Foreign Minister.

52 Quote from Vice Admiral Paul Maddison (Ret'd), former head of the Canadian Navy and former Canadian High Commissioner in Canberra on "Deep Dive on AUKUS," Defence Deconstructed podcast for October 1, 2021. https://www.cgai.ca/deep_dive_on_aukus.

53 Joint Leaders Statement on AUKUS, issued in Washington, D.C. on September 15, 2021.

54 "U.S. ...FDI in China (stock) was $123.9 billion in 2020, a 9.4 percent increase from 2019 ...led by manufacturing, wholesale trade, and finance and insurance." "The People's Republic of China," Office of the United States Trade Representative. Accessed December 2021. https://ustr.gov/countries-regions/china-mongolia-taiwan/peoples-republic-china.

55 World Economic League Table 2021: A World Economic League Table with Forecasts for 193 Countries to 2035, *Centre for Economics and Business Research*, December 26, 2020, p 8. https://cebr.com/service/macroeconomic-forecasting/.

56 International Monetary Fund, World Economic Outlook 2021, World Economic Outlook (October 2021) - GDP, current prices (imf.org). Accessed December 2021.

57 Homi Kharas, *The Unprecedented Expansion of the Global Middle Class: An Update, Global Economy & Development* Working Paper 100, Brookings Institution, February 2017. https://www.brookings.edu/wp-content/uploads/2017/02/global_20170228_global-middle-class.pdf.

58 Statistics Canada, Accessed January 2022, Table 12-10-0104-01 Trade in goods by exporter characteristics, by country of destination.

59 Alyssa Leng and Roland Rajah, "Chart of the Week: Global Trade Through a US-China Lens," Lowy Institute, December 18, 2019. https://www.lowyinstitute.org/the-interpreter/chart-week-global-trade-through-us-china-lens.

60 Asia Pacific Foundation of Canada, Accessed December 2021, 2021 *National Opinion Poll*: Canada's Generational Perspectives on Asia (asiapacific.ca).

61 Laura Silver, Kat Devlin and Christine Huang, "Unfavorable Views of China Reach Historic Highs in Many Countries," Pew Research Center, October 6, 2020. https://www.pewresearch.org/global/2020/10/06/unfavorable-views-of-china-reach-historic-highs-in-many-countries/.

62 See: International Trade Centre Investment Map. https://www.investmentmap.org/home

63 Statista, Accessed December 2021. China: direct investment capital stock leading countries and regions 2020 | Statista.

64 "Chinese," The Language Flagship, Accessed December 2021. https://www.thelanguageflagship.org/chinese.

65 "New Colombo Plan," Australian Government, Department of Foreign Affairs and Trade, Accessed December 2021. https://www.dfat.gov.au/people-to-people/new-colombo-plan.

66 Ibid.

67 The Comprehensive and Progressive Agreement for Trans-Pacific Partnership. One of the benefits of such multilateral agreements is that they offer a mutual liberalization vehicle for pairs of countries for whom a bilateral agreement would be politically untenable. A case in point is the adherence of both Japan and South Korea to the 15-country Regional Comprehensive Economic Partnership (RCEP) trade agreement in 2020, at a time when a bilateral Japan-South Korea agreement would have been unthinkable.

68 https://duihua.org/resources/death-penalty-reform/. Accessed November 2021.

69 The University of Toronto has piloted a good example of this in its security-considerations checklist for federal research grant applicants.

70 A national opinion poll undertaken by the APFC in September 2021 revealed a strong interest among young Canadians in learning more about Asia in school, and in learning an Asia language, with Chinese (Mandarin/Cantonese) being the top choice among Asian languages (and second choice overall, after Spanish). Asia Pacific Foundation of Canada, 2021 National Opinion Poll: Canada's Generational Perspectives on

Asia, December 7, 2021. https://www.asiapacific.ca/sites/default/files/publication-pdf/NOP%202021_Generational%20Perspectives.pdf.

**71** Asia Pacific Foundation of Canada, Asia Pacific Curriculum. https://asiapacificcurriculum.ca/.

**72** https://globalskillsopportunity.ca/about-us/.

**73** World Population Review. "ASEAN Countries | Association of Southeast Asian Nations." 2021. Accessed October 27, 2021. https://worldpopulationreview.com/country-rankings/asean-countries.

**74** Ibid.

**75** Statista. "Gross domestic product (GDP) of the ASEAN countries from 2011 to 2021." 2021. Accessed October 27, 2021. https://Ibid.statista.com/statistics/796245/gdp-of-the-asean-countries/.

**76** University of Toronto. "Mapping Canada in Asia." 2021. Accessed January 8, 2021. https://munkschool.uto-ronto.ca/canasiafootprint/.

**77** Ministry of Trade and Industry Singapore. "RCEP." 2021. Accessed October 27, 2021. https://Ibid.mti.gov.sg/Improving-Trade/Free-Trade-Agreements/RCEP.

**78** Government of Canada. "Canada and the Association of Southeast Asian Nations (ASEAN)." 2021. Accessed October 27, 2021. https://Ibid.international.gc.ca/world-monde/international_relations-relations_internatio-nales/asean/index.aspx?lang=eng#a2.

**79** Canada-ASEAN Business Council. ASEAN Commercial Opportunities Study for Canadian Business. 2013. Accessed October 27, 2021. https://Ibid.canasean.com/wp-content/uploads/2017/07/Canada-ASEAN-Opportunities-Study_April-2013-1.pdf.

**80** Asian Development Bank. "The Rise of Asia's Middle Class" in Key Indicators for Asia and the Pacific 2010 (Mandaluyong City, Philippines: Asian Development Bank, 2010). 3–4.

**81** Canada Agri-food Trade Alliance. "CAFTA Canada-ASEAN Briefing Note." 2018. Accessed October 25, 2021. https://cafta.org/trade-agreements/canada-asean-free-trade-agreement/attachment/cafta-canada-asean-briefing/.

**82** Government of Canada. "Exporting your Canadian agri-food to the ASEAN region." 2021. Accessed October 25, 2021. https://agriculture.canada.ca/en/international-trade/market-intelligence/exporting-your-canadian-agri-food-asean-region.

**83** Ibid.

**84** Asia Pacific Foundation of Canada. "The ASEAN Advantage: Exploring Canada's Trade Potential." May 12, 2017. Accessed October 25, 2021. https://Ibid.asiapacific.ca/research-report/asean-advantage-exploring-canadas-trade-potential.

**85** Ciuriak, Dan, Lucy Ciuriak, and Yingkang Lyu. "The Case for an ASEAN-Canada Free Trade Agreement Revisited." 2022. CD Howe Institute (forthcoming).

**86** Ibid.

**87** Ibid.

**88** Ibid.

**89** Ibid.

**90** The researchers calculated the economic implications of a Canada-ASEAN FTA based on simulations carried out on a dynamic computable general equilibrium (CGE) model. ASEAN's commitments under the Regional Comprehensive Economic Partnership (RCEP) were used in the analysis, which came into force at the beginning of 2022, to calibrate a realistic outcome.

**91** Ciuriak, Op.Cit.

**92** Ibid.

**93** Government of Canada. "Global defence engagement." 2019. Accessed November 6, 2021. https://Ibid.canada.ca/en/department-national-defence/corporate/reports-publications/canada-defence-policy/global-defence-engagement.html.

**94** OECD. "Overview of challenges and opportunities for improving food security in Southeast Asia" in Building Food Security and Managing Risk in Southeast Asia. (Paris: OECD Publishing, 2017), 13.

**95** FAO. "New Scenarios on Global Food Security based on Russia-Ukraine Conflict." Accessed April 14, 2022. https://www.fao.org/director-general/news/news-article/en/c/1476480/.

**96** Ibid.

**97** International Energy Agency. "Russia's War on Ukraine." 2022. Accessed April 18, 2022. https://www.iea.org/topics/russia-s-war-on-ukraine.

**98** Government of Canada. "Oil, Natural Gas & Coal." 2022. Accessed April 18, 2022. https://www.nrcan.gc.ca/science-and-data/data-and-analysis/energy-data-and-analysis/energy-facts/oil-natural-gas-and-coal/23936.

**99** Government of Canada. "Budget 2022." 2022. Accessed April 18, 2022. https://www.budget.gc.ca/2022/home-accueil-en.html.

**100** International Energy Agency. Electricity Market Report. Paris: International Energy Agency, 2020. Accessed October 27, 2021. https://www.iea.org/reports/electricity-market-report-december-2020.

**101** Galang, Jessica. "Toronto Region Board of Trade and City of Toronto Launch Smart Cities Initiative." 2016. Accessed October 27, 2021. https://betakit.com/toronto-region-board-of-trade-and-city-of-toronto-launch-smart-cities-initiative/.

**102** Environment Journal. "Brookfield's New $7.5 billion Climate-Focused Fund." 2021. Accessed November 6, 2021. https://environmentjournal.ca/brookfields-new-7-5-billion-climate-focused-fund/.

**103** Bank of Montreal. "Sustainable Banking in the ASEAN Region." 2020. Accessed November 6, 2021. https://www.bmogam.com/ca-en/institutional/news-and-insights/sustainable-banking-in-the-asean-region/.

**104** Asian Development Bank. Meeting Asia's Infrastructure Needs. Mandaluyong City, Philippines: Asian Development Bank, 2010. Accessed October 28, 2021. https://Ibid.adb.org/sites/default/files/publication/227496/special-report-infrastructure.pdf.

**105** CPP Investments. "Canada Pension Plan Investment Board to Invest in Cipali Toll Road in Indonesia." 2019. Accessed November 6, 2021. https://Ibid.cppinvestments.com/public-media/headlines/2019/cppib-invest-cipali-toll-road-indonesia.

**106** Canadian Commercial Corporation. "How G2G contracting reduces risk for your foreign government buyers (and makes your bid stand out)." 2021. Accessed November 6, 2021. https://info.ccc.ca/insights-for-exporters/how-g2g-contracting-reduces-risk-for-your-foreign-government-buyers-and-makes-your-bid-stand-out.

**107** El-Assal, Kareem. "642,000 international students: Canada now ranks 3rd globally in foreign student attraction." 2020. Accessed November 8, 2021. https://Ibid.cicnews.com/2020/02/642000-international-students-canada-now-ranks-3rd-globally-in-foreign-student-attraction-0213763.html#gs.epo56o.

**108** Canada-ASEAN Business Council. Strengthening the Canada-ASEAN Connection: Business Mobility. 2020. Accessed October 28, 2021. https://Ibid.canasean.com/wp-content/uploads/2020/08/CABC-2020_report_2020-08-14.pdf?x12140.

**109** Allison-Reumann, Laura, and Philomena Murray. "What Does The ASEAN-EU Strategic Partnership Mean?" Diplomat 2021. https://thediplomat.com/2021/01/what-does-the-asean-eu-strategic-partnership-mean.

**110** Goh, Gayle. "Singapore is looking to sign a digital economy agreement with the EU: Chan." 2020. Accessed November 6, 2021. https://Ibid.businesstimes.com.sg/government-economy/singapore-is-looking-to-sign-a-digital-economy-agreement-with-the-eu-chan.

**111** Allison-Reumann, Op.Cit.

**112** Australian Government Department of Foreign Affairs and Trade. "New Colombo Plan." n.d. Accessed November 6, 2021. https://Ibid.dfat.gov.au/people-to-people/new-colombo-plan

**113** European Commission. "Horizon Europe." 2021. Accessed November 6, 2021. https://ec.europa.eu/info/research-and-innovation/funding/funding-opportunities/funding-programmes-and-open-calls/horizon-europe_en.

**114** University of Saskatchewan. "Saskatchewan government announces $3.2M in funding to the Global Institute for Food Security." 2021. Accessed November 6, 2021. https://news.usask.ca/articles/research/2021/saskatchewan-government-announces-3.2m-in-funding-to-the-global-institute-for-food-security.php.

115 Government of Canada. "Canada and the Association of Southeast Asian Nations (ASEAN)." 2021. Accessed October 27, 2021. https://Ibid.international.gc.ca/world-monde/international_relations-relations_internationales/asean/index.aspx?lang=eng#a2.

116 Ciuriak, Op.Cit.

117 The "shared Canada-Japan priorities" under FOIP were announced following a meeting between the two Foreign Ministers on the margins of a G7 Ministerial in London in May 2021. The six agreed areas are: the rule of law, security cooperation, energy security, health, trade promotion, and the environment and climate change.

118 The Joint Statement issued after the Summit meeting between President Biden and then PM Suga in April 2021, which underscored "the importance of peace and stability across the Taiwan Straight," was the first direct reference to Taiwan by the United States and Japan at the leaders level since 1969, which was before either had established diplomatic relations with the PRC. More recently, former PM Shinzo Abe has been publicly sounding the alarm over possible Chinese military intervention in Taiwan, for example in remarks to a Taipei-based think tank on December 1, 2021, in which he argued that "military adventure would lead to economic suicide," predictably drawing a sharp rebuke from China.

119 The FOIP concept was initially advanced by former Prime Minister Abe during his first term in power, in a 2007 speech to the Indian Parliament entitled "Confluence of Two Seas." It failed to get traction in the geo-strategic environment of the day, but was reintroduced by Abe in 2017 in the wake of China's active BRI overtures and its rejection of the 2016 decision of the Permanent Court of Arbitration against China's claims in the South China Seas. Abe successfully sold it to the Trump Administration and subsequently attracted widespread buy-in within the region and beyond, aided by heightened concerns about the security threat posed by China, not least its proclivity for using coercive behaviour to achieve its aims.

120 World Bank, "World Development Indicators Database," 1 July 2021. https://databank.worldbank.org/data/download/GDP.pdf.

121 Jesper Koll, "Japan's cash reserves are now a great source of advantage," *Financial Times,* May 14, 2020.

122 Pharmaceutical goods, machinery and optical components each landed in Canada's top ten exports to Japan in 2020, according to data from Statistics Canada, as reported in the Global Trade Atlas on the HIS Markit-Connect platform.

123 Global Affairs Canada, "State of Trade 2021 - A Closer Look at Foreign Direct Investment (FDI)," Table 2.1. https://www.international.gc.ca/transparency-transparence/state-trade-commerce-international/2021.aspx?lang=eng#a2_2.

124 World Bank, "World Development Indicators Database," 1 July 2021. https://databank.worldbank.org/data/download/GDP.pdf.

125 Based on Statistics Canada data, as reported in the Global Trade Atlas on the HIS Markit—Connect platform, Canada was Japan's 18th largest export market through the first 11 months of 2021, ahead of France, Italy, Russia and Brazil, but behind China, the United States, other Asian economies, as well as Germany, Australia, the Netherlands, Mexico and the United Kingdom.

126 Prime Minister Trudeau attended the G20 Summit in Osaka in June 2019, but there was no bilateral component to that visit.

127 This includes our 2+2 mechanism involving the deputy ministers of GAC and DND, along with their Japanese counterparts, and the Canada-Japan Joint Economic Committee, co-chaired by Canada's deputy trade minister and the senior deputy minister (economic) in MOFA. Both are meant to meet annually, but in practice often do not, particularly the 2+2, which most recently met virtually in March 2022, more than 3 years after the last session in December 2018. Ironically, the argument often presented for not elevating our mechanisms to the political level is that it would make scheduling more difficult.

128 On January 6, 2022, Prime Ministers Kishida and Morrison signed the "Japan-Australia Reciprocal Access Agreement," Japan's first such agreement with a country other than the United States. Hailed as a "landmark" development by both sides, the agreement will significantly expand defence cooperation and military

inter-operability between the two countries. Negotiations for a similar agreement between Japan and the United Kingdom were launched in September 2021.

129 The Digital Economic Partnership Agreement (DEPA) involving Chile, New Zealand, and Singapore was concluded in June 2020 and entered into force on January 7, 2021. The Canadian government carried out public consultations on the possibility of acceding to the DEPA in the spring of 2021 and is reportedly engaged in exploratory discussions with the DEPA membership. In October 2021, South Korea became the first non-party to formally submit its application to accede to the DEPA.

130 Japan's manga and anime are ever more popular with Canada's youth, while Japan has been a very successful market for a wide variety of Canadian cultural offerings, from our iconic Cirque de Soleil performers and classical and jazz giants like Glenn Gould and Oscar Peterson, to pop superstars of the likes of Celine Dion, Justin Bieber and Shawn Mendes.

131 Canada participated in all four past expos in Japan, beginning with the 1970 expo in Osaka itself, which featured a visit by the then Prime Minister Pierre Trudeau, and subsequently at expos in Okinawa in 1975, Tsukuba in 1985 and Aichi (Nagoya) in 2005.

132 The Japanese Government has in recent years made significant investments in the promotion of the study of Japan abroad, including a $5 million donation in 2017 to establish the Centre for the Study of Global Japan at the Munk School at the University of Toronto.

133 The JCCC is co-chaired on the Japanese side by Mr. Tatsuo Yasunaga, Representative Director and Chair of the Board of Directors, Mitsui & Co., Ltd., and on the Canadian side by Mr. Steve Dechka, former President and CEO of Canpotex Ltd and the Honourable Perrin Beatty, President and CEO of the Canadian Chamber of Commerce.

134 Japan and Canada will mark the 100th anniversary of diplomatic relations in 2028 and 2029 respectively, given that Japan first established its diplomatic presence in Ottawa in 1928, while Canada followed suit with its "legation" in Tokyo in 1929.

135 The Canada-Japan Forum was initially launched by our then Prime Ministers in 1991 and co-chaired in its first iteration by Peter Lougheed and Yoshio Okawara. A follow-up committee operated from 1993-95, and then a new standing mechanism ran from 1996-2000. It was most recently reconstituted from 2003–2006, and issued its report in June 2006: "Toward a Renewed Canada Japan Partnership."

136 Raoul Oberman, Richard Doobs, Arief Budiman, Fraser Thompson and Morten Rossé, "The archipelago economy: Unleashing Indonesia's potential," McKinsey Global Institute, 2012. https://www.mckinsey.com/featured-insights/asia-pacific/the-archipelago-economy; John Hawksworth, Rob Clarry, and Hannah Audino, "The Long View: How will the global economic order change by 2050?" PricewaterhouseCoopers, 2017. https://www.pwc.com/gx/en/research-insights/economy/the-world-in-2050.html.

137 Hawksworth, Clarry and Audino, Op.Cit, "The Long View."

138 "Indonesia Population," Worldometer 2021. https://www.worldometers.info/world-population/indonesia-population/.

139 "Future of Indonesia: Trends & Age-Cohort Analysis," ProximityOne, 2021. http://proximityone.com/future_of_indonesia.htm.

140 Hanadian Nurhayati-Wolff, "Smartphone users in Indonesia 2017-2026," Statista, 2021. https://www.statista.com/statistics/266729/smartphone-users-in-indonesia/#:~:text=The%20number%20of%20smartphone%20users,India%20and%20the%20United%20States.

141 Regina Asariotis, Hassiba Benamara, Hannes Finkenbrink, Jan Hoffmann, Jennier Lavelle, Maria Misovicova, Vincent Valentine and Frida Youssef, "Review of Maritime Transport 2011," United Nations Conference on Trade and Development, 2011. https://unctad.org/system/files/official-document/rmt2011_en.pdf.

142 Witada Anukoonwattaka and Pedro Romao, "Asia-Pacific Trade and Investment Trends 2020/21: Trade in Goods Outlook in Asia and the Pacific," The United Nations Economic and Social Commission for Asia and the Pacific, 2021. https://www.unescap.org/resources/trade-goods-outlook-asia-and-pacific-20202021.

143 Leonard J. Edwards, "Innovation and Change: Forging the New Canada-Indonesia Partnership," Centre for International Governance Innovation, 2016. https://www.cigionline.org/publications/innovation-and-change-forging-new-canada-indonesia-partnership/.

144 Ibid.

145 Ibid.

146 Ibid.

147 Ibid.

148 Ibid.

149 Ibid.

150 Leonard J. Edwards, "Innovation and Change: Forging the New Canada-Indonesia Partnership," Centre for International Governance Innovation, 2016. https://www.cigionline.org/publications/innovation-and-change-forging-new-canada-indonesia-partnership/.

151 "Recruiting from Indonesia in a context of increased competition," ICEF Monitor, 2019. https://monitor.icef.com/2019/09/recruiting-from-indonesia-in-a-context-of-increased-competition/.

152 "Past Rankings," Global Firepower, 2017, Accessed January 5, 2022. https://www.globalfirepower.com/global-ranks-previous.php.

153 Leonard J. Edwards, "Innovation and Change: Forging the New Canada-Indonesia Partnership," Centre for International Governance Innovation, 2016. https://www.cigionline.org/publications/innovation-and-change-forging-new-canada-indonesia-partnership/.

154 Ibid.

155 The author wishes to thank Randy Hanbyul Lee for his research assistance for this chapter.

156 Christian Davies, "South Korea forges ahead with end-of-war declaration despite US reservations," Financial Times, January 4, 2022, Accessed January 10, 2022. https://www.ft.com/content/8f00d054-d66a-409c-9a8e-cd6b0a1012f4.

157 Government of Canada. "Defense Relations: Canada-Korea," Last modified October 19, 2020. Accessed December 11, 2021. https://www.canadainternational.gc.ca/korea-coree/bilateral_relations_bilaterales/defence_relations_defense.aspx?lang=eng.

158 Senate of Canada, "Honoring the Veterans of the Korean War," August 5, 2016. Accessed December 10, 2021. https://sencanada.ca/en/sencaplus/news/honouring-veterans-of-the-korean-war/.

159 The CIA World Factbook, "South Korea: Country Overview," Last updated January 12, 2022, Accessed January 15, 2022. https://www.cia.gov/the-world-factbook/countries/korea-south/#geography.

160 Paulina Sajnach, "The Korean Wave: From PSY to BTS -The Impact of K-Pop on the South Korean Economy," Asia Scotland Institute, January 22, 2021, Accessed January 2, 2022. https://www.asiascot.com/news/2021/01/22/the-korean-wave-from-psy-to-bts-the-impact-of-k-pop-on-the-south-korean-economy/.

161 Jiyeun Lee and Sam Kim, "The 'Squid Game' Takes Korean Soft Power Up a Notch, And It's Good for Economy Too," Bloomberg, October 6, 2021, Accessed January 8, 2022. https://www.bloomberg.com/news/articles/2021-10-07/k-pop-to-squid-game-lift-korean-soft-power-and-the-economy.

162 Government of Canada, "Market Overview: South Korea," Last modified December 22, 2021, Accessed January 10, 2022. https://agriculture.canada.ca/en/international-trade/market-intelligence/reports/market-overview-south-korea-0.

163 "South Korea's fertility rate is the lowest in the world," The Economist, June 30, 2018, Accessed January 12, 2022. https://www.economist.com/asia/2018/06/30/south-koreas-fertility-rate-is-the-lowest-in-the-world.

164 Government of Canada, "Market Overview: South Korea," Last modified December 22, 2021, Accessed January 10, 2022. https://agriculture.canada.ca/en/international-trade/market-intelligence/reports/market-overview-south-korea-0.

165 "The pandemic has accentuated South Korea's two-speed economy," The Economist, May 1, 2021, Accessed January 10, 2022. https://www.economist.com/asia/2021/05/01/the-pandemic-has-accentuated-south-koreas-two-speed-economy.

**166** "South Korea Demonstrates Asia's Economic Resilience During Pandemic," *The Wall Street Journal,* January 26, 2021. Accessed January 10, 2022. https://www.wsj.com/articles/south-korea-demonstrates-asias-economic-resilience-to-pandemic-11611664966.

**167** "South Korea 2021: Leading the Way: Resilience, Perspectives and Innovations," *IPSOS GAME CHANGER,* 2021. https://www.ipsos.com/sites/default/files/ct/publication/documents/2021-04/South%20Korean%2010%20key%20things.pdf.

**168** The summary of final Canada-Korea Free Trade Agreement can be found here: https://www.international.gc.ca/trade-commerce/assets/pdfs/agreements-accords/ckfta-fas-saf-eng.pdf.

**169** Trade Commissioner Services Canada, "The Canada-Korea Free Trade Agreement: Benefits and Opportunities for the Canadian Services Sector," Last modified May 10, 2021. Accessed January 12, 2022. https://www.tradecommissioner.gc.ca/korea-republic-coree-republique/157133.aspx?lang=eng.

**170** https://www.canadainternational.gc.ca/korea-coree/bilateral_relations_bilaterales/index.aspx?lang=eng.

**171** Government of Canada, "How the CKFTA Will Benefit Canada's Key Economic Sectors," May 10, 2021, Accessed January 2, 2022. https://www.tradecommissioner.gc.ca/korea-republic-coree-republique/157174.aspx?lang=eng.

**172** In 2018 alone, for instance, international students in Canada contributed some CAD $21.6 billion to Canada's GDP and supported almost 170,000 jobs for the Canadian economy. For more details, see Government of Canada, "Building on Success: International Education Strategy (2019-2024)," Last modified October 19, 2020, Accessed January 10, 2022. https://www.international.gc.ca/education/strategy-2019-2024-strategie.aspx?lang=eng.

**173** Nicholas Eberstadt, "Korea" in Richard J. Ellings and Aaron L. Friedberg eds. *Strategic Asia: Power and Purpose 2001-2002,* (Seattle: National Bureau of Asian Research, 2001), 138.

**174** David Brunnstrom, "U.S. accuses China of 'flagrant' N.Korea violations, offers $5 million reward," *Reuters,* December 1, 2020 https://www.reuters.com/article/usa-northkorea-china-idUSKBN28B540.

**175** In fact, this is only part of some 70,000 to 100,000 laborers that the DPRK regime sends to over thirty countries all over the world to earn foreign currency. For more details, see: https://www.forbes.com/sites/ewelinaochab/2019/07/01/trafficking-of-north-korean-women-in-china/?sh=8d66ad37af07. Also see: Yeo-sang Yoon & Seung-ju Lee, *Human Rights and North Korea's Overseas Labourers: Dilemmas and Policy Changes.* Seoul: Database Centre for North Korean Human Rights, 22, (2015).

**176** Yew Lun Tian and Josh Smith, "North Korea-China trade by rail to resume on Monday as border closures end," Reuters, January 16, 2022, Accessed January 16, 2022. https://www.reuters.com/world/china/nkorea-train-makes-rare-arrival-china-during-border-lockdown-yonhap-2022-01-16/.

**177** Human-Centered Artificial Intelligence Institute, "Artificial Intelligence Index Report 2021," Stanford University, 2021, Accessed January 13, 2022. https://aiindex.stanford.edu/wp-content/uploads/2021/11/2021-AI-Index-Report_Master.pdf.

**178** Jaeyong Lee, "KERI-Waterloo Collaboration Hub for Manufacturing AI," *Electric Power Journal,* Nov 17, 2021, Accessed January 10, 2022. http://www.epj.co.kr/news/articleView.html?idxno=29228.

**179** International Trade Administration, "Korea- Artificial Intelligence," Privacy Shield Framework, 2021. Accessed January 5, 2022. https://www.privacyshield.gov/article?id=Korea-Artificial-Intelligence. Also see this article from Joong-Ang Daily for a detailed overview of Samsung's global AI network. https://www.joongang.co.kr/article/25023861#home.

**180** Jungsoo Hwang, "AI 전진기지'를 캐나다에 세우는 이유(Why Canada is an attractive hub for AI)," *Hankyung Economic News,* October 18, 2020, Accessed January 17, 2022. https://www.hankyung.com/economy/article/2020101811741.

**181** The Asia Pacific Foundation of Canada, "APF Canada & Korea Artificial Intelligence Ethics Association Sign MoU for Co-operation on AI-related Projects," October 14, 2020, Accessed January 2, 2022. https://www.asiapacific.ca/media/news-releases/55380.

**182** Hyungjun Woo, "홍남기 '2025년까지 반도체, 미래차, 바이오 등 BIG3 산업 세계 1위 위해 역량 투입'" *SBS Biz,* December 21, 2021. https://news.naver.com/main/read.naver?mode=LSD&mid=sec&sid1=101&oid=3 74&aid=0000268594.

**183** Soojin Kim, "2021년 바이오 헬스 R&D 예산, 올해보다 30% 증가한 1조 7천억 원 투입," *BioTimes,* November 17, 2020. http://www.biotimes.co.kr/news/articleView.html?idxno=4664.

**184** Sung-Kyung Lee, "The Bio Industry to Become a New Growth Engine in Korea," *Invest KOREA,* August 6, 2021. https://www.investkorea.org/ik-en/bbs/i-308/detail.do?ntt_sn=490759.

**185** Sung-Kyung Lee, "The Bio Industry to Become a New Growth Engine in Korea."; Also see: "Samsung Biologics rises as global supply chain for COVID-19 vaccines," *Korea Herald,* December 28, 2021.

**186** Chan-hyuk Kim, "CMO emerges as key biz for Korean drugmakers," Korea BioMedical Journal, Apr 19, 2021. Accessed January 15, 2022. https://www.koreabiomed.com/news/articleView.html?idxno=10960.

**187** "Korea's Bio-Healthcare Industry to Make a Huge Leap Forward," *BIO Magazine,* May 28, 2021. Accessed January 2, 2022. https://www.bio.org/blogs/koreas-bio-healthcare-industry-make-huge-leap-forward.

**188** Sunyoung Lim, "[단독]韓 백신접종 완료 OECD 꼴찌...콜롬비아에도 뒤졌다." *Joongang Ilbo,* August 9, 2021, Accessed January 2, 2022. https://www.joongang.co.kr/article/24123650#home.

**189** Remarks by President Moon Jae-in at Presentation on Korea's Vision and Strategy for Becoming Global Vaccine Hub," Cheongwadae (Blue House), August 5, 2021. Accessed January 15, 2022. https://english1.president.go.kr/briefingspeeches/speeches/1041.

**190** Ibid.

**191** ROK Ministry of Culture, Sports and Tourism. "글로벌 백신허브화 (The Global Vaccine Hub Strategy)," Korea.kr, last modified on December 17, 2021. Accessed January 15, 2022. https://www.korea.kr/special/policyCurationView.do?newsId=148897096.

**192** Jess Craig, "Your next vaccine could be grown in a tobacco plant," July 8, 2021, Accessed January 3, 2022. https://www.nationalgeographic.com/science/article/your-next-vaccine-could-be-grown-in-a-tobacco-plant.

**193** Ibid.

**194** Natalie Béchamp, "Canada: A Playground for Cleantech Companies," Invest in Canada, accessed December 5, 2021, Accessed January 7, 2022. https://www.investcanada.ca/blog/canada-playground-cleantech-companies.

**195** Statistics Canada, "The Daily — Environmental and Clean Technology Products Sector Grew at Twice the Pace as the Total Economy in 2019," December 18, 2020, Accessed January 4, 2022. https://www150.statcan.gc.ca/n1/daily-quotidien/201218/dq201218d-eng.htm.

**196** For the latest Hydrogen Strategy for Canada, issued by Natural Resources Canada on Dec 2020, check: https://www.nrcan.gc.ca/sites/www.nrcan.gc.ca/files/environment/hydrogen/NRCan_Hydrogen-Strategy-Canada-na-en-v3.pdf.

**197** Isabelle Gerretsen, "South Korea 2050 Net Zero Pledge Spurs Renewables Investment," Climate Home News, January 14, 2021, Accessed January 5, 2022. https://www.climatechangenews.com/2021/01/14/south-korea-2050-net-zero-pledge-spurs-renewables-investment/.

**198** Trade Commissioner Service of Canada, "The Canada-Korea Free Trade Agreement: Benefits and Opportunities for the Canadian Sustainable Technologies Sector," Last modified on May 10, 2021, Accessed January 8, 2022. https://www.tradecommissioner.gc.ca/korea-republic-coree-republique/157157.aspx?lang=eng.

**199** Yonhap News Agency, "S. Korea to Close 30 Coal Plants by 2034 amid Shift to Renewable Energy," Yonhap News, December 24, 2020, Accessed January 4, 2022. https://en.yna.co.kr/view/AEN2020122400 5300320.

**200** Ministry of Economy and Finance, "Government Announces Korean New Deal 2.0," July 14, 2021, Accessed January 9, 2022. https://english.moef.go.kr/pc/selectTbPressCenterDtl.do?boardCd=N0001&seq=5173.

**201** World Nuclear Association, "Nuclear Power in Canada," July 2021, Accessed January 4. 2022. https://www.world-nuclear.org/information-library/country-profiles/countries-a-f/canada-nuclear-power.aspx.

**202** Natural Resources Canada, "Uranium and Nuclear Power Facts," March 22, 2021, Accessed January 10, 2022. https://www.nrcan.gc.ca/science-and-data/data-and-analysis/energy-data-and-analysis/energy-facts/uranium-and-nuclear-power-facts/20070.

**203** World Nuclear Association, Op.Cit.

**204** "Canada-South Korea MoU to leverage used fuel experience," *World Nuclear News,* October 18, 2021, Accessed January 15, 2022. https://www.world-nuclear-news.org/Articles/Canada-South-Korea-MoU-to-leverage-used-fuel-exper.

**205** "SNC-Lavalin awarded four contracts by Korea Hydro & Nuclear Power (KHNP)," SNC-Lavalin Press Release, February 4, 2020, Accessed January 15, 2022. https://www.snclavalin.com/en/media/press-releases/2020/04a-02-2020.

**206** Trade Commissioner Service of Canada, "The Canada-Korea Free Trade Agreement: Benefits and Opportunities for the Canadian Sustainable Technologies Sector," Op.Cit.

**207** International Energy Agency, January 2022, Canada Report.

**208** https://sdgs.un.org/goals.

**209** In 2021 Canada produced over 4.7 million barrels a day of crude oil and equivalent(https://www.cer-rec.gc.ca/en/data-analysis/energy-commodities/crude-oil-petroleum-products/statistics/estimated-production-canadian-crude-oil-equivalent.html). In 2019 we exported about 3.7 million barrels a day (https://www.cer-rec.gc.ca/en/data-analysis/energy-commodities/crude-oil-petroleum-products/statistics/crude-oil-summary/crude-oil-annual-export-summary.html)almost all of which goes to the US (and much of that destined to the refineries on the Gulf Coast, for either use in the US or for further export abroad.). In 2019 Canada imported almost 700 thousand barrels per day (Mb/d) (over 70% of that from the US, much of it to feed refineries in Ontario, Quebec and New Brunswick (https://www.cer-rec.gc.ca/en/data-analysis/energy-markets/market-snapshots/2021/market-snapshot-crude-oil-imports-decreased-in-2020-and-so-did-the-cost.html).

**210** Canada produces around 160,000 Bm3 of natural gas a year (https://www.cer-rec.gc.ca/en/data-analysis/energy-commodities/natural-gas/statistics/marketable-natural-gas-production-in-canada.html) but, like oil, we use some domestically; we export and we import. In 2019 Canada exported 76.6 Bm3 of natural gas, imported 25.6 Bm3 (about a third of what we exported.) Virtually all exports are from various parts of Canada to the US (because of infrastructure (pipeline availability) and most of the gas imported came from the US into Ontario (again, due to infrastructure (pipeline) limits/availability. (https://www.cer-rec.gc.ca/en/data-analysis/energy-commodities/natural-gas/report/natural-gas-summary/natural-gas-annual-trade-summary.html).

**211** For residential and industrial heat, cooking, etc. and for replacing coal-fired electricity generation. Various countries are looking to alternate, reliable sources of supply for energy security reasons.

**212** Stats on LNG.

**213** Note the progress on LNG Canada and hopes, but also __ projects cancelled due to regulatory barriers.

**214** https://www.eia.gov/todayinenergy/detail.php?id=50598.

**215** In 2018 Canada produced 648 terawatt hours (TW.h) of electricity: 61% from hydro; 15% from nuclear: 9% from natural gas; 8% from coal and coke: 5% from wind; less than 1% from solar. We exported about 7% of that production, and imported about 1/6 of what we exported (https://www.cer-rec.gc.ca/en/data-analysis/energy-markets/provincial-territorial-energy-profiles/provincial-territorial-energy-profiles-canada.html).

**216** https://www.theglobeandmail.com/business/article-maine-voters-poised-to-reject-hydropower-line-from-canada-to-new/.

**217** https://eralberta.ca/projects/details/alberta-zero-emissions-truck-electrification-collaboration-azetec/.

**218** https://www.nrcan.gc.ca/climate-change/canadas-green-future/the-hydrogen-strategy/23080.

**219** https://www.cer-rec.gc.ca/en/data-analysis/energy-markets/provincial-territorial-energy-profiles/provincial-territorial-energy-profiles-canada.html.

**220** https://www.wcap.ca/sustainability/co2-sequestration.

**221** https://www.saskpower.com/Our-Power-Future/Infrastructure-Projects/Carbon-Capture-and-Storage/ Boundary-Dam-Carbon-Capture-Project.

**222** https://www.shell.ca/en_ca/about-us/projects-and-sites/quest-carbon-capture-and-storage-project.html.

**223** IPCC: https://www.ipcc.ch/site/assets/uploads/2018/03/srccs_summaryforpolicymakers-1.pdf; IEA: other quotes.

**224** https://www.iea.org/reports/carbon-capture-utilisation-and-storage-the-opportunity-in-southeast-asia.

**225** In 2015, Canada signed on to the Paris Agreement and set an ambitious Nationally Determined Contribution (NDC) target, now pledging emission reductions of 40–45% below 2005 levels. To achieve this objective Canada has implemented 64 different federal regulations and policies to date, including: carbon pricing, started in 2007 in Alberta and now nationally, with incremental increases to $170t/CO2 by 2030, the most aggressive carbon pricing regime in the world; some of the most stringent methane regulations in the world; a phase out of coal for electricity by 2030, and stringent national clean fuel standards.

**226** Oil Sands Pathways to Net Zero by 2050 initiative: www.pathways.ca.

**227** https://www.iea.org/reports/canada-2022.

**228** See chart at end of doc with summary of many projections, from Cenovus Energy Report on Sustainability.

**229** Carbon Engineering as a great Canadian example of this technology

**230** https://carbonengineering.com/.

**231** https://www.sdtc.ca/en/ ; https://cleanresourceinnovation.com/ ; https://cosia.ca/ ;

**232** International Energy Agency, IEA Press Release Jan 2022.

**233** OECD (2019), "Measuring the Digital Transformation: A Roadmap for the Future," OECD Publishing, Paris, p.56. https://doi.org/10.1787/9789264311992-en.

**234** Riccardo Bassoli, Frank H.P. Fitzek, and Emilio Calvanese Strinati, "Why do we need 6G?," *ITU Journal on Future and Evolving Technologies*, Volume 2, Issue 6, 13 September 2021. https://www.itu.int/dms_pub/ itu-s/opb/jnl/S-JNL-VOL2.ISSUE6-2021-A01-PDF-E.pdf; Naoki Watanabe, "Race for 6G: South Korea and China off to early leads," *Nikkei Asia*, June 3, 2020. https://asia.nikkei.com/Business/Technology/ Race-for-6G-South-Korea-and-China-off-to-early-leads.

**235** Deanna Horton, "Mapping Canadian Tech Companies in International Markets: Wrap-up Report to CDO 2019," *Munk School of Global Affairs and Public Policy*, April 22, 2019. https://munkschool.utoronto.ca/ipl/ files/2019/04/Horton_Mapping-CanadianTechCo_Summary-22AP2019.pdf.

**236** World Bank, "Individuals using the Internet (% of population) - Korea, Rep.," *The World Bank Group*, 2021. https://data.worldbank.org/indicator/IT.NET.USER.ZS?locations=KR.

**237** GSMA, "GSMA Mobile Connectivity Index," *GSMA*, 2020. https://www.mobileconnectivityindex.com.

**238** World Bank, "Fixed broadband subscriptions (per 100 people)," *The World Bank Group*, Accessed October 10, 2021. https://data.worldbank.org/indicator/IT.NET.BBND.P2.

**239** World Bank, "Fixed broadband subscriptions (per 100 people)," *The World Bank Group*, Accessed October 10, 2021. https://data.worldbank.org/indicator/IT.NET.BBND.P2.

**240** World Bank, "Mobile cellular subscriptions," *The World Bank Group*, Accessed November 27, 2021. https:// data.worldbank.org/indicator/IT.CEL.SETS?name_desc=true.

**241** International Telecommunications Union, "Digital inclusion of all," *International Telecommunications Union*, April 2021. https://www.itu.int/en/mediacentre/backgrounders/Pages/digital-inclusion-of-all.aspx.

**242** Deanna Horton, "Promoting global digital connectivity and inclusion," Policy Options, *Institute for Research on Public Policy*, April 22, 2021. https://policyoptions.irpp.org/magazines/april-2021/promoting- global-digital-connectivity-and-inclusion/.

**243** Ian Fogg, "Benchmarking the 5G Experience — Asia Pacific — June 2021," *OpenSignal*, June 14, 2021. https://www.opensignal.com/2021/06/14/benchmarking-the-5g-experience-asia-pacific-june-2021.

**244** United Nations Conference on Trade and Development, "Estimates of Global E-Commerce 2019 and Preliminary Assessment of COVID-19 Impact on Online Retail 2020," *United Nations Conference on*

*Trade and Development*, p. 2, May 3, 2020. https://unctad.org/system/files/official-document/tn_unctad_ict4d18_en.pdf.

245 United Nations Conference on Trade and Development, "Estimates of Global E-Commerce 2019 and Preliminary Assessment of COVID-19 Impact on Online Retail 2020," *United Nations Conference on Trade and Development*, p.1, May 3, 2020. https://unctad.org/system/files/official-document/tn_unctad_ict4d18_en.pdf.

246 United Nations Conference on Trade and Development, "Estimates of Global E-Commerce 2019 and Preliminary Assessment of COVID-19 Impact on Online Retail 2020," *United Nations Conference on Trade and Development*, p.1, May 3, 2020. https://unctad.org/system/files/official-document/tn_unctad_ict4d18_en.pdf.

247 Statistics Bureau of Japan, "Statistics Today No. 162," *Statistics Bureau of Japan*, September 7, 2020. https://www.stat.go.jp/info/today/162.html.

248 United Nations Conference on Trade and Development, "International trade in digitally-deliverable services, value, shares and growth, annual," *United Nations Conference on Trade and Development*, September 7, 2021. https://unctadstat.unctad.org/wds/TableViewer/tableView.aspx?ReportId=158358.

249 United Nations Conference on Trade and Development, "Share of ICT goods as percentage of total trade, annual," *United Nations Conference on Trade and Development*, September 30, 2021. https://unctadstat.unctad.org/wds/TableViewer/tableView.aspx?ReportId=195158&IF_Language=eng.

250 United Nations Conference on Trade and Development, "International trade in ICT services, value, shares and growth, annual," *United Nations Conference on Trade and Development*, September 7, 2021. https://unctadstat.unctad.org/wds/TableViewer/tableView.aspx?ReportId=158359.

251 United Nations Conference on Trade and Development, "International trade in ICT services, value, shares and growth, annual," *United Nations Conference on Trade and Development*, September 7, 2021. https://unctadstat.unctad.org/wds/TableViewer/tableView.aspx?ReportId=158359.

252 United Nations Conference on Trade and Development, "International trade in ICT services, value, shares and growth, annual," *United Nations Conference on Trade and Development*, September 7, 2021. https://unctadstat.unctad.org/wds/TableViewer/tableView.aspx?ReportId=158359.

253 United Nations Conference on Trade and Development, "Share of ICT goods as percentage of total trade, annual," *United Nations Conference on Trade and Development*, September 30, 2021. https://unctadstat.unctad.org/wds/TableViewer/tableView.aspx?ReportId=195158&IF_Language=eng.

254 Jae-yeon Lee, "Vietnam is another Samsung republic," *The Hankyoreh*, June 27, 2019. https://www.hani.co.kr/arti/society/society_general/899511.html.

255 United Nations Conference on Trade and Development, "Digital Economy Report 2021," *United Nations Conference on Trade and Development*, p. 22, September 29, 2021. https://unctad.org/webflyer/digital-economy-report-2021.

256 United Nations Conference on Trade and Development, "Digital Economy Report 2021," *United Nations Conference on Trade and Development*, p. 27, September 29, 2021. https://unctad.org/webflyer/digital-economy-report-2021.

257 Arjun Kharpal, "Alibaba, JD smash Singles Day record with $139 billion of sales and focus on 'social responsibility,'" *CNBC*, November 12, 2021. https://www.cnbc.com/2021/11/12/china-singles-day-2021-alibaba-jd-hit-record-139-billion-of-sales.html.

258 Arjun Kharpal, "JD.com plans to boost overseas investment as China's e-commerce giants look to challenge Amazon," *CNBC*, November 10, 2021. https://www.cnbc.com/2021/11/11/china-jdcom-plans-to-boost-investment-overseas-in-challenge-to-amazon.html.

259 Mynt, "Mynt Secures $300m in Funding from Lead Investors Warburg Pincus, Insight Partners and Bow Wave," *Cision*, November 2, 2021. https://www.prnewswire.com/news-releases/mynt-secures-300m-in-funding-from-lead-investors-warburg-pincus-insight-partners-and-bow-wave-301413410.html.

260 Ken Koyanagi, "Southeast Asia hosting more unicorns as internet economy takes off," *Nikkei Asia*, October 15, 2021. https://asia.nikkei.com/Spotlight/Comment/Southeast-Asia-hosting-more-unicorns-as-internet-economy-takes-off.

261 CBInsights, "The Complete List of Unicorn Companies," *CBInsights*, Accessed November 29, 2021. https://www.cbinsights.com/research-unicorn-companies.

262 Shagun Karki, "A horse of another: Here's the complete list of Southeast Asia's 26 unicorns," E27, *Optimatic Pte Ltd.*, November 2, 2021. https://e27.co/a-horse-of-another-heres-the-full-list-of-southeast-asias-20-unicorns-20210730/.

263 Organisation for Economic Co-operation and Development, "Southeast Asia Going Digital: Connecting SMEs," *Organisation for Economic Co-operation and Development*, p. 77, 2019. https://www.oecd.org/going-digital/southeast-asia-connecting-SMEs.pdf.

264 Kentaro Iwamoto, "How Singapore's Sea is surfing Southeast Asia's digital wave," *Nikkei Asia*, October 2, 2020. https://asia.nikkei.com/Business/Business-Spotlight/How-Singapore-s-Sea-is-surfing-Southeast-Asias-s-digital-wave.

265 Faris Mokhtar, "China's Tencent ops for co-working space for first office in Singapore," *DealStreetAsia*, October 16, 2020. https://www.dealstreetasia.com/stories/tencent-singapore-office-211666/.

266 Reuters, "Bytedance to invest billions, recruit hundreds in Singapore in 3 years – source," *Reuters*, September 10, 2020. https://www.reuters.com/article/china-bytedance-singapore/bytedance-to-invest-billions-recruit-hundreds-in-singapore-in-3-years-source-idUSFWN2G70IG.

267 Jon Russell, "Alibaba gets serious in Southeast Asia in preparation for battle with Amazon," *TechCrunch*, March 24, 2017. https://techcrunch.com/2017/03/24/alibaba-gets-serious-in-southeast-asia/.

268 Phred Dvorak and Liza Lin, "Alibaba switches Lazada CEO again in tough e-commerce market," *The Wall Street Journal*, June 26, 2020. https://www.wsj.com/articles/alibaba-switches-lazada-ceo-again-in-tough-e-commerce-market-11593173345.

269 P.R. Venkat and Quentin Webb, "Tencent-backed tech giant Sea taps investors for $6 billion," *The Wall Street Journal*, September 10, 2021. https://www.wsj.com/articles/tencent-backed-tech-giant-sea-taps-investors-for-about-6-billion-11631170423.

270 Julia Fioretti, "Tencent-backed Sea raises $6 billion in fresh capital," *Bloomberg*, September 9, 2021. https://www.bloomberg.com/news/articles/2021-09-10/tencent-backed-sea-is-said-to-raise-6-billion-in-fresh-capital.

271 P.R. Venkat and Quentin Webb, "Tencent-backed tech giant Sea taps investors for $6 billion," *The Wall Street Journal*, September 10, 2021. https://www.wsj.com/articles/tencent-backed-tech-giant-sea-taps-investors-for-about-6-billion-11631170423.

272 新商业派, "Tencent Emerges as Winner in its Proxy War with Alibaba, For Now," *TMTPost*, June 16, 2021. https://en.tmtpost.com/post/5402876.

273 Shotaro Tani, "SoftBank and Alibaba take top stakes in Indonesia's GoTo," *Nikkei Asia*, May 20, 2021. https://asia.nikkei.com/Business/Technology/SoftBank-and-Alibaba-take-top-stakes-in-Indonesia-s-GoTo.

274 Jon Russell, "Alibaba plays politics with new cross-border e-commerce initiative in Malaysia," *TechCrunch*, March 22, 2017. https://techcrunch.com/2017/03/22/alibaba-malaysia/.

275 Alibaba Group, "Malaysia Airports and Alibaba Announce Operation Commencement of Cainiao Aeropolis eWTP Hub, Malaysia," *Alibaba Group*, November 3, 2020. https://www.alibabagroup.com/en/news/article?news=p201103.

276 Xinmei Shen, "Alibaba Cloud doubles down on Southeast Asia amid competition at home after clearing antitrust uncertainty," *South China Morning Post*, June 8, 2021. https://www.scmp.com/tech/big-tech/article/3136475/alibaba-cloud-doubles-down-southeast-asia-amid-competition-home-after.

277 Ministry of Economy and Finance, "Government Releases an English Booklet on the Korean New Deal," *Ministry of Economy and Finance*, July 28, 2020. https://english.moef.go.kr/pc/selectTbPressCenterDtl.do?boardCd=N0001&seq=4948.

**278** Ministry of Planning and Finance, "Myanmar Digital Economy Roadmap," *Ministry of Planning and Finance*, February 26, 2019. https://www.mopfi.gov.mm/en/ministry-article/publication/myanmar-digital-economy-roadmap.

**279** Economic Planning Unit, Prime Minister's Department, "Malaysia Digital Economy Blueprint," *Economic Planning Unit, Prime Minister's Department*, February, 2021. https://www.epu.gov.my/sites/default/files/2021-02/malaysia-digital-economy-blueprint.pdf.

**280** Association of Southeast Asian Nations, "ASEAN Digital Masterplan 2025," *Association of Southeast Asian Nations*, Accessed November 27, 2021. https://asean.org/book/asean-digital-masterplan-2025/.

**281** Singapore Ministry of Trade and Industry, "Digital Economy Agreements," *Singapore Ministry of Trade and Industry*, November 25, 2021. https://www.mti.gov.sg/Improving-Trade/Digital-Economy-Agreements.

**282** GSMA, "GSMA Mobile Connectivity Index," *GSMA*, 2020. https://www.mobileconnectivityindex.com.

**283** Xiaomeng Lu, "Is China Changing Its Thinking on Data Localization?," *The Diplomat*, June 4, 2020. https://thediplomat.com/2020/06/is-china-changing-its-thinking-on-data-localization/.

**284** Mugdha Variyar, "Alibaba backs data localization in India," *The Economic Times*, September 20, 2018. https://economictimes.indiatimes.com/small-biz/startups/newsbuzz/alibaba-backs-data-localisation-in-india/articleshow/65869841.cms?from=mdr.

**285** Eliza Gkritsi, "Insights | Data localization is going global," *TechNode*, October 19, 2020. https://technode.com/2020/10/19/insights-data-localization-is-going-global/.

**286** East Asia Forum, "Digital trade integral to East Asia's recovery and dynamism," *East Asia Forum*, April 19, 2021. https://www.eastasiaforum.org/2021/04/19/digital-trade-integral-to-east-asias-recovery-and-dynamism/.

**287** Google, Temasek, and Bain & Company, "e-conomy SEA 2019," *Google, Temasek, and Bain & Company*, Accessed November 27, 2021. https://www.blog.google/documents/47/SEA_Internet_/.

# Index

# Authors

**Derek H. Burney** is a former, 30 year career diplomat who served as Ambassador to the United States of America from 1989–1993.

**Ian Burney**'s distinguished, 34-year diplomatic career culminated with his appointment as Ambassador to Japan from 2016–21. He currently serves on various corporate boards.

**The Honourable Jean Charest** is the former Deputy Prime Minister of Canada, a former Premier of Québec, and Partner at McCarthy Tétrault.

**Dr. Fen Osler Hampson** is Chancellor's Professor at Carleton University, President of the World Refugee & Migration Council and a Fellow of the Royal Society of Canada.

**Leonard Edwards** served as Canada's deputy minister of both International Trade and Foreign Affairs. His several Asia assignments included ambassador to Japan and the Republic of Korea.

**Wayne Farmer** is the President of the Canada-ASEAN Business Council. Wayne has over 20 years of experience in pan-Asian and global private equity.

**Martha Hall Findlay** is the Chief Climate Officer at Suncor Energy, Canada's leading fully integrated energy company. She leads Suncor's efforts to address the nexus of climate and energy.

**Deanna Horton** is a former Canadian diplomat with extensive experience in Asia, now affiliated with the Munk School of Global Affairs & Public Policy and the Asia-Pacific Foundation of Canada.

**Goldy Hyder** is President and CEO of the Business Council of Canada and chair of the Asia Business Leaders Advisory Council, a high-level group of business leaders convened by the Asia Pacific Foundation of Canada.

**Dr. Meredith Lilly** is Associate Professor at the Norman Paterson School of International Affairs, Carleton University, where she holds the Simon Reisman Chair in International Economic Policy.

**Amily Li** earned a B.A. in International Relations from Western University and an M.A. from the Norman Paterson School of International Affairs.

**Dr. Jim Mitchell** is an Adjunct Professor at Carleton University. A former foreign service officer, he later headed the Machinery of Government unit in the Privy Council Office.

**Jeff Nankivell** joined the Asia Pacific Foundation of Canada as President and CEO in September 2021. Prior to this role, he had a distinguished career in Canada's Foreign Service over 33 years.

**Dr. Tina J. Park** is the Chief Executive Officer of The Park Group and Vice-President of the NATO Association of Canada.

**Nadir Patel** held a series of high-level positions over a distinguished career in Canada's public service. Most recently, he served as Canada's longest-serving High Commissioner to the Republic of India.

**Michael Small** was a senior official and career diplomat in the Canadian Foreign Service, notably as Canada's High Commissioner to Australia (2010 – 2014). He is now a Fellow at Simon Fraser University's Morris J. Wosk Centre for Dialogue.

The editors wish to thank **Trevor Kennedy** of the Business Council of Canada and **Kenneth Whyte** of Sutherland House for their outstanding contributions to this collective endeavour.